What Readers Are Saying About
Programming Clojure, Second Edition

Clojure is one of the most interesting languages out there right now, and the best way of learning Clojure just got better. The second edition of *Programming Clojure* adds up-to-date information, plenty of practical examples, and a ton of useful tips on how to learn, work with, and succeed with Clojure.

➤ **Ola Bini**
   Creator of Ioke language, developer, ThoughtWorks

Intimidated by Clojure? You won't be after you read this book. Written in a clear and enjoyable style, it teaches the language one small piece at a time in a very accessible way.

➤ **Tim Berglund**
   Founder and Principal, August Technology Group

The authors have charted the smoothest path yet to Clojure fluency with this well-organized and easy-to-read book. They have a knack for creating simple and effective examples that demonstrate how the language's unique features fit together.

➤ **Chris Houser**
   Primary Clojure contributor and library author

Clojure is a beautiful, elegant, and very powerful language on the JVM. It's like a cathedral: you could wander into it, but you'd prefer the company of a knowledgeable guide who can give you their perspectives, to help you grasp and appreciate the architecture and the art. In this book you can enjoy and benefit from the company of not one, but two seasoned developers who have the depth of knowledge and the perspective you need.

➤ **Dr. Venkat Subramaniam**
Award-winning author and founder, Agile Developer, Inc.

Programming Clojure

Second Edition

Stuart Halloway

Aaron Bedra

The Pragmatic Bookshelf

Dallas, Texas • Raleigh, North Carolina

Many of the designations used by manufacturers and sellers to distinguish their products are claimed as trademarks. Where those designations appear in this book, and The Pragmatic Programmers, LLC was aware of a trademark claim, the designations have been printed in initial capital letters or in all capitals. The Pragmatic Starter Kit, The Pragmatic Programmer, Pragmatic Programming, Pragmatic Bookshelf, PragProg and the linking *g* device are trademarks of The Pragmatic Programmers, LLC.

Every precaution was taken in the preparation of this book. However, the publisher assumes no responsibility for errors or omissions, or for damages that may result from the use of information (including program listings) contained herein.

Our Pragmatic courses, workshops, and other products can help you and your team create better software and have more fun. For more information, as well as the latest Pragmatic titles, please visit us at *http://pragprog.com*.

The team that produced this book includes:

Michael Swaine (editor)
Potomac Indexing, LLC (indexer)
Kim Wimpsett (copyeditor)
David J Kelly (typesetter)
Janet Furlow (producer)
Juliet Benda (rights)
Ellie Callahan (support)

Printed in the United States of America.
ISBN-13: 978-1-934356-86-9
Printed on acid-free paper.
Book version: P1.0—April 2012

In loving memory of my father and mentor, Craig Bedra, who taught me the value of learning by exploration and that there is no such thing as magic.—Aaron

Contents

Foreword for the Second Edition

A lot has changed since the first edition of the book. Yes, the language has had some enhancements, such as protocols and records. Most significant, though, is that Clojure has seen adoption across a wide variety of domains. People are building start-ups, analyzing large data sets, and doing communications, financial, web, and database work in Clojure. A large and supportive community has grown up around Clojure and, with it, a ton of libraries. These libraries are particularly exciting, not just in the facilities they provide. The best of them embrace the Clojure approach and mechanisms and, in doing so, reach new levels of simplicity and interoperability.

In this second edition, Stuart and Aaron make sure to cover the language enhancements and include a taste of what it's like to leverage some of the community libraries, while taking care to convey the concepts that make it all work. The book remains an exhilarating introduction to Clojure, and I hope it inspires you to join the community and, eventually, contribute to the library ecosystem.

—Rich Hickey
Creator of Clojure

Foreword for the First Edition

We are drowning in complexity. Much of it is incidental—arising from the way we are solving problems, instead of the problems themselves. Object-oriented programming seems easy, but the programs it yields can often be complex webs of interconnected mutable objects. A single method call on a single object can cause a cascade of change throughout the object graph. Understanding what is going to happen when, how things got into the state they did, and how to get them back into that state in order to try to fix a bug are all very complex. Add concurrency to the mix, and it can quickly become unmanageable. We throw mock objects and test suites at our programs but too often fail to question our tools and programming models.

Functional programming offers an alternative. By emphasizing pure functions that take and return immutable values, it makes side effects the exception rather than the norm. This is only going to become more important as we face increasing concurrency in multicore architectures. Clojure is designed to make functional programming approachable and practical for commercial software developers. It recognizes the need for running on trusted infrastructure like the JVM and supporting existing customer investments in Java frameworks and libraries, as well as the immense practicality of doing so.

What is so thrilling about Stuart's book is the extent to which he "gets" Clojure, because the language is targeted to professional developers just like himself. He clearly has enough experience of the pain points Clojure addresses, as well as an appreciation of its pragmatic approach. This book is an enthusiastic tour of the key features of Clojure, well grounded in practical applications, with gentle introductions to what might be new concepts. I hope it inspires you to write software in Clojure that you can look back at and say, "Not only does this do the job, but it does so in a robust and simple way, and writing it was fun too!"

—Rich Hickey
Creator of Clojure

Acknowledgments

Many people have contributed to what is good in this book. The problems and errors that remain are ours alone.

Thanks to the awesome team at Relevance and Clojure/core for creating an atmosphere in which good ideas can grow and thrive.

Thanks to the kind folks on the Clojure mailing list[1] for all their help and encouragement.

Thanks to everyone at the Pragmatic Bookshelf. Thanks especially to our editor, Michael Swaine, for good advice delivered on a very aggressive schedule. Thanks to Dave Thomas and Andy Hunt for creating a fun platform for writing technical books and for betting on the passions of their authors.

Thanks to all the people who posted suggestions on the book's errata page.[2]

Thanks to our technical reviewers for all your comments and helpful suggestions, including Kevin Beam, Ola Bini, Sean Corfield, Fred Daoud, Steven Huwig, Tibor Simic, David Sletten, Venkat Subramaniam, and Stefan Turalski.

A very special thanks to David Liebke who wrote the original content for Chapter 6, *Protocols and Datatypes*, on page 143. He provided a fantastic guide through the new ideas and this book would not be the same without his contributions.

Thanks to Rich Hickey for creating the excellent Clojure language and fostering a community around it.

Thanks to my wife, Joey, and my daughters, Hattie, Harper, and Mabel Faire. You all make the sun rise.—*Stuart*

Thanks to my wife, Erin, for endless love and encouragement.—*Aaron*

---

1. http://groups.google.com/group/clojure
2. http://www.pragprog.com/titles/shcloj2/errata

Preface

Clojure is a dynamic programming language for the Java Virtual Machine (JVM), with a compelling combination of features:

- *Clojure is elegant.* Clojure's clean, careful design lets you write programs that get right to the essence of a problem, without a lot of clutter and ceremony.

- *Clojure is Lisp reloaded.* Clojure has the power inherent in Lisp but is not constrained by the history of Lisp.

- *Clojure is a functional language.* Data structures are immutable, and most functions are free from side effects. This makes it easier to write correct programs and to compose large programs from smaller ones.

- *Clojure simplifies concurrent programming.* Many languages build a concurrency model around locking, which is difficult to use correctly. Clojure provides several alternatives to locking: software transactional memory, agents, atoms, and dynamic variables.

- *Clojure embraces Java.* Calling from Clojure to Java is direct and fast, with no translation layer.

- *Unlike many popular dynamic languages, Clojure is fast.* Clojure is written to take advantage of the optimizations possible on modern JVMs.

Many other languages cover *some* of the features described in the previous list. Of all these languages, Clojure stands out. The individual features listed earlier are powerful and interesting. Their clean synergy in Clojure is *compelling.* We will cover all these features and more in Chapter 1, *Getting Started*, on page 1.

Who This Book Is For

Clojure is a powerful, general-purpose programming language. As such, this book is for experienced programmers looking for power and elegance. This book will be useful for anyone with experience in a modern programming language such as C#, Java, Python, or Ruby.

Clojure is built on top of the Java Virtual Machine, and it is *fast*. This book will be of particular interest to Java programmers who want the expressiveness of a dynamic language without compromising on performance.

Clojure is helping to redefine what features belong in a general-purpose language. If you program in Lisp, use a functional language such as Haskell, or write explicitly concurrent programs, you will enjoy Clojure. Clojure combines ideas from Lisp, functional programming, and concurrent programming and makes them more approachable to programmers seeing these ideas for the first time.

Clojure is part of a larger phenomenon. Languages such as Erlang, F#, Haskell, and Scala have garnered attention recently for their support of functional programming or their concurrency model. Enthusiasts of these languages will find much common ground with Clojure.

What Is in This Book

Chapter 1, *Getting Started*, on page 1 demonstrates Clojure's elegance as a general-purpose language, plus the functional style and concurrency model that make Clojure unique. It also walks you through installing Clojure and developing code interactively at the REPL.

Chapter 2, *Exploring Clojure*, on page 21 is a breadth-first overview of all of Clojure's core constructs. After this chapter, you will be able to read most day-to-day Clojure code.

The next two chapters cover functional programming. Chapter 3, *Unifying Data with Sequences*, on page 55 shows how all data can be unified under the powerful sequence metaphor.

Chapter 4, *Functional Programming*, on page 85 shows you how to write functional code in the same style used by the sequence library.

Chapter 5, *State*, on page 113 delves into Clojure's concurrency model. Clojure provides four powerful models for dealing with concurrency, plus all of the goodness of Java's concurrency libraries.

Chapter 6, *Protocols and Datatypes*, on page 143 walks through records, types, and protocols in Clojure. These concepts were introduced in Clojure 1.2.0 and enhanced in 1.3.0.

Chapter 7, *Macros*, on page 165 shows off Lisp's signature feature. Macros take advantage of the fact that Clojure code is data to provide metaprogramming abilities that are difficult or impossible in anything but a Lisp.

Chapter 8, *Multimethods*, on page 187 covers one of Clojure's answers to polymorphism. Polymorphism usually means "take the *class* of the *first* argument and dispatch a method based on that." Clojure's multimethods let you choose *any function* of *all* the arguments and dispatch based on that.

Chapter 9, *Java Down and Dirty*, on page 203 shows you how to call Java from Clojure and call Clojure from Java. You will see how to take Clojure straight to the metal and get Java-level performance.

Finally, Chapter 10, *Building an Application*, on page 227 provides a view into a complete Clojure workflow. You will build an application from scratch, working through solving the various parts to a problem and thinking about simplicity and quality. You will use a set of helpful Clojure libraries to produce and deploy a web application.

Appendix 1, *Editor Support*, on page 253 lists editor support options for Clojure, with links to setup instructions for each.

How to Read This Book

All readers should begin by reading the first two chapters in order. Pay particular attention to Section 1.1, *Why Clojure?*, on page 2, which provides an overview of Clojure's advantages.

Experiment continuously. Clojure provides an interactive environment where you can get immediate feedback; see *Using the REPL*, on page 12 for more information.

After you read the first two chapters, skip around as you like. But read Chapter 3, *Unifying Data with Sequences*, on page 55 before you read Chapter 5, *State*, on page 113. These chapters lead you from Clojure's immutable data structures to a powerful model for writing correct concurrency programs.

As you make the move to longer code examples in the later chapters, make sure you use an editor that provides Clojure indentation for you. Appendix 1, *Editor Support*, on page 253 will point you to common editor options. If you can, try to use an editor that supports parentheses balancing, such as Emacs' paredit mode or the CounterClockWise plug-in for eclipse. This feature will be a huge help as you are learning to program in Clojure.

For Functional Programmers

- Clojure's approach to FP strikes a balance between academic purity and the realities of execution on the current generation of JVMs. Read Chapter 4, *Functional Programming*, on page 85 carefully to understand how Clojure idioms differ from languages such as Haskell.

- The concurrency model of Clojure (Chapter 5, *State*, on page 113) provides several explicit ways to deal with side effects and state and will make FP appealing to a broader audience.

For Java/C# Programmers

- Read Chapter 2, *Exploring Clojure*, on page 21 carefully. Clojure has very little syntax (compared to Java or C#), and we cover the ground rules fairly quickly.

- Pay close attention to macros in Chapter 7, *Macros*, on page 165. These are the most alien part of Clojure when viewed from a Java or C# perspective.

For Lisp Programmers

- Some of Chapter 2, *Exploring Clojure*, on page 21 will be review, but read it anyway. Clojure preserves the key features of Lisp, but it breaks with Lisp tradition in several places, and they are covered here.

- Pay close attention to the lazy sequences in Chapter 4, *Functional Programming*, on page 85.

- Get an Emacs mode for Clojure that makes you happy before working through the code examples in later chapters.

For Perl/Python/Ruby Programmers

- Read Chapter 5, *State*, on page 113 carefully. Intraprocess concurrency is very important in Clojure.

- Embrace macros (Chapter 7, *Macros*, on page 165). But do not expect to easily translate metaprogramming idioms from your language into macros. Remember always that macros execute at read time, not runtime.

Notation Conventions

The following notation conventions are used throughout the book.

Literal code examples use the following font:

```
(+ 2 2)
```

The result of executing a code example is preceded by ->.

```
(+ 2 2)
-> 4
```

Where console output cannot easily be distinguished from code and results, it is preceded by a pipe character (|).

```
(println "hello")
| hello
-> nil
```

When introducing a Clojure form for the first time, we will show the grammar for the form like this:

```
(example-fn required-arg)
(example-fn optional-arg?)
(example-fn zero-or-more-arg*)
(example-fn one-or-more-arg+)
(example-fn & collection-of-variable-args)
```

The grammar is informal, using ?, *, +, and & to document different argument-passing styles, as shown previously.

Clojure code is organized into *libs* (libraries). Where examples in the book depend on a library that is not part of the Clojure core, we document that dependency with a use or require form:

```
(use '[lib-name :only (var-names+)])
(require '[lib-name :as alias])
```

This form of use brings in only the names in var-names, while require creates an alias, making each function's origin clear. For example, a commonly used function is file, from the clojure.java.io library:

```
(use '[clojure.java.io :only (file)])
(file "hello.txt")
-> #<File hello.txt>
```

or the require-based counterpart:

```
(require '[clojure.java.io :as io])
(io/file "hello.txt")
-> #<File hello.txt>
```

Clojure returns nil from a successful call to use. For brevity, this is omitted from the example listings.

While reading the book, you will enter code in an interactive environment called the REPL. The REPL prompt looks like this:

```
user=>
```

The user before the prompt tells the namespace you are currently working in. For most of the book's examples, the current namespace is irrelevant. Where the namespace is irrelevant, we will use the following syntax for interaction with the REPL:

```
(+ 2 2)          ; input line without namespace prompt
-> 4             ; return value
```

In those few instances where the current namespace is important, we will use this:

```
user=> (+ 2 2)  ; input line with namespace prompt-> 4                ; return value
```

Web Resources and Feedback

Programming Clojure's official home on the Web is the *Programming Clojure* home page[1] at the Pragmatic Bookshelf website. From there you can order electronic or paper copies of the book and download sample code. You can also offer feedback by submitting errata entries[2] or posting in the forum[3] for the book.

Downloading Sample Code

The sample code for the book is available from one of two locations:

- The *Programming Clojure* home page[4] links to the official copy of the source code and is updated to match each release of the book.

- The *Programming Clojure* git repository[5] is updated in real time. This is the latest, greatest code and may sometimes be *ahead* of the prose in the book.

Individual examples are in the examples directory, unless otherwise noted.

---

1. http://www.pragprog.com/titles/shcloj2/programming-clojure
2. http://www.pragprog.com/titles/shcloj2/errata
3. http://forums.pragprog.com/forums/207
4. http://www.pragprog.com/titles/shcloj2
5. http://github.com/stuarthalloway/programming-clojure

Throughout the book, listings begin with their filename, set apart from the actual code by a gray background. For example, the following listing comes from src/examples/preface.clj:

```
src/examples/preface.clj
(println "hello")
```

If you are reading the book in PDF form, you can click the little gray box preceding a code listing and download that listing directly.

With the sample code in hand, you are ready to get started. We will begin by meeting the combination of features that make Clojure unique.

CHAPTER 1

Getting Started

Many factors have contributed to Clojure's quick rise. A quick web search will likely tell you that Clojure:

- is a functional language,
- is a Lisp for the JVM, and
- has special features for dealing with concurrency.

All of these things are important, but none of them is the key to thinking in Clojure. In our opinion, there are two key concepts that drive everything else in Clojure: simplicity and power.

Simplicity has several meanings that are relevant in software, but the definition we mean is the original and best one: a thing is simple if it is not compound. Simple components allow systems to do what their designers intend, without also doing other things irrelevant to the task at hand. In our experience, irrelevant complexity quickly becomes dangerous complexity.

Power also has many meanings. The one we care about here is sufficiency to the tasks we want to undertake. To feel powerful as a programmer, you need to build on a substrate that is itself capable and widely deployed, e.g., the JVM. Then, your tools must give you full, unrestricted access to that power. Power is often a gatekeeping requirement for projects that must get the most out of their platform.

As programmers, we have spent years tolerating baroquely complex tools that were the only way to get the power we needed or accepting reduced power for a sanity-enhancing simplification of the programming model. Some trade-offs are truly fundamental, but power vs. simplicity is not one of them. Clojure shows that power and simplicity can go hand in hand.

1.1 Why Clojure?

All of the distinctive features in Clojure are there to provide simplicity, power, or both. Here are a few examples:

- Functional programming is simple, in that it isolates calculation from state and identity. Benefits: functional programs are easier to understand, write, test, optimize, and parallelize.

- Clojure's Java interop forms are powerful, giving you direct access to the semantics of the Java platform. Benefits: you can have performance and semantic equivalence to Java. Most importantly, you will never need to "drop down" to a lower-level language for a little extra power.

- Lisp is simple in two critical ways: it separates reading from evaluation, and the language syntax is made from a tiny number of orthogonal parts. Benefits: syntactic abstraction captures design patterns, and S-expressions are XML, JSON, and SQL as they should have been.

- Lisp is also powerful, providing a compiler and macro system at runtime. Benefits: Lisp has late-bound decision making and easy DSLs.

- Clojure's time model is simple, separating values, identities, state, and time. Benefits: programs can perceive and remember information, without fear that somebody is about to scribble over the past.

- Protocols are simple, separating polymorphism from derivation. Benefits: you get safe, ad hoc extensibility of type and abstractions, without a tangle of design patterns or fragile monkey patching.

This list of features acts as a road map for the rest of the book, so don't worry if you don't follow every little detail here. Each feature gets an entire chapter later.

Let's see some of these features in action by building a small application. Along the way, you will learn how to load and execute the larger examples we will use later in the book.

Clojure Is Elegant

Clojure is high-signal, low-noise. As a result, Clojure programs are short programs. Short programs are cheaper to build, cheaper to deploy, and cheaper to maintain.[1] This is particularly true when the programs are concise

---

1. *Software Estimation: Demystifying the Black Art* [McC06] is a great read and makes the case that smaller is cheaper.

rather than merely terse. As an example, consider the following Java code, from Apache Commons:

data/snippets/isBlank.java
```java
public class StringUtils {
    public static boolean isBlank(String str) {
        int strLen;
        if (str == null || (strLen = str.length()) == 0) {
            return true;
        }
        for (int i = 0; i < strLen; i++) {
            if ((Character.isWhitespace(str.charAt(i)) == false)) {
                return false;
            }
        }
        return true;
    }
}
```

The isBlank() method checks to see whether a string is *blank*: either empty or consisting of only whitespace. Here is a similar implementation in Clojure:

src/examples/introduction.clj
```clojure
(defn blank? [str]
  (every? #(Character/isWhitespace %) str))
```

The Clojure version is shorter. But even more important, it is *simpler*: it has no variables, no mutable state, and no branches. This is possible thanks to *higher-order functions*. A higher-order function is a function that takes functions as arguments and/or returns functions as results. The every? function takes a function and a collection as its arguments and returns true if that function returns true for every item in the collection.

Because the Clojure version has no branches, it is easier to read and test. These benefits are magnified in larger programs. Also, while the code is concise, it is still readable. In fact, the Clojure program reads like a *definition* of blank: a string is blank if every character in it is whitespace. This is much better than the Commons method, which hides the definition of blank behind the implementation detail of loops and if statements.

As another example, consider defining a trivial Person class in Java:

data/snippets/Person.java
```java
public class Person {
    private String firstName;
    private String lastName;

    public Person(String firstName, String lastName) {
        this.firstName = firstName;
```

```
            this.lastName = lastName;
    }

    public String getFirstName() {
        return firstName;
    }

    public void setFirstName(String firstName) {
        this.firstName = firstName;
    }

    public String getLastName() {
        return lastName;
    }

    public void setLastName(String lastName) {
        this.lastName = lastName;
    }
}
```

In Clojure, you would define Person with a single line:

```
(defrecord Person [first-name last-name])
```

and work with the record like so:

```
(def foo (->Person "Aaron" "Bedra"))
-> #'user/foo
foo
-> #:user.Person{:first-name "Aaron", :last-name "Bedra"}
```

defrecord and related functions are covered in Section 6.3, *Protocols*, on page 147.

Other than being an order of magnitude shorter, the Clojure approach differs in that a Clojure Person is *immutable*. Immutable data structures are naturally thread safe, and update capabilities can be layered when using Clojure's references, agents, and atoms, which are covered in Chapter 5, *State*, on page 113. Because records are immutable, Clojure also provides correct implementations of hashCode() and equals() automatically.

Clojure has a lot of elegance baked in, but if you find something missing, you can add it yourself, thanks to the power of Lisp.

Clojure Is Lisp Reloaded

Clojure is a Lisp. For decades, Lisp advocates have pointed out the advantages that Lisp has over, well, everything else. At the same time, Lisp's world domination plan seems to be proceeding slowly.

Like any other Lisp, Clojure faces two challenges:

- Clojure must succeed as a Lisp by persuading Lisp programmers that Clojure embraces the critical parts of Lisp.

- At the same time, Clojure needs to succeed *where past Lisps have failed* by winning support from the broader community of programmers.

Clojure meets these challenges by providing the metaprogramming capabilities of Lisp and at the same time embracing a set of syntax enhancements that make Clojure friendlier to non-Lisp programmers.

Why Lisp?

Lisps have a tiny language core, almost no syntax, and a powerful macro facility. With these features, you can bend Lisp to meet your design, instead of the other way around. By contrast, consider the following snippet of Java code:

```
public class Person {
  private String firstName;
  public String getFirstName() {
  // continues
```

In this code, getFirstName() is a method. Methods are polymorphic and can bend to meet your needs. But the interpretation of *every other word* in the example is *fixed by the language*. Sometimes you really need to change what these words mean. So, for example, you might do the following:

- Redefine private to mean "private for production code but public for serialization and unit tests."

- Redefine class to automatically generate getters and setters for private fields, unless otherwise directed.

- Create a subclass of class that provides callback hooks for life-cycle events. For example, a life cycle–aware class could fire an event whenever an instance of the class is created.

We have seen programs that needed all these features. Without them, programmers resort to repetitive, error-prone workarounds. Literally *millions* of lines of code have been written to work around missing features in programming languages.

In most languages, you would have to petition the language implementer to add the kinds of features mentioned earlier. In Clojure, you can add your own language features with *macros* (Chapter 7, *Macros*, on page 165). Clojure itself is built out of macros such as defrecord:

```
(defrecord name [arg1 arg2 arg3])
```

If you need different semantics, write your own macro. If you want a variant of records with strong typing and configurable null-checking for all fields, you can create your own defrecord macro, to be used like this:

```
(defrecord name [Type :arg1 Type :arg2 Type :arg3]
  :allow-nulls false)
```

This ability to reprogram the language from within the language is the unique advantage of Lisp. You will see facets of this idea described in various ways:

- Lisp is homoiconic.[2] That is, Lisp code is just Lisp data. This makes it easy for programs to write other programs.

- The whole language is there, all the time. Paul Graham's essay "Revenge of the Nerds"[3] explains why this is so powerful.

Lisp syntax also eliminates rules for operator precedence and associativity. You will not find a table documenting operator precedence or associativity anywhere in this book. With fully parenthesized expressions, there is no possible ambiguity.

The downside of Lisp's simple, regular syntax, at least for beginners, is Lisp's fixation on parentheses and on lists as the core datatype. Clojure offers an interesting combination of features that makes Lisp more approachable for non-Lispers.

Lisp, with Fewer Parentheses

Clojure offers significant advantages for programmers coming to it from other Lisps:

- Clojure generalizes Lisp's physical list into an abstraction called a *sequence*. This preserves the power of lists, while extending that power to a variety of other data structures.

- Clojure's reliance on the JVM provides a standard library and a deployment platform with great reach.

- Clojure's approach to symbol resolution and syntax quoting makes it easier to write many common macros.

---

2.   http://en.wikipedia.org/wiki/Homoiconicity
3.   http://www.paulgraham.com/icad.html

Many Clojure programmers will be new to Lisp, and they have probably heard bad things about all those parentheses. Clojure keeps the parentheses (and the power of Lisp!) but improves on traditional Lisp syntax in several ways:

- Clojure provides a convenient literal syntax for a wide variety of data structures besides just lists: regular expressions, maps, sets, vectors, and metadata. These features make Clojure code less "listy" than most Lisps. For example, function parameters are specified in a vector: [] instead of a list: ().

```
src/examples/introduction.clj
(defn hello-world [username]
  (println (format "Hello, %s" username)))
```

The vector makes the argument list jump out visually and makes Clojure function definitions easy to read.

- In Clojure, unlike most Lisps, commas are whitespace.

```
; make vectors look like arrays in other languages
[1, 2, 3, 4]
-> [1 2 3 4]
```

- Idiomatic Clojure does not nest parentheses more than necessary. Consider the cond macro, present in both Common Lisp and Clojure. cond evaluates a set of test/result pairs, returning the first result for which a test form yields true. Each test/result pair is grouped with parentheses, like so:

```
; Common Lisp cond
(cond ((= x 10) "equal")
((> x 10) "more"))
```

Clojure avoids the extra parentheses:

```
; Clojure cond
(cond (= x 10) "equal"
(> x 10) "more")
```

This is an aesthetic decision, and both approaches have their supporters. The important thing is that Clojure takes the opportunity to be less Lispy when it can do so without compromising Lisp's power.

Clojure is an excellent Lisp, both for Lisp experts and for Lisp beginners.

Clojure Is a Functional Language

Clojure is a functional language but not a pure functional language like Haskell. Functional languages have the following properties:

- Functions are *first-class objects*. That is, functions can be created at runtime, passed around, returned, and in general used like any other datatype.

- Data is immutable.

- Functions are *pure*; that is, they have no side effects.

For many tasks, functional programs are easier to understand, less error-prone, and *much* easier to reuse. For example, the following short program searches a database of compositions for every composer who has written a composition named "Requiem":

```
(for [c compositions :when (= "Requiem" (:name c))] (:composer c))
-> ("W. A. Mozart" "Giuseppe Verdi")
```

The name for does not introduce a loop but a *list comprehension*. Read the earlier code as "For each c in compositions, where the name of c is "Requiem", yield the composer of c." List comprehension is covered more fully in *Transforming Sequences*, on page 66.

This example has four desirable properties:

- It is *simple*; it has no loops, variables, or mutable state.

- It is *thread safe*; no locking is needed.

- It is *parallelizable*; you could farm out individual steps to multiple threads without changing the code for each step.

- It is *generic*; compositions could be a plain set or XML or a database result set.

Contrast functional programs with *imperative* programs, where explicit statements alter program state. Most object-oriented programs are written in an imperative style and have *none* of the advantages listed earlier; they are unnecessarily complex, not thread safe, not parallelizable, and difficult to generalize. (For a head-to-head comparison of functional and imperative styles, skip forward to Section 2.7, *Where's My for Loop?*, on page 48.)

People have known about the advantages of functional languages for a while now. And yet, pure functional languages like Haskell have not taken over the world, because developers find that not everything fits easily into the pure functional view.

There are four reasons that Clojure can attract more interest now than functional languages have in the past:

- Functional programming is more urgent today than ever before. Massively multicore hardware is right around the corner, and functional languages provide a clear approach for taking advantage of it. Functional programming is covered in Chapter 4, *Functional Programming*, on page 85.

- Purely functional languages can make it awkward to model state that really needs to change. Clojure provides a structured mechanism for working with changeable state via software transactional memory and refs (on page 115), agents (on page 123), atoms (on page 122), and dynamic binding (on page 127).

- Many functional languages are statically typed. Clojure's dynamic typing makes it more accessible for programmers learning functional programming.

- Clojure's Java invocation approach is *not* functional. When you call Java, you enter the familiar, mutable world. This offers a comfortable haven for beginners learning functional programming and a pragmatic alternative to functional style when you need it. Java invocation is covered in Chapter 9, *Java Down and Dirty*, on page 203.

Clojure's approach to changing state enables concurrency without explicit locking and complements Clojure's functional core.

Clojure Simplifies Concurrent Programming

Clojure's support for functional programming makes it easy to write thread-safe code. Since immutable data structures cannot *ever* change, there is no danger of data corruption based on another thread's activity.

However, Clojure's support for concurrency goes beyond just functional programming. When you need references to mutable data, Clojure protects them via software transactional memory (STM). STM is a higher-level approach to thread safety than the locking mechanisms that Java provides. Rather than creating fragile, error-prone locking strategies, you can protect shared state with transactions. This is much more productive, because many programmers have a good understanding of transactions based on experience with databases.

For example, the following code creates a working, thread-safe, in-memory database of accounts:

```
(def accounts (ref #{}))
(defrecord Account [id balance])
```

The ref function creates a transactionally protected reference to the current state of the database. Updating is trivial. The following code adds a new account to the database:

```
(dosync
  (alter accounts conj (->Account "CLJ" 1000.00)))
```

The dosync causes the update to accounts to execute inside a transaction. This guarantees thread safety, and it is easier to use than locking. With transactions, you never have to worry about which objects to lock or in what order. The transactional approach will also perform better under some common usage scenarios, because (for example) readers will never block.

Although the example here is trivial, the technique is general, and it works on real-world problems. See Chapter 5, *State*, on page 113 for more on concurrency and STM in Clojure.

Clojure Embraces the Java Virtual Machine

Clojure gives you clean, simple, direct access to Java. You can call any Java API directly:

```
(System/getProperties)
-> {java.runtime.name=Java(TM) SE Runtime Environment
... many more ...
```

Clojure adds a lot of syntactic sugar for calling Java. We won't get into the details here (see Section 2.5, *Calling Java*, on page 43), but notice that in the following code the Clojure version has both fewer dots *and fewer parentheses* than the Java version:

```
// Java
"hello".getClass().getProtectionDomain()

; Clojure
(.. "hello" getClass getProtectionDomain)
```

Clojure provides simple functions for implementing Java interfaces and sub-classing Java classes. Also, Clojure functions all implement Callable and Runnable. This makes it trivial to pass the following anonymous function to the constructor for a Java Thread.

```
(.start (new Thread (fn [] (println "Hello" (Thread/currentThread)))))
-> Hello #<Thread Thread[Thread-0,5,main]>
```

The funny output here is Clojure's way of printing a Java instance. Thread is the class name of the instance, and Thread[Thread-0,5,main] is the instance's toString representation.

(Note that in the preceding example the new thread will run to completion, but its output may interleave in some strange way with the REPL prompt. This is not a problem with Clojure but simply the result of having more than one thread writing to an output stream.)

Because the Java invocation syntax in Clojure is clean and simple, it is idiomatic to use Java directly, rather than to hide Java behind Lispy wrappers.

Now that you have seen a few of the reasons to use Clojure, it is time to start writing some code.

1.2 Clojure Coding Quick Start

To run Clojure and the code in this book, you need two things:

- *A Java runtime.* Download[4] and install Java version 5 or greater. Java version 6 has significant performance improvements and better exception reporting, so prefer this if possible.
- *Leiningen.*[5] Leiningen is a tool for managing dependencies and launching tasks against your code. It is also the most common tool for this job in the Clojure space.

You will use Leiningen to install Clojure and all of the dependencies for the sample code in this book. If you already have Leiningen installed, you should be familiar with the basics. If not, you should take a quick tour of Leiningen's GitHub page,[6] where you will find install instructions as well as basic usage instructions. Don't worry about learning everything now, though, because this book will guide you through the commands necessary to follow along at home.

While you are working through the book, use the version of Clojure tied to the book's sample code. After you read the book, you can follow the instructions in *Building Clojure Yourself*, on page 12 to build an up-to-the-minute version of Clojure.

See Section 6, *Downloading Sample Code*, on page xxii for instructions on downloading the sample code. Once you have downloaded the sample code, you will need to use Leiningen to fetch the dependencies. From the root of the example code folder, run this:

```
lein deps
```

---

4. http://www.oracle.com/technetwork/java/javase/downloads/index.html
5. http://github.com/technomancy/leiningen
6. http://github.com/technomancy/leiningen

Building Clojure Yourself

You may want to build Clojure from source to get access to newer features and bug fixes. Here's how:

```
git clone git://github.com/clojure/clojure.git
cd clojure
mvn package
```

The sample code is regularly updated to match the current development head of Clojure. Check the README file in the sample code to see the revision numbers that the samples were most recently tested with.

The dependencies will be downloaded and placed in the proper location. You can test your install by navigating to the directory where you placed the sample code and running a Clojure *read-eval-print loop* (REPL). Leiningen contains a REPL launch script that loads Clojure along with the dependencies that we will need later in the book.

```
lein repl
```

When you successfully launch the REPL, it should prompt you with user=>:

```
Clojure
user=>
```

Now you are ready for "Hello World."

Using the REPL

To see how to use the REPL, let's create a few variants of "Hello World." First, type (println "hello world") at the REPL prompt:

```
user=> (println "hello world")
-> hello world
```

The second line, hello world, is the console output you requested.

Next, encapsulate your "Hello World" into a function that can address a person by name:

```
(defn hello [name] (str "Hello, " name))
-> #'user/hello
```

Let's break this down:

- defn defines a function.

- hello is the function name.

- hello takes one argument, name.

- str is a function call that concatenates an arbitrary list of arguments into a string.

- defn, hello, name, and str are all *symbols*, which are names that refer to things. Legal symbols are defined in *Symbols*, on page 25.

Look at the return value, #'user/hello. The prefix #' indicates that the function was stored in a Clojure *var*, and user is the *namespace* of the function. (The user namespace is the REPL default, like the default package in Java.) You do not need to worry about vars and namespaces yet; they are covered in Section 2.4, *Vars, Bindings, and Namespaces*, on page 36.

Now you can call hello, passing in your name:

```
user=> (hello "Stu")
-> "Hello, Stu"
```

If you get your REPL into a state that confuses you, the simplest fix is to kill the REPL with CTRL+C on Windows or CTRL+D on *nix and then start another one.

Special Variables

The REPL includes several useful special variables. When you are working in the REPL, the results of evaluating the three most recent expressions are stored in the special variables *1, *2, and *3, respectively. This makes it easy to work iteratively. Say hello to a few different names:

```
user=> (hello "Stu")
-> "Hello, Stu"
```

```
user=> (hello "Clojure")
-> "Hello, Clojure"
```

Now, you can use the special variables to combine the results of your recent work:

```
(str *1 " and " *2)
-> "Hello, Clojure and Hello, Stu"
```

If you make a mistake in the REPL, you will see a Java exception. The details are often omitted for brevity. For example, dividing by zero is a no-no:

```
user=> (/ 1 0)
-> ArithmeticException Divide by zero  clojure.lang.Numbers.divide
```

Here the problem is obvious, but sometimes the problem is more subtle and you want the detailed stack trace. The *e special variable holds the last exception. Because Clojure exceptions are Java exceptions, you can ask for the stacktrace by calling pst (print stacktrace).[7]

```
user=> (pst)
-> ArithmeticException Divide by zero
|   clojure.lang.Numbers.divide
|   sun.reflect.NativeMethodAccessorImpl.invoke0
|   sun.reflect.NativeMethodAccessorImpl.invoke
|   sun.reflect.DelegatingMethodAccessorImpl.invoke
|   java.lang.reflect.Method.invoke
|   clojure.lang.Reflector.invokeMatchingMethod
|   clojure.lang.Reflector.invokeStaticMethod
|   user/eval1677
|   clojure.lang.Compiler.eval
|   clojure.lang.Compiler.eval
|   clojure.core/eval
```

Java interop is covered in Chapter 9, *Java Down and Dirty*, on page 203.

If you have a block of code that is too large to conveniently type at the REPL, save the code into a file, and then load that file from the REPL. You can use an absolute path or a path relative to where you launched the REPL:

```
; save some work in temp.clj, and then ...
user=> (load-file "temp.clj")
```

The REPL is a terrific environment for trying ideas and getting immediate feedback. For best results, keep a REPL open at all times while reading this book.

Adding Shared State

The hello function of the previous section is *pure*; that is, it has no side effects. Pure functions are easy to develop, test, and understand, and you should prefer them for many tasks.

That said, most programs have some shared state and will use impure functions to manage that shared state. Let's extend hello to keep track of past visitors. First, you will need a data structure to track the visitors. A set will do the trick:

```
#{}
-> #{}
```

The #{} is a literal for an empty set. Next, you will need conj:

```
(conj coll item)
```

---

7.   pst is available only in Clojure 1.3.0 and greater.

conj is short for conjoin, and it builds a new collection with an item added. conj an element onto a set to see that a new set is created:

```
(conj #{} "Stu")
-> #{"Stu"}
```

Now that you can build new sets, you need some way to keep track of the *current* set of visitors. Clojure provides several *reference types* (refs) for this purpose. The most basic reference type is the atom:

```
(atom initial-state)
```

To name your atom, you can use def:

```
(def symbol initial-value?)
```

def is like defn but more general. A def can define functions *or* data. Use atom to create an atom, and use def to bind the atom to the name visitors:

```
(def visitors (atom #{}))
-> #'user/visitors
```

To update a reference, you must use a function such as swap!:

```
(swap! r update-fn & args)
```

swap! applies an update-fn to reference r, with optional args if necessary. Try to swap! a visitor into visitors, using conj as the update function:

```
(swap! visitors conj "Stu")
-> #{"Stu"}
```

atom is one of several reference types in Clojure. Choosing the appropriate reference type requires care (discussed in Chapter 5, *State*, on page 113).

At any time, you can peek inside the ref with deref or with the shorter @:

```
(deref visitors)
-> #{"Stu"}

@visitors
-> #{"Stu"}
```

Now you are ready to build the new, more elaborate version of hello:

src/examples/introduction.clj
```
(defn hello
  "Writes hello message to *out*. Calls you by username.
  Knows if you have been here before."
  [username]
  (swap! visitors conj username)
  (str "Hello, " username))
```

Next, check that visitors are correctly tracked in memory:

```
(hello "Rich")
-> "Hello, Rich"

@visitors
-> #{"Aaron" "Stu" "Rich"}
```

In all probability, your visitors list is different from the one shown here. That's the problem with state! Your results will vary, depending on when things happened. You can reason about a function with direct local knowledge. Reasoning about state requires a full understanding of history.

Avoid state where possible. But when you need it, make it sane and manageable by using refs such as atoms. Atoms (and all other Clojure reference types) are safe for multiple threads and processors. Better yet, this safety comes without any need for locks, which are notoriously tricky to use.

At this point, you should feel comfortable entering small bits of code at the REPL. Larger units of code aren't that different; you can load and run Clojure libraries from the REPL as well. Let's explore that next.

1.3 Exploring Clojure Libraries

Clojure code is packaged in *libraries*. Each Clojure library belongs to a *namespace*, which is analogous to a Java package. You can load a Clojure library with require:

```
(require quoted-namespace-symbol)
```

When you require a library named clojure.java.io, Clojure looks for a file named clojure/java/io.clj on the CLASSPATH. Try it:

```
user=> (require 'clojure.java.io)
-> nil
```

The leading single quote (') is required, and it *quotes* the library name (quoting is covered in Section 2.2, *Reader Macros*, on page 30). The nil returned indicates success. While you are at it, test that you can load the sample code for this chapter, examples.introduction:

```
user=> (require 'examples.introduction)
-> nil
```

The examples.introduction library includes an implementation of the Fibonacci numbers, which is the traditional "Hello World" program for functional languages. We will explore the Fibonacci numbers in more detail in Section 4.2,

How to Be Lazy, on page 90. For now, just make sure that you can execute the sample function fibs. Enter the following line of code at the REPL to take the first ten Fibonacci numbers:

```
(take 10 examples.introduction/fibs)
-> (0 1 1 2 3 5 8 13 21 34)
```

If you see the first ten Fibonacci numbers as listed here, you have successfully installed the book samples.

The book samples are all unit tested, with tests located in the examples/test directory. The tests for the samples themselves are not explicitly covered in the book, but you may find them useful for reference. You can run the unit tests yourself with lein test.

Require and Use

When you require a Clojure library, you must refer to items in the library with a namespace-qualified name. Instead of fibs, you must say examples.introduction/fibs. Make sure to launch a new REPL,[8] and then try it:

```
(require 'examples.introduction)
-> nil

(take 10 examples.introduction/fibs)
-> (0 1 1 2 3 5 8 13 21 34)
```

Fully qualified names get old quickly. You can refer a namespace, creating mappings for all its names in your current namespace:

```
(refer quoted-namespace-symbol)
```

Call refer on examples.introduction, and verify that you can then call fibs directly:

```
(refer 'examples.introduction)
-> nil

(take 10 fibs)
-> (0 1 1 2 3 5 8 13 21 34)
```

For convenience, the use function will require and refer a library in a single step:

```
(use quoted-namespace-symbol)
```

From a new REPL you should be able to do the following:

---

8. Creating a new REPL will prevent name collisions between your previous work and the sample code functions of the same name. This is not a problem in real-world development, as you will see in *Namespaces*, on page 40.

```
(use 'examples.introduction)
-> nil

(take 10 fibs)
-> (0 1 1 2 3 5 8 13 21 34)
```

As you are working through the book samples, you can call require or use with a :reload flag to force a library to reload:

```
(use :reload 'examples.introduction)
-> nil
```

The :reload flag is useful if you are making changes and want to see results without restarting the REPL.

Finding Documentation

Often you can find the documentation you need right at the REPL. The most basic helper function[9] is doc:

`(doc name)`

Use doc to print the documentation for str:

```
user=> (doc str)
-------------------------
clojure.core/str
([] [x] [x & ys])
With no args, returns the empty string. With one arg x, returns
x.toString().  (str nil) returns the empty string. With more than
one arg, returns the concatenation of the str values of the args.
```

The first line of doc's output contains the fully qualified name of the function. The next line contains the possible argument lists, generated directly from the code. (Some common argument names and their uses are explained in *Conventions for Parameter Names*, on page 19.) Finally, the remaining lines contain the function's *doc string*, if the function definition included one.

You can add a doc string to your own functions by placing it immediately after the function name:

src/examples/introduction.clj
```
(defn hello
  "Writes hello message to *out*. Calls you by username"
  [username]
  (println (str "Hello, " username)))
```

---

9. doc is actually a Clojure macro.

Conventions for Parameter Names

The documentation strings for reduce and areduce show several terse parameter names. Here are some parameter names and how they are normally used:

Parameter	Usage
a	A Java array
agt	An agent
coll	A collection
expr	An expression
f	A function
idx	Index
r	A ref
v	A vector
val	A value

These names may seem a little terse, but there is a good reason for them: the "good names" are often taken by Clojure functions! Naming a parameter that collides with a function name is legal but considered bad style: the parameter will shadow the function, which will be unavailable while the parameter is in scope. So, don't call your refs ref, your agents agent, or your counts count. Those names refer to functions.

Sometimes you will not know the exact name you want documentation for. The find-doc function will search for anything whose doc output matches a regular expression or string you pass in:

```
(find-doc s)
```

Use find-doc to explore how Clojure does reduce:

```
user=> (find-doc "reduce")
-------------------------
clojure/areduce
([a idx ret init expr])
Macro
... details elided ...
-------------------------
clojure/reduce
([f coll] [f val coll])
... details elided ...
```

reduce reduces Clojure collections and is covered in *Transforming Sequences*, on page 66. areduce is for interoperation with Java arrays and is covered in *Using Java Collections*, on page 216.

Much of Clojure is written in Clojure, and it is instructive to read the source code. You can view the source of a Clojure function using the repl library.

```
(clojure.repl/source a-symbol)
```

Try viewing the source of the simple identity function:

```
(use 'clojure.repl)
(source identity)

-> (defn identity
     "Returns its argument."
     {:added "1.0"
      :static true}
     [x] x)
```

Of course, you can also use Java's Reflection API. You can use methods such as class, ancestors, and instance? to reflect against the underlying Java object model and tell, for example, that Clojure's collections are also Java collections:

```
(ancestors (class [1 2 3]))

-> #{clojure.lang.ILookup clojure.lang.Sequential
     java.lang.Object clojure.lang.Indexed
     java.lang.Iterable clojure.lang.IObj
     clojure.lang.IPersistentCollection
     clojure.lang.IPersistentVector clojure.lang.AFn
     java.lang.Comparable java.util.RandomAccess
     clojure.lang.Associative
     clojure.lang.APersistentVector clojure.lang.Counted
     clojure.lang.Reversible clojure.lang.IPersistentStack
     java.util.List clojure.lang.IEditableCollection
     clojure.lang.IFn clojure.lang.Seqable
     java.util.Collection java.util.concurrent.Callable
     clojure.lang.IMeta java.io.Serializable java.lang.Runnable}
```

Clojure's complete API is documented online at http://clojure.github.com/clojure. The right sidebar links to all functions and macros by name, and the left sidebar links to a set of overview articles on various Clojure features.

1.4 Wrapping Up

You have just gotten the whirlwind tour of Clojure. You have seen Clojure's expressive syntax, learned about Clojure's approach to Lisp, and seen how easy it is to call Java code from Clojure.

You have Clojure running in your own environment, and you have written short programs at the REPL to demonstrate functional programming and the reference model for dealing with state. Now it is time to explore the entire language.

CHAPTER 2

Exploring Clojure

Clojure offers great power through functional style, concurrency support, and clean Java interop. But before you can appreciate all these features, you have to start with the language basics. In this chapter, you will take a quick tour of the Clojure language, including the following:

- Forms
- Reader macros
- Functions
- Bindings and namespaces
- Flow control
- Metadata

If your background is primarily in imperative languages, this tour may seem to be missing key language constructs, such as variables and for loops. Section 2.7, *Where's My for Loop?*, on page 48 will show you how you can *live better* without for loops and variables.

Clojure is very expressive, and this chapter covers many concepts quite quickly. Don't worry if you don't understand every detail; we will revisit these topics in more detail in later chapters. If possible, bring up a REPL, and follow along with the examples as you read.

2.1 Forms

Clojure is *homoiconic*,[1] which is to say that Clojure code is composed of Clojure data. When you run a Clojure program, a part of Clojure called the *reader* reads the text of the program in chunks called *forms* and translates them

---

1. http://en.wikipedia.org/wiki/Homoiconicity

into Clojure data structures. Clojure then compiles and executes the data structures.

The Clojure forms covered in this book are summarized in Table 1, *Clojure forms*, on page 23. To see forms in action, let's start with some simple forms supporting numeric types.

Using Numeric Types

Numeric literals are forms. Numbers simply evaluate to themselves. If you enter a number, the REPL will give it back to you:

```
42
-> 42
```

A vector of numbers is another kind of form. Create a vector of the numbers 1, 2, and 3:

```
[1 2 3]
-> [1 2 3]
```

A list is also a kind of form. A list is "just data," but it is also used to call functions. Create a list whose first item names a Clojure function, like the symbol +:

```
(+ 1 2)
-> 3
```

As you can see, Clojure evaluates the list as a function call. The style of placing the function first is called *prefix notation*,[2] as opposed to the more familiar *infix notation* $1 + 2 = 3$. Of course, prefix notation is perfectly familiar for functions whose names are words. For example, most programmers would correctly expect concat to come first in this expression:

```
(concat [1 2] [3 4])
-> (1 2 3 4)
```

Clojure is simply being consistent in treating mathematical operators like all other functions and placing them first.

A practical advantage of prefix notation is that you can easily extend it for arbitrary numbers of arguments:

```
(+ 1 2 3)
-> 6
```

---

2. More specifically, it's called Cambridge Polish notation.

Form	Example(s)	Primary Coverage
Boolean	true, false	*Booleans and nil*, on page 27
Character	\a	*Strings and Characters*, on page 25
Keyword	:tag, :doc	*Maps, Keywords, and Records*, on page 28
List	(1 2 3), (println "foo")	Chapter 3, *Unifying Data with Sequences*, on page 55
Map	{:name "Bill", :age 42}	*Maps, Keywords, and Records*, on page 28
Nil	nil	*Booleans and nil*, on page 27
Number	1, 4.2	*Using Numeric Types*, on page 22
Set	#{:snap :crackle :pop}	Chapter 3, *Unifying Data with Sequences*, on page 55
String	"hello"	*Strings and Characters*, on page 25
Symbol	user/foo, java.lang.String	*Symbols*, on page 25
Vector	[1 2 3]	Chapter 3, *Unifying Data with Sequences*, on page 55

Table 1—Clojure forms

Even the degenerate case of no arguments works as you would expect, returning zero. This helps to eliminate fragile, special-case logic for boundary conditions:

```
(+)
-> 0
```

Many mathematical and comparison operators have the names and semantics that you would expect from other programming languages. Addition, subtraction, multiplication, comparison, and equality all work as you would expect:

```
(- 10 5)
-> 5

(* 3 10 10)
-> 300

(> 5 2)
-> true

(>= 5 5)
-> true
```

```
(< 5 2)
-> false
```

```
(= 5 2)
-> false
```

Division may surprise you:

```
(/ 22 7)
-> 22/7
```

As you can see, Clojure has a built-in Ratio type:

```
(class (/ 22 7))
-> clojure.lang.Ratio
```

If what you actually want is decimal division, use a floating-point literal for the dividend:

```
(/ 22.0 7)
-> 3.142857142857143
```

If you want to stick to integers, you can get the integer quotient and remainder with quot and rem:

```
(quot 22 7)
-> 3
```

```
(rem 22 7)
-> 1
```

If you need to do arbitrary-precision floating-point math, append M to a number to create a BigDecimal literal:

```
(+ 1 (/ 0.00001 1000000000000000000))
-> 1.0
```

```
(+ 1 (/ 0.00001M 1000000000000000000))
-> 1.0000000000000000000000001M
```

For arbitrary precision integers, you can append N to create a BigInt literal:

```
(* 1000N 1000 1000 1000 1000 1000 1000)
-> 1000000000000000000000N
```

Notice that only one BigInt literal is needed and is contagious to the entire calculation.

Symbols

Forms such as +, concat, and java.lang.String are called *symbols* and are used to name things. For example, + names the function that adds things together. Symbols name all sorts of things in Clojure:

- Functions like str and concat
- "Operators" like + and -, which are, after all, just functions
- Java classes like java.lang.String and java.util.Random
- Namespaces like clojure.core and Java packages like java.lang
- Data structures and references

Symbols cannot start with a number but can consist of alphanumeric characters, plus +, -, *, /, !, ?, ., and _. The list of legal symbol characters is a minimum set that Clojure promises to support. You should stick to these characters in your own code, but do not assume the list is exhaustive. Clojure can use other, undocumented characters in symbols that it employs internally and may add more legal symbol characters in the future. See Clojure's online documentation[3] for updates to the list of legal symbol characters.

Clojure treats / and . specially in order to support namespaces; see *Namespaces*, on page 40 for details.

Strings and Characters

Strings are another kind of reader form. Clojure strings are Java strings. They are delimited by double quotes, and they can span multiple lines:

```
"This is a\nmultiline string"
-> "This is a\nmultiline string"

"This is also
a multiline string"
-> "This is also\na multiline string"
```

As you can see, the REPL always shows string literals with escaped newlines. If you actually print a multiline string, it will print on multiple lines:

```
(println "another\nmultiline\nstring")
| another
| multiline
| string
-> nil
```

Clojure does not wrap most of Java's string functions. Instead, you can call them directly using Clojure's Java interop forms:

---

3. http://clojure.org/reader

```
(.toUpperCase "hello")
-> "HELLO"
```

The dot before toUpperCase tells Clojure to treat it as the name of a Java method instead of a Clojure function.

One string function that Clojure *does* wrap is toString. You do not need to call toString directly. Instead of calling toString, use Clojure's str function:

(str & args**)**

str differs from toString in two ways. It smashes together multiple arguments, and it skips nil without error:

```
(str 1 2 nil 3)
-> "123"
```

Clojure characters are Java characters. Their literal syntax is \{letter}, where letter can be a letter or the name of a character: backspace, formfeed, newline, return, space, or tab:

```
(str \h \e \y \space \y \o \u)
-> "hey you"
```

As is the case with strings, Clojure does not wrap Java's character functions. Instead, you can use a Java interop form such as Character/toUpperCase:

```
(Character/toUpperCase \s)
-> \S
```

The Java interop forms are covered in Section 2.5, *Calling Java*, on page 43. For more on Java's Character class, see the API documentation at http://tinyurl.com/java-character.

Strings are sequences of characters. When you call Clojure sequence functions on a string, you get a sequence of characters back. Imagine that you wanted to conceal a secret message by interleaving it with a second, innocuous message. You could use interleave to combine the two messages:

```
(interleave "Attack at midnight" "The purple elephant chortled")
-> (\A \T \t \h \t \e \a \space \c \p \k \u \space \r
\a \p \t \l \space \e \m \space \i \e \d \l \n \e
\i \p \g \h \h \a \t \n)
```

That works, but you probably want the resulting sequence as a string for transmission. It is tempting to use str to pack the characters back into a string, but that doesn't quite work:

```
(str (interleave "Attack at midnight" "The purple elephant chortled"))
-> "clojure.lang.LazySeq@d4ea9f36"
```

The problem is that str works with a variable number of arguments, and you are passing it a *single* argument that contains the argument list. The solution is apply:

```
(apply f args* argseq)
```

apply takes a function f, some optional args, and a sequence of args called argseq. It then calls f, unrolling args and argseq into an argument list. Use (apply str ...) to build a string from a sequence of characters:

```
(apply str (interleave "Attack at midnight" "The purple elephant chortled"))
-> "ATthtea cpku raptl em iedlneipghhatn"
```

You can use (apply str ...) again to reveal the message:

```
(apply str (take-nth 2 "ATthtea cpku raptl em iedlneipghhatn"))
-> "Attack at midnight"
```

The call to (take-nth 2 ...) takes every second element of the sequence, extracting the obfuscated message.

Booleans and nil

Clojure's rules for booleans are easy to understand:

- true is true, and false is false.

- In addition to false, nil also evaluates to false when used in a boolean context.

- Other than false and nil, *everything else* evaluates to true in a boolean context.

Lisp programmers be warned: the empty list is not false in Clojure:

```
;           (if part)                (else part)
(if () "We are in Clojure!" "We are in Common Lisp!")
-> "We are in Clojure!"
```

C programmers be warned: zero is not false in Clojure, either:

```
;           (if part)      (else part)
(if 0 "Zero is true" "Zero is false")
-> "Zero is true"
```

A *predicate* is a function that returns either true or false. In Clojure, it is idiomatic to name predicates with a trailing question mark, for example true?, false?, nil?, and zero?:

```
(true? expr)
```

```
(false? expr)
```

```
(nil? expr)
```

```
(zero? expr)
```

true? tests whether a value is actually true, *not* whether the value evaluates to true in a boolean context. The only thing that is true? is true itself:

```
(true? true)
-> true

(true? "foo")
-> false
```

nil? and false? work the same way. Only nil is nil?, and only false is false?.

zero? works with any numeric type, returning true if it is zero:

```
(zero? 0.0)
-> true

(zero? (/ 22 7))
-> false
```

There are many more predicates in Clojure. To review them, enter (find-doc #"\?$") at the REPL.

Maps, Keywords, and Records

A Clojure *map* is a collection of key/value pairs. Maps have a literal form surrounded by curly braces. You can use a map literal to create a lookup table for the inventors of programming languages:

```
(def inventors {"Lisp" "McCarthy" "Clojure" "Hickey"})
-> #'user/inventors
```

The value "McCarthy" is associated with the key "Lisp", and the value "Hickey" is associated with the key "Clojure".

If you find it easier to read, then you can use commas to delimit each key/value pair. Clojure doesn't care. It treats commas as whitespace:

```
(def inventors {"Lisp" "McCarthy", "Clojure" "Hickey"})
-> #'user/inventors
```

Maps are functions. If you pass a key to a map, it will return that key's value, or it will return nil if the key is not found:

```
(inventors "Lisp")
-> "McCarthy"

(inventors "Foo")
-> nil
```

You can also use the more verbose get function:

```
(get the-map key not-found-val?)
```

get allows you to specify a different return value for missing keys:

```
(get inventors "Lisp" "I dunno!")
-> "McCarthy"

(get inventors "Foo"  "I dunno!")
-> "I dunno!"
```

Because Clojure data structures are immutable and implement hashCode correctly, *any Clojure data structure can be a key in a map*. That said, a very common key type is the Clojure keyword.

A *keyword* is like a symbol, except that keywords begin with a colon (:). Keywords resolve to themselves:

```
:foo
-> :foo
```

This is different from symbols, which want to refer *to* something:

```
foo
-> CompilerException java.lang.RuntimeException:
   Unable to resolve symbol: foo in this context
```

The fact that keywords resolve to themselves makes keywords useful as keys. You could redefine the inventors map using keywords as keys:

```
(def inventors {:Lisp "McCarthy" :Clojure "Hickey"})
-> #'user/inventors
```

Keywords are also functions. They take a map argument and look themselves up in the map. Having switched to keyword keys for the inventors, you can look up an inventor by calling the map or by calling a key:

```
(inventors :Clojure)
-> "Hickey"

(:Clojure inventors)
-> "Hickey"
```

This flexibility in ordering comes in handy when calling higher-order functions, such as the reference and agent APIs in Chapter 5, *State*, on page 113.

If several maps have keys in common, you can document (and enforce) this fact by creating a record with defrecord:

```
(defrecord name [arguments])
```

The argument names are converted to keys that have the values passed in when creating the record. Use defrecord to create a Book record:

```
(defrecord Book [title author])
-> user.Book
```

Then, you can instantiate a record with user.Book.:

```
(->Book "title" "author")
```

Once you instantiate a Book, it behaves almost like any other map:

```
(def b (->Book "Anathem" "Neal Stephenson"))
-> #'user/b

b
-> #:user.Book{:title "Anathem", :author "Neal Stephenson"}

(:title b)
-> "Anathem"
```

Records also have alternative invocations. There is the original syntax that you may have already seen:

```
(Book. "Anathem" "Neal Stephenson")
-> #user.Book{:title "Anathem", :author "Neal Stephenson"}
```

You can also instantiate a record using the literal syntax. This is done by typing in exactly what you have seen returned to you at the REPL. The only difference you will notice is that record literals have to be fully qualified:

```
#user.Book{:title "Infinite Jest", :author "David Foster Wallace"}
-> #user.Book{:title "Infinite Jest", :author "David Foster Wallace"}
```

So far, you have seen numeric literals, lists, vectors, symbols, strings, characters, booleans, records, and nil. The remaining forms are covered later in the book, as they are needed. For your reference, see Table 1, *Clojure forms*, on page 23, which lists all the forms used in the book, a brief example of each, and a pointer to more complete coverage.

2.2 Reader Macros

Clojure forms are read by the *reader*, which converts text into Clojure data structures. In addition to the basic forms, the Clojure reader also recognizes a set of *reader macros*.[4] Reader macros are special reader behaviors triggered by prefix *macro characters*.

---

4. Reader macros are totally different from macros, which are discussed in Chapter 7, *Macros*, on page 165.

The most familiar reader macro is the comment. The macro character that triggers a comment is the semicolon (;), and the special reader behavior is "ignore everything else up to the end of this line."

Reader macros are abbreviations of longer list forms and are used to reduce clutter. You have already seen one of these. The quote character (') prevents evaluation:

```
'(1 2)
-> (1 2)
```

'(1 2) is equivalent to the longer (quote (1 2)):

```
(quote (1 2))
-> (1 2)
```

The other reader macros are covered later in the book. In the following table, you'll find a quick syntax overview and references to where each reader macro is covered.

Reader Macro	Example(s)	Primary Coverage
Anonymous function	#(.toUpperCase %)	Section 2.3, *Functions*, on page 32
Comment	; single-line comment	Section 2.2, *Reader Macros*, on page 30
Deref	@form => (deref form)	Chapter 5, *State*, on page 113
Metadata	^metadata form	Section 2.8, *Metadata*, on page 51
Quote	'form => (quote form)	Section 2.1, *Forms*, on page 21
Regex pattern	#"foo" => a java.util.regex.Pattern	*Seq-ing Regular Expressions*, on page 72
Syntax-quote	`x	Section 7.3, *Making Macros Simpler*, on page 172
Unquote	~	Section 7.3, *Making Macros Simpler*, on page 172
Unquote-splicing	~@	Section 7.3, *Making Macros Simpler*, on page 172
Var-quote	#'x => (var x)	Chapter 5, *State*, on page 113

Clojure does not allow programs to define new reader macros. The rationale for this has been explained (and debated) on the Clojure mailing list.[5] If you

---

5. http://tinyurl.com/clojure-reader-macros

come from a Lisp background, this may be frustrating. We feel your pain. But this compromise in flexibility gives Clojure a more stable core. Custom reader macros could make Clojure programs less interoperable and more difficult to read.

2.3 Functions

In Clojure, a function call is simply a list whose first element resolves to a function. For example, this call to str concatenates its arguments to create a string:

```
(str "hello" " " "world")
-> "hello world"
```

Function names are typically hyphenated, as in clear-agent-errors. If a function is a predicate, then by convention its name should end with a question mark. As an example, the following predicates test the type of their argument, and all end with a question mark:

```
(string? "hello")
-> true

(keyword? :hello)
-> true

(symbol? 'hello)
-> true
```

To define your own functions, use defn:

```
(defn name doc-string? attr-map? [params*] body)
```

The attr-map associates metadata with the function's var. It's covered separately in Section 2.8, *Metadata*, on page 51. To demonstrate the other components of a function definition, create a greeting function that takes a name and returns a greeting preceded by "Hello":

src/examples/exploring.clj
```
(defn greeting
  "Returns a greeting of the form 'Hello, username.'"
  [username]
  (str "Hello, " username))
```

You can call greeting:

```
(greeting "world")
-> "Hello, world"
```

You can also consult the documentation for greeting:

```
user=> (doc greeting)
-----------------------
exploring/greeting
([username])
  Returns a greeting of the form 'Hello, username.'
```

What does greeting do if the caller omits username?

```
(greeting)
-> ArityException Wrong number of args (0) passed to: user$greeting
   clojure.lang.AFn.throwArity (AFn.java:437)
```

Clojure functions enforce their *arity*, that is, their expected number of arguments. If you call a function with an incorrect number of arguments, Clojure will throw an ArityException. If you want to make greeting issue a generic greeting when the caller omits username, you can use this alternate form of defn, which takes multiple argument lists and method bodies:

```
(defn name doc-string? attr-map?
  ([params*] body)+)
```

Different arities of the same function can call one another, so you can easily create a zero-argument greeting that delegates to the one-argument greeting, passing in a default username:

```
src/examples/exploring.clj
(defn greeting
  "Returns a greeting of the form 'Hello, username.'
  Default username is 'world'."
  ([] (greeting "world"))
  ([username] (str "Hello, " username)))
```

You can verify that the new greeting works as expected:

```
(greeting)
-> "Hello, world"
```

You can create a function with variable arity by including an ampersand in the parameter list. Clojure will bind the name after the ampersand to a sequence of all the remaining parameters.

The following function allows two people to go on a date with a variable number of chaperones:

```
src/examples/exploring.clj
(defn date [person-1 person-2 & chaperones]
  (println person-1 "and" person-2
           "went out with" (count chaperones) "chaperones."))

(date "Romeo" "Juliet" "Friar Lawrence" "Nurse")
| Romeo and Juliet went out with 2 chaperones.
```

Variable arity is very useful in recursive definitions. See Chapter 4, *Functional Programming*, on page 85 for examples.

Writing function implementations differing by arity is useful. But if you come from an object-oriented background, you'll want *polymorphism*, that is, different implementations that are selected by *type*. Clojure can do this and a whole lot more. See Chapter 8, *Multimethods*, on page 187 and Chapter 6, *Protocols and Datatypes*, on page 143 for details.

defn is intended for defining functions at the top level. If you want to create a function from within another function, you should use an anonymous function form instead.

Anonymous Functions

In addition to named functions with defn, you can also create anonymous functions with fn. There are at least three reasons to create an anonymous function:

- The function is so brief and self-explanatory that giving it a name makes the code harder to read, not easier.

- The function is being used only from inside another function and needs a local name, not a top-level binding.

- The function is created inside another function for the purpose of closing over some data.

Filter functions are often brief and self-explanatory. For example, imagine that you want to create an index for a sequence of words, and you do not care about words shorter than three characters. You can write an indexable-word? function like this:

src/examples/exploring.clj
```
(defn indexable-word? [word]
  (> (count word) 2))
```

Then, you can use indexable-word? to extract indexable words from a sentence:

```
(require '[clojure.string :as str])
(filter indexable-word? (str/split "A fine day it is" #"\W+"))
-> ("fine" "day")
```

The call to split breaks the sentence into words, and then filter calls indexable-word? once for each word, returning those for which indexable-word? returns true.

Anonymous functions let you do the same thing in a single line. The simplest anonymous fn form is the following:

```
(fn [params*] body)
```

With this form, you can plug the implementation of indexable-word? directly into the call to filter:

```
(filter (fn [w] (> (count w) 2)) (str/split "A fine day" #"\W+"))
-> ("fine" "day")
```

There is an even shorter syntax for anonymous functions, using implicit parameter names. The parameters are named %1, %2, and so on. You can also use % for the first parameter. This syntax looks like this:

```
#(body)
```

You can rewrite the call to filter with the shorter anonymous form:

```
(filter #(> (count %) 2) (str/split "A fine day it is" #"\W+"))
-> ("fine" "day")
```

A second motivation for anonymous functions is wanting a named function but only inside the scope of another function. Continuing with the indexable-word? example, you could write this:

src/examples/exploring.clj
```
(defn indexable-words [text]
  (let [indexable-word? (fn [w] (> (count w) 2))]
    (filter indexable-word? (str/split text #"\W+"))))
```

The let binds the name indexable-word? to the same anonymous function you wrote earlier, this time inside the lexical scope of indexable-words. (let is covered in more detail under Section 2.4, *Vars, Bindings, and Namespaces*, on page 36.) You can verify that indexable-words works as expected:

```
(indexable-words "a fine day it is")
-> ("fine" "day")
```

The combination of let and an anonymous function says the following to readers of your code: "The function indexable-word? is interesting enough to have a name but is relevant only inside indexable-words."

A third reason to use anonymous functions is when you create a function dynamically at runtime. Earlier, you implemented a simple greeting function. Extending this idea, you can create a make-greeter function that creates greeting functions. make-greeter will take a greeting-prefix and return a new function that composes greetings from the greeting-prefix and a name.

src/examples/exploring.clj
```
(defn make-greeter [greeting-prefix]
  (fn [username] (str greeting-prefix ", " username)))
```

It makes no sense to name the fn, because it is creating a *different* function each time make-greeter is called. However, you may want to name the results of specific calls to make-greeter. You can use def to name functions created by make-greeter:

```
(def hello-greeting (make-greeter "Hello"))
-> #'user/hello-greeting

(def aloha-greeting (make-greeter "Aloha"))
-> #'user/aloha-greeting
```

Now, you can call these functions, just like any other functions:

```
(hello-greeting "world")
-> "Hello, world"

(aloha-greeting "world")
-> "Aloha, world"
```

Moreover, there is no need to give each greeter a name. You can simply create a greeter and place it in the first (function) slot of a form:

```
((make-greeter "Howdy") "pardner")
-> "Howdy, pardner"
```

As you can see, the different greeter functions remember the value of greeting-prefix at the time they were created. More formally, the greeter functions are *closures* over the value of greeting-prefix.

When to Use Anonymous Functions

Anonymous functions have a terse syntax that is not always appropriate. You may actually prefer to be explicit and create named functions such as indexable-word?. That's perfectly fine and will certainly be the right choice if indexable-word? needs to be called from more than one place.

Anonymous functions are an option, not a requirement. Use the anonymous forms only when you find that they make your code more readable. They take a little getting used to, so don't be surprised if you gradually use them more and more.

2.4 Vars, Bindings, and Namespaces

When you define an object with def or defn, that object is stored in a Clojure *var*. For example, the following def creates a var named user/foo:

```
(def foo 10)
-> #'user/foo
```

The symbol user/foo refers to a var that is *bound* to the value 10. If you ask Clojure to evaluate the symbol foo, it will return the value of the associated var:

```
foo
-> 10
```

The initial value of a var is called its *root binding*. Sometimes it is useful to have thread-local bindings for a var; this is covered in Section 5.5, *Managing Per-Thread State with Vars*, on page 127.

You can refer to a var directly. The var special form returns a var itself, not the var's value:

```
(var a-symbol)
```

You can use var to return the var bound to user/foo:

```
(var foo)
-> #'user/foo
```

You will almost never see the var form directly in Clojure code. Instead, you will see the equivalent reader macro #', which also returns the var for a symbol:

```
#'foo
-> #'user/foo
```

Why would you want to refer to a var directly? Most of the time, you won't, and you can often simply ignore the distinction between symbols and vars.

But keep in the back of your mind that vars have many abilities other than just storing a value:

- The same var can be aliased into more than one namespace (*Namespaces*, on page 40). This allows you to use convenient short names.

- Vars can have metadata (Section 2.8, *Metadata*, on page 51). Var metadata includes documentation (*Finding Documentation*, on page 18), type hints for optimization, and unit tests.

- Vars can be dynamically rebound on a per-thread basis (Section 5.5, *Managing Per-Thread State with Vars*, on page 127).

Bindings

Vars are bound to names, but there are other kinds of bindings as well. For example, in a function call, argument values bind to parameter names. In the following call, 10 binds to the name number inside the triple function:

```
(defn triple [number] (* 3 number))
-> #'user/triple

(triple 10)
-> 30
```

A function's parameter bindings have a *lexical* scope: they are visible only inside the text of the function body. Functions are not the only way to create a lexical binding. The special form let does nothing other than create a set of lexical bindings:

```
(let [bindings*] exprs*)
```

The bindings are then in effect for exprs, and the value of the let is the value of the last expression in exprs.

Imagine that you want coordinates for the four corners of a square, given the bottom, left, and size. You can let the top and right coordinates, based on the values given:

src/examples/exploring.clj
```
(defn square-corners [bottom left size]
  (let [top (+ bottom size)
        right (+ left size)]
    [[bottom left] [top left] [top right] [bottom right]]))
```

The let binds top and right. This saves you the trouble of calculating top and right more than once. (Both are needed twice to generate the return value.) The let then returns its last form, which in this example becomes the return value of square-corners.

Destructuring

In many programming languages, you bind a variable to an *entire* collection when you need to access only *part* of the collection.

Imagine that you are working with a database of book authors. You track both first and last names, but some functions need to use only the first name:

src/examples/exploring.clj
```
(defn greet-author-1 [author]
  (println "Hello," (:first-name author)))
```

The greet-author-1 function works fine:

```
(greet-author-1 {:last-name "Vinge" :first-name "Vernor"})
| Hello, Vernor
```

Having to bind author is unsatisfying. You don't need the author; all you need is the first-name. Clojure solves this with *destructuring*. Any place that you bind names, you can nest a vector or a map in the binding to reach into a collection and bind only the part you want. Here is a variant of greet-author that binds only the first name:

src/examples/exploring.clj
```
(defn greet-author-2 [{fname :first-name}]
  (println "Hello," fname))
```

The binding form {fname :first-name} tells Clojure to bind fname to the :first-name of the function argument. greet-author-2 behaves just like greet-author-1:

```
(greet-author-2 {:last-name "Vinge" :first-name "Vernor"})
| Hello, Vernor
```

Just as you can use a map to destructure any associative collection, you can use a vector to destructure any sequential collection. For example, you could bind only the first two coordinates in a three-dimensional coordinate space:

```
(let [[x y] [1 2 3]]
  [x y])
-> [1 2]
```

The expression [x y] destructures the vector [1 2 3], binding x to 1 and y to 2. Since no symbol lines up with the final element 3, it is not bound to anything.

Sometimes you want to skip elements at the start of a collection. Here's how you could bind only the z coordinate:

```
(let [[_ _ z] [1 2 3]]
  z)
-> 3
```

The underscore (_) is a legal symbol and is used idiomatically to indicate "I don't care about this binding." Binding proceeds from left to right, so the _ is actually bound twice:

```
; *not* idiomatic!
(let [[_ _ z] [1 2 3]]
  _)
-> 2
```

It is also possible to simultaneously bind both a collection and elements within the collection. Inside a destructuring expression, an :as clause gives you a binding for the entire enclosing structure. For example, you could capture the x and y coordinates individually, plus the entire collection as coords, in order to report the total number of dimensions:

```
(let [[x y :as coords] [1 2 3 4 5 6]]
  (str "x: " x ", y: " y ", total dimensions " (count coords)))
-> "x: 1, y: 2, total dimensions 6"
```

Try using destructuring to create an ellipsize function. ellipsize should take a string and return the first three words followed by ....

src/examples/exploring.clj
```
(require '[clojure.string :as str])
(defn ellipsize [words]
  (let [[w1 w2 w3] (str/split words #"\s+")]
    (str/join " " [w1 w2 w3 "..."])))

(ellipsize "The quick brown fox jumps over the lazy dog.")
-> "The quick brown ..."
```

split splits the string around whitespace, and then the destructuring form [w1 w2 w3] grabs the first three words. The destructuring ignores any extra items, which is exactly what we want. Finally, join reassembles the three words, adding the ellipsis at the end.

Destructuring has several other features not shown here and is a mini-language in itself. The Snake game in Section 5.6, *A Clojure Snake*, on page 132 makes heavy use of destructuring. For a complete list of destructuring options, see the online documentation for let.[6]

Namespaces

Root bindings live in a namespace. You can see evidence of this when you start the Clojure REPL and create a binding:

```
user=> (def foo 10)
-> #'user/foo
```

The user=> prompt tells you that you are currently working in the user namespace.[7] You should treat user as a scratch namespace for exploratory development.

When Clojure resolves the name foo, it namespace-qualifies foo in the current namespace user. You can verify this by calling resolve:

```
(resolve sym)
```

resolve returns the var or class that a symbol will resolve to in the current namespace. Use resolve to explicitly resolve the symbol foo:

```
(resolve 'foo)
-> #'user/foo
```

---

6. http://clojure.org/special_forms
7. Most of the REPL session listings in the book omit the REPL prompt for brevity. In this section, the REPL prompt will be included whenever the current namespace is important.

You can switch namespaces, creating a new one if needed, with in-ns:

```
(in-ns name)
```

Try creating a myapp namespace:

```
user=> (in-ns 'myapp)
-> #<Namespace myapp>
myapp=>
```

Now you are in the myapp namespace, and anything you def or defn will belong to myapp.

When you create a new namespace with in-ns, the java.lang package is automatically available to you:

```
myapp=> String
-> java.lang.String
```

While you are learning Clojure, you should use the clojure.core namespace whenever you move to a new namespace, making Clojure's core functions available in the new namespace as well:

```
myapp=> (clojure.core/use 'clojure.core)
-> nil
```

By default, class names outside java.lang must be fully qualified. You cannot just say File:

```
myapp=> File/separator
-> java.lang.Exception: No such namespace: File
```

Instead, you must specify the fully qualified java.io.File. Note that your file separator character may be different from that shown here:

```
myapp=> java.io.File/separator
-> "/"
```

If you do not want to use a fully qualified class name, you can map one or more class names from a Java package into the current namespace using import.

```
(import '(package Class+))
```

Once you import a class, you can use its short name:

```
(import '(java.io InputStream File))
-> java.io.File

(.exists (File. "/tmp"))
-> true
```

import is only for Java classes. If you want to use a Clojure var from another namespace, you must use its fully qualified name or map the name into the current namespace. Take, for example, Clojure's split function that resides in clojure.string:

```
(require 'clojure.string)
(clojure.string/split "Something,separated,by,commas" #",")
-> ["Something" "separated" "by" "commas"]

(split "Something,separated,by,commas" #",")
-> Unable to resolve symbol: split in this context
```

To alias split in the current namespace, call require on split's namespace and give it the alias str:

```
(require '[clojure.string :as str])
(str/split "Something,separated,by,commas" #",")
-> ["Something" "separated" "by" "commas"]
```

The simple form of require shown earlier causes the current namespace to reference *all* public vars in clojure.string and provide access to them under the alias str. This can be confusing, because it does not make explicit which names are being referred to.

It is idiomatic to import Java classes and require namespaces at the top of a source file, using the ns macro:

```
(ns name & references)
```

The ns macro sets the current namespace (available as *ns*) to name, creating the namespace if necessary. The references can include :import, :require, and :use, which work like the similarly named functions to set up the namespace mappings in a single form at the top of a source file. For example, this call to ns appears at the top of the sample code for this chapter:

src/examples/exploring.clj
```
(ns examples.exploring
  (:require [clojure.string :as str])
  (:import (java.io File)))
```

Clojure's namespace functions can do quite a bit more than I have shown here.

You can reflectively traverse namespaces and add or remove mappings at any time. To find out more, issue this command at the REPL. Since we have moved around a bit in the REPL, we will also ensure that we are in the user namespace so that our REPL utilities are available to us:

```
(in-ns 'user)
(find-doc "ns-")
```

Alternately, browse the documentation at http://clojure.org/namespaces.

2.5 Calling Java

Clojure provides simple, direct syntax for calling Java code: creating objects, invoking methods, and accessing static methods and fields. In addition, Clojure provides syntactic sugar that makes calling Java from Clojure more concise than calling Java from Java!

Not all types in Java are created equal: the primitives and arrays work differently. Where Java has special cases, Clojure gives you direct access to these as well. Finally, Clojure provides a set of convenience functions for common tasks that would be unwieldy in Java.

Accessing Constructors, Methods, and Fields

The first step in many Java interop scenarios is creating a Java object. Clojure provides the new special form for this purpose:

```
(new classname)
```

Try creating a new Random:

```
(new java.util.Random)
-> <Random java.util.Random@667cbde6>
```

The REPL simply prints out the new Random instance by calling its toString() method. To use a Random instance, you will need to save it away somewhere. For now, simply use def to save the Random into a Clojure Var:

```
(def rnd (new java.util.Random))
-> #'user/rnd
```

Now you can call methods on rnd using Clojure's dot (.) special form:

```
(. class-or-instance member-symbol & args)
(. class-or-instance (member-symbol & args))
```

The . can call methods. For example, the following code calls the no-argument version of nextInt():

```
(. rnd nextInt)
-> -791474443
```

Random also has a nextInt() that takes an argument. You can call that version by simply adding the argument to the list:

```
(. rnd nextInt 10)
-> 8
```

In the previous call, the . form is used to access an instance method. But . works with all kinds of class members: fields as well as methods, and statics as well as instances. Here you can see the . used to get the value of pi:

```
(. Math PI)
-> 3.141592653589793
```

Notice that Math is not fully qualified. It doesn't have to be, because Clojure imports java.lang automatically. To avoid typing java.util.Random everywhere, you could explicitly import it:

```
(import [& import-lists])
; import-list => (package-symbol & class-name-symbols)
```

import takes a variable number of lists, with the first part of each list being a package name and the rest being names to import from that package. The following import allows unqualified access to Random, Locale, and MessageFormat:

```
(import '(java.util Random Locale)
        '(java.text MessageFormat))
-> java.text.MessageFormat

Random
-> java.util.Random

Locale
-> java.util.Locale

MessageFormat
-> java.text.MessageFormat
```

At this point, you have almost everything you need to call Java from Clojure. You can do the following:

- Import class names
- Create instances
- Access fields
- Invoke methods

However, there isn't anything particularly exciting about the syntax. It is just "Java with different parentheses."

Javadoc

Although reaching into Java from Clojure is easy, remembering how all of the Java bits underneath work can be daunting. Clojure provides a javadoc function that will make your life much easier. This provides a pleasant experience from REPL when exploring.

```
(javadoc java.net.URL)
->
```

2.6   Flow Control

Clojure has very few flow control forms. In this section, you will meet if, do, and loop/recur. As it turns out, this is almost all you will ever need.

Branch with if

Clojure's if evaluates its first argument. If the argument is logically true, it returns the result of evaluating its second argument:

```
src/examples/exploring.clj
(defn is-small? [number]
  (if (< number 100) "yes"))

(is-small? 50)
-> "yes"
```

If the first argument to if is logically false, it returns nil:

```
(is-small? 50000)
-> nil
```

If you want to define a result for the "else" part of if, add it as a third argument:

```
src/examples/exploring.clj
(defn is-small? [number]
  (if (< number 100) "yes" "no"))

(is-small? 50000)
-> "no"
```

The when and when-not control flow macros are built on top of if and are described in *when and when-not*, on page 171.

Introduce Side Effects with do

Clojure's if allows only one form for each branch. What if you want to do more than one thing on a branch? For example, you might want to log that a certain branch was chosen. do takes any number of forms, evaluates them all, and returns the last.

You can use a do to print a logging statement from within an if:

```
src/examples/exploring.clj
(defn is-small? [number]
  (if (< number 100)
    "yes"
    (do
      (println "Saw a big number" number)
      "no")))
```

which results in:

```
(is-small? 200)
| Saw a big number 200
-> "no"
```

This is an example of a *side effect*. The println doesn't contribute to the return value of is-small? at all. Instead, it reaches out into the world outside the function and actually *does something*.

Many programming languages mix pure functions and side effects in a completely ad hoc fashion. Not Clojure. In Clojure, side effects are explicit and unusual. do is one way to say "side effects to follow." Since do ignores the return values of all its forms save the last, those forms must have side effects to be of any use at all.

Recur with loop/recur

The Swiss Army knife of flow control in Clojure is loop:

```
(loop [bindings *] exprs*)
```

The loop special form works like let, establishing bindings and then evaluating exprs. The difference is that loop sets a recursion point, which can then be targeted by the recur special form:

```
(recur exprs*)
```

recur binds new values for loop's bindings and returns control to the top of the loop. For example, the following loop/recur returns a countdown:

```
src/examples/exploring.clj
(loop [result [] x 5]
  (if (zero? x)
    result
    (recur (conj result x) (dec x))))

-> [5 4 3 2 1]
```

The first time through, loop binds result to an empty vector and binds x to 5. Since x is not zero, recur then rebinds the names x and result:

- result binds to the previous result conjoined with the previous x.
- x binds to the decrement of the previous x.

Control then returns to the top of the loop. Since x is again not zero, the loop continues, accumulating the result and decrementing x. Eventually, x reaches zero, and the if terminates the recurrence, returning result.

Instead of using a loop, you can recur back to the top of a function. This makes it simple to write a function whose entire body acts as an implicit loop:

```
src/examples/exploring.clj
(defn countdown [result x]
  (if (zero? x)
    result
    (recur (conj result x) (dec x))))

(countdown [] 5)
-> [5 4 3 2 1]
```

recur is a powerful building block. But you may not use it very often, because many common recursions are provided by Clojure's sequence library.

For example, countdown could also be expressed as any of these:

```
(into [] (take 5 (iterate dec 5)))
-> [5 4 3 2 1]

(into [] (drop-last (reverse (range 6))))
-> [5 4 3 2 1]

(vec (reverse (rest (range 6))))
-> [5 4 3 2 1]
```

Do not expect these forms to make sense yet—just be aware that there are often alternatives to using recur directly. The sequence library functions used here are described in Section 3.2, *Using the Sequence Library*, on page 60. Clojure *will not* perform automatic tail-call optimization (TCO). However, it will optimize calls to recur. Chapter 4, *Functional Programming*, on page 85 defines TCO and explores recursion and TCO in detail.

At this point, you have seen quite a few language features but still no variables. Some things really do vary, and Chapter 5, *State*, on page 113 will show you how Clojure deals with changeable *references*. But most variables in traditional languages are unnecessary and downright dangerous. Let's see how Clojure gets rid of them.

2.7 Where's My for Loop?

Clojure has no for loop and no direct mutable variables.[8] So, how do you write all that code you are accustomed to writing with for loops?

Rather than create a hypothetical example, we decided to grab a piece of open source Java code (sort of) randomly, find a method with some for loops and variables, and port it to Clojure. We opened the Apache Commons project, which is very widely used. We selected the StringUtils class in Commons Lang, assuming that such a class would require little domain knowledge to understand. We then browsed for a method that had multiple for loops and local variables and found indexOfAny:

data/snippets/StringUtils.java
```java
// From Apache Commons Lang, http://commons.apache.org/lang/
public static int indexOfAny(String str, char[] searchChars) {
    if (isEmpty(str) || ArrayUtils.isEmpty(searchChars)) {
        return -1;
    }
    for (int i = 0; i < str.length(); i++) {
        char ch = str.charAt(i);
        for (int j = 0; j < searchChars.length; j++) {
            if (searchChars[j] == ch) {
                return i;
            }
        }
    }
    return -1;
}
```

indexOfAny walks str and reports the index of the first char that matches any char in searchChars, returning -1 if no match is found.

Here are some example results from the documentation for indexOfAny:

```
StringUtils.indexOfAny(null, *)                = -1
StringUtils.indexOfAny("", *)                  = -1
StringUtils.indexOfAny(*, null)                = -1
StringUtils.indexOfAny(*, [])                  = -1
StringUtils.indexOfAny("zzabyycdxx",['z','a']) =  0
StringUtils.indexOfAny("zzabyycdxx",['b','y']) =  3
StringUtils.indexOfAny("aba", ['z'])           = -1
```

---

8. Clojure provides *indirect* mutable references, but these must be explicitly called out in your code. See Chapter 5, *State*, on page 113 for details.

There are two ifs, two fors, three possible points of return, and three mutable local variables in indexOfAny, and the method is fourteen lines long, as counted by David A. Wheeler's SLOCCount.[9]

Now let's build a Clojure index-of-any, step by step. If we just wanted to find the matches, we could use a Clojure filter. But we want to find the *index* of a match. So, we create indexed, a function that takes a collection and returns an indexed collection:

```
src/examples/exploring.clj
(defn indexed [coll] (map-indexed vector coll))
```

indexed returns a sequence of pairs of the form [idx elt]. Try indexing a string:

```
(indexed "abcde")
-> ([0 \a] [1 \b] [2 \c] [3 \d] [4 \e])
```

Next, we want to find the indices of all the characters in the string that match the search set.

Create an index-filter function that is similar to Clojure's filter but that returns the indices instead of the matches themselves:

```
src/examples/exploring.clj
(defn index-filter [pred coll]
  (when pred
    (for [[idx elt] (indexed coll) :when (pred elt)] idx)))
```

Clojure's for is *not* a loop but a sequence comprehension (see *Transforming Sequences*, on page 66). The index/element pairs of (indexed coll) are bound to the names idx and elt but only when (pred elt) is true. Finally, the comprehension yields the value of idx for each matching pair.

Clojure sets are functions that test membership in the set. So, you can pass a set of characters and a string to index-filter and get back the indices of all characters in the string that belong to the set. Try it with a few different strings and character sets:

```
(index-filter #{\a \b} "abcdbbb")
-> (0 1 4 5 6)

(index-filter #{\a \b} "xyz")
-> ()
```

At this point, we have accomplished *more* than the stated objective. index-filter returns the indices of all the matches, and we need only the first index. So, index-of-any simply takes the first result from index-filter:

---

9.   http://www.dwheeler.com/sloccount/

src/examples/exploring.clj
```
(defn index-of-any [pred coll]
  (first (index-filter pred coll)))
```

Test that index-of-any works correctly with a few different inputs:

```
(index-of-any #{\z \a} "zzabyycdxx")
-> 0
(index-of-any #{\b \y} "zzabyycdxx")
-> 3
```

The Clojure version is simpler than the imperative version by every metric (see Table 2, *Relative complexity of imperative and functional indexOfAny*, on page 51). What accounts for the difference?

- The imperative indexOfAny must deal with several special cases: null or empty strings, a null or empty set of search characters, and the absence of a match. These special cases add branches and exits to the method. With a functional approach, most of these kinds of special cases just work without any explicit code.

- The imperative indexOfAny introduces local variables to traverse collections (both the string and the character set). By using higher-order functions such as map and sequence comprehensions such as for, the functional index-of-any avoids all need for variables.

Unnecessary complexity tends to snowball. For example, the special case branches in the imperative indexOfAny use the magic number -1 to indicate a nonmatch. Should the magic number be a symbolic constant? Whatever you think the right answer is, *the question itself disappears* in the functional version. While shorter and simpler, the functional index-of-any is also *vastly more general*:

- indexOfAny searches a string, while index-of-any can search any sequence.

- indexOfAny matches against a set of characters, while index-of-any can match against any predicate.

- indexOfAny returns the first match, while index-filter returns all the matches and can be further composed with other filters.

As an example of how much more general the functional index-of-any is, you could use code like we just wrote to find the third occurrence of "heads" in a series of coin flips:

```
(nth (index-filter #{:h} [:t :t :h :t :h :t :t :t :h :h])
2)
-> 8
```

Metric	LOC	Branches	Exits/Method	Variables
Imperative version	14	4	3	3
Functional version	6	1	1	0

Table 2—Relative complexity of imperative and functional indexOfAny

So, it turns out that writing index-of-any in a functional style, without loops or variables, is simpler, less error prone, and more general than the imperative indexOfAny.[10] On larger units of code, these advantages become even more telling.

2.8 Metadata

The Wikipedia entry on metadata[11] begins by saying that metadata is "data about data." That is true but not usably specific. In Clojure, metadata is data that is *orthogonal to the logical value of an object*. For example, a person's first and last names are plain old data. The fact that a person object can be serialized to XML has nothing to do with the person and is metadata. Likewise, the fact that a person object is dirty and needs to be flushed to the database is metadata.

Reader Metadata

The Clojure language itself uses metadata in several places. For example, vars have a metadata map containing documentation, type information, and source information. Here is the metadata for the str var:

```
(meta #'str)
-> {:ns #<Namespace clojure.core>,
    :name str,
    :file "core.clj",
    :line 313,
    :arglists ([] [x] [x & ys]),
    :tag java.lang.String,
    :doc "With no args, ... etc."}
```

Some common metadata keys and their uses are shown in Table 3, *Common metadata keys*, on page 52.

---

10. It is worth mentioning that you could write a functional indexOfAny in plain Java, although it would not be idiomatic. It may become more idiomatic when closures are added to the language. See http://functionaljava.org/ for more information.

11. http://en.wikipedia.org/wiki/Metadata

Metadata Key	Used For
:arglists	Parameter info used by doc
:doc	Documentation used by doc
:file	Source file
:line	Source line number
:macro	True for macros
:name	Local name
:ns	Namespace
:tag	Expected argument or return type

Table 3—Common metadata keys

Much of the metadata on a var is added automatically by the Clojure compiler. To add your own key/value pairs to a var, use the metadata reader macro:

```
^metadata form
```

For example, you could create a simple shout function that upcases a string and then document that shout both expects and returns a string, using the :tag key:

```
; see also shorter form below
(defn ^{:tag String} shout [^{:tag String} s] (.toUpperCase s))
-> #'user/shout
```

You can inspect shout's metadata to see that Clojure added the :tag:

```
(meta #'shout)
-> {:arglists ([s]),
    :ns #<Namespace user>,
    :name shout,
    :line 32,
    :file "NO_SOURCE_FILE",
    :tag java.lang.String}
```

You provided the :tag, and Clojure provided the other keys. The :file value NO_SOURCE_FILE indicates that the code was entered at the REPL.

Because :tag metadata is so common, you can also use the short-form ^Classname, which expands to ^{:tag Classname}. Using the shorter form, you can rewrite shout as follows:

```
(defn ^String shout [^String s] (.toUpperCase s))
-> #'user/shout
```

If you find the metadata disruptive when you are reading the definition of a function, you can place the metadata last. Use a variant of defn that wraps one or more body forms in parentheses, followed by a metadata map:

```
(defn shout
  ([s] (.toUpperCase s))
  {:tag String})
```

2.9 Wrapping Up

This has been a long chapter. But think about how much ground you have covered: you can instantiate basic literal types, define and call functions, manage namespaces, and read and write metadata. You can write purely functional code, and yet you can easily introduce side effects when you need to do so. You have also met Lisp concepts including reader macros, special forms, and destructuring.

The material here would take hundreds of pages to cover in most other languages. Is the Clojure way really that much simpler? Yes, in part. Half the credit for this chapter belongs to Clojure. Clojure's elegant design and abstraction choices make the language much easier to learn than most.

That said, the language may not *seem* so easy to learn right now. That's because we are taking advantage of Clojure's power to move much faster than most programming language books.

So, the other half of the credit for this chapter belongs to you, the reader. Clojure will give back what you put in, and then some. Take the time you need to feel comfortable with the chapter's examples and with using the REPL. The rest of the book will give you the opportunity to do that.

CHAPTER 3

Unifying Data with Sequences

Programs manipulate data. At the lowest level, programs work with structures such as strings, lists, vectors, maps, sets, and trees. At a higher level, these same data structure abstractions crop up again and again. For example:

- XML data is a tree.
- Database result sets can be viewed as lists or vectors.
- Directory hierarchies are trees.
- Files are often viewed as one big string or as a vector of lines.

In Clojure, all these data structures can be accessed through a single abstraction: the sequence (or *seq*).

A seq (pronounced "seek") is a *logical* list. It's logical because Clojure does not tie sequences to *implementation details* of a list such as a Lisp cons cell (see *The Origin of Cons*, on page 58 for the history of cons). Instead, the seq is an abstraction that can be used everywhere.

Collections that can be viewed as seqs are called *seq-able* (pronounced "SEEK-a-bull"). In this chapter, you will meet a variety of seq-able collections:

- All Clojure collections
- All Java collections
- Java arrays and strings
- Regular expression matches
- Directory structures
- I/O streams
- XML trees

You will also meet the sequence library, a set of functions that can work with any seq-able. Because so many things are sequences, the sequence library is much more powerful and general than the collection APIs in most languages. The sequence library includes functions to create, filter, and transform data.

These functions act as the Collections API for Clojure, and they also replace many of the loops you would write in an imperative language.

In this chapter, you will become a power user of Clojure sequences. You will see how to use a common set of very expressive functions with an incredibly wide range of datatypes. Then, in the next chapter (Chapter 4, *Functional Programming*, on page 85), you will learn the functional style in which the sequence library is written.

3.1 Everything Is a Sequence

Every aggregate data structure in Clojure can be viewed as a sequence. A sequence has three core capabilities:

- You can get the first item in a sequence:

  ```
  (first aseq)
  ```

  first returns nil if its argument is empty or nil.

- You can get everything after the first item, in other words, the rest of a sequence:

  ```
  (rest aseq)
  ```

  rest returns an empty seq (not nil) if there are no more items.

- You can construct a new sequence by adding an item to the front of an existing sequence. This is called consing:

  ```
  (cons elem aseq)
  ```

Under the hood, these three capabilities are declared in the Java interface clojure.lang.ISeq. (Keep this in mind when reading about Clojure, because the name ISeq is often used interchangeably with seq.)

The seq function will return a seq on any seq-able collection:

```
(seq coll)
```

seq will return nil if its coll is empty or nil. The next function will return the seq of items after the first:

```
(next aseq)
```

(next aseq) is equivalent to (seq (rest aseq)). Table 4, *Clarifying rest/next behavior*, on page 57 clarifies the rest/next behavior.

If you have a Lisp background, you expect to find that the seq functions work for lists:

Form	Result
(rest ())	()
(next ())	nil
(seq (rest ()))	nil

Table 4—Clarifying rest/next behavior

```
(first '(1 2 3))
-> 1

(rest '(1 2 3))
-> (2 3)

(cons 0 '(1 2 3))
-> (0 1 2 3)
```

In Clojure, the same functions will work for other data structures as well. You can treat vectors as seqs:

```
(first [1 2 3])
-> 1

(rest [1 2 3])
-> (2 3)

(cons 0 [1 2 3])
-> (0 1 2 3)
```

When you apply rest or cons to a vector, the result is a seq, not a vector. In the REPL, seqs print just like lists, as you can see in the earlier output. You can check the actual returned type by taking its class:

```
(class (rest [1 2 3]))
-> clojure.lang.PersistentVector$ChunkedSeq
```

The $ChunkedSeq at the end of the class name is Java's way of mangling nested class names. Seqs that you produce from a specific collection type are often implemented as a ChunkedSeq class nested inside the original collection class (PersistentVector in this example).

The generality of seqs is very powerful, but sometimes you want to produce a specific implementation type. This is covered in Section 3.5, *Calling Structure-Specific Functions*, on page 76.

You can treat maps as seqs, if you think of a key/value pair as an item in the sequence:

The Origin of Cons

Clojure's sequence is an abstraction based on Lisp's concrete lists. In the original implementation of Lisp, the three fundamental list operations were named car, cdr, and cons. car and cdr are acronyms that refer to implementation details of Lisp on the original IBM 704 platform. Many Lisps, including Clojure, replace these esoteric names with the more meaningful names first and rest.

The third function, cons, is short for construct. Lisp programmers use cons as a noun, verb, and adjective. You use cons to create a data structure called a *cons cell*, or just a *cons* for short.

Most Lisps, including Clojure, retain the original cons name, since "construct" is a pretty good mnemonic for what cons does. It also helps remind you that sequences are immutable. For convenience, you might say that cons adds an element to a sequence, but it is more accurate to say that cons *constructs* a new sequence, which is like the original sequence but with one element added.

```
(first {:fname "Aaron" :lname "Bedra"})
-> [:lname "Bedra"]

(rest {:fname "Aaron" :lname "Bedra"})
-> ([:fname "Aaron"])

(cons [:mname "James"] {:fname "Aaron" :lname "Bedra"})
-> ([:mname "James"] [:lname "Bedra"] [:fname "Aaron"])
```

You can also treat sets as seqs:

```
(first #{:the :quick :brown :fox})
-> :brown

(rest #{:the :quick :brown :fox})
-> (:quick :fox :the)

(cons :jumped #{:the :quick :brown :fox})
-> (:jumped :brown :quick :fox :the)
```

Maps and sets have a stable traversal order, but that order depends on implementation details, and you should not rely on it. Elements of a set will not necessarily come back in the order that you put them in:

```
#{:the :quick :brown :fox}
-> #{:brown :quick :fox :the}
```

If you want a reliable order, you can use this:

```
(sorted-set & elements)
```

sorted-set will sort the values by their natural sort order:

```
(sorted-set :the :quick :brown :fox)
-> #{:brown :fox :quick :the}
```

Likewise, key/value pairs in maps won't necessarily come back in the order you put them in:

```
{:a 1 :b 2 :c 3}
-> {:a 1, :c 3, :b 2}
```

You can create a sorted map with sorted-map:

(sorted-map & elements**)**

sorted-maps won't come back in the order you put them in either, but they *will* come back sorted by key:

```
(sorted-map :c 3 :b 2 :a 1)
-> {:a 1, :b 2, :c 3}
```

In addition to the core capabilities of seq, two other capabilities are worth meeting immediately: conj and into.

(conj coll element & elements**)**

(into to-coll from-coll**)**

conj adds one or more elements to a collection, and into adds all the items in one collection to another. Both conj and into add items at an efficient insertion spot for the underlying data structure. For lists, conj and into add to the front:

```
(conj '(1 2 3) :a)
-> (:a 1 2 3)

(into '(1 2 3) '(:a :b :c))
-> (:c :b :a 1 2 3)
```

For vectors, conj and into add elements to the back:

```
(conj [1 2 3] :a)
-> [1 2 3 :a]

(into [1 2 3] [:a :b :c])
-> [1 2 3 :a :b :c]
```

Because conj (and related functions) do the efficient thing for the underlying data structure, you can often write code that is both efficient and completely decoupled from a specific underlying implementation.

The Clojure sequence library is particularly suited for large (or even infinite) sequences. Most Clojure sequences are *lazy*: they generate elements only

Joe asks:

Why Do Functions on Vectors Return Lists?

When you try examples at the REPL, the results of rest and cons appear to be lists, even when the inputs are vectors, maps, or sets. Does this mean that Clojure is converting everything to a list internally? No! The sequence functions always return a seq, regardless of their inputs. You can verify this by checking the Java type of the returned objects:

```
(class '(1 2 3))
-> clojure.lang.PersistentList

(class (rest [1 2 3]))
-> clojure.lang.PersistentVector$ChunkedSeq
```

As you can see, the result of (rest [1 2 3]) is some kind of Seq, not a List. So, why does the result appear to be a list?

The answer lies in the REPL. When you ask the REPL to display a sequence, all it knows is that it has a sequence. It does not know what kind of collection the sequence was built from. So, the REPL prints all sequences the same way: it walks the entire sequence, printing it as a list.

when they are actually needed. Thus, Clojure's sequence functions can process sequences too large to fit in memory.

Clojure sequences are *immutable*: they never change. This makes it easier to reason about programs and means that Clojure sequences are safe for concurrent access. It does, however, create a small problem for human language. English-language descriptions flow much more smoothly when describing mutable things. Consider the following two descriptions for a hypothetical sequence function triple:

- triple triples each element of a sequence.
- triple takes a sequence and returns a new sequence with each element of the original sequence tripled.

The latter version is specific and accurate. The former is much easier to read, but it might lead to the mistaken impression that a sequence is actually changing. Don't be fooled: *sequences never change*. If you see the phrase "foo changes x," mentally substitute "foo returns a changed copy of x."

3.2 Using the Sequence Library

The Clojure sequence library provides a rich set of functionality that can work with any sequence. If you come from an object-oriented background where nouns rule, the sequence library is truly "Revenge of the Verbs."[1] The functions provide a rich backbone of functionality that can take advantage of any data structure that obeys the basic first/rest/cons contract.

The following functions are grouped into four broad categories:

- Functions that create sequences
- Functions that filter sequences
- Sequence predicates
- Functions that transform sequences

These divisions are somewhat arbitrary. Since sequences are immutable, *most* of the sequence functions create new sequences. Some of the sequence functions both filter and transform. Nevertheless, these divisions provide a rough road map through a large library.

Creating Sequences

In addition to the sequence literals, Clojure provides a number of functions that create sequences. range produces a sequence from a start to an end, incrementing by step each time.

```
(range start? end step?)
```

Ranges include their start but not their end. If you do not specify them, start defaults to zero, and step defaults to 1. Try creating some ranges at the REPL:

```
(range 10)
-> (0 1 2 3 4 5 6 7 8 9)

(range 10 20)
-> (10 11 12 13 14 15 16 17 18 19)
(range 1 25 2)
-> (1 3 5 7 9 11 13 15 17 19 21 23)
```

The repeat function repeats an element x n times:

```
(repeat n x)
```

Try to repeat some items from the REPL:

```
(repeat 5 1)
-> (1 1 1 1 1)

(repeat 10 "x")
-> ("x" "x" "x" "x" "x" "x" "x" "x" "x" "x")
```

---

1. Steve Yegge's "Execution in the Kingdom of Nouns" (http://tinyurl.com/the-kingdom-of-nouns) argues that object-oriented programming has pushed nouns into an unrealistically dominant position and that it is time for a change.

Both range and repeat represent ideas that can be extended infinitely. You can think of iterate as the infinite extension of range:

`(iterate f x)`

iterate begins with a value x and continues forever, applying a function f to each value to calculate the next.

If you begin with 1 and iterate with inc, you can generate the whole numbers:

```
(take 10 (iterate inc 1))
-> (1 2 3 4 5 6 7 8 9 10)
```

Since the sequence is infinite, you need another new function to help you view the sequence from the REPL.

`(take n sequence)`

take returns a lazy sequence of the first n items from a collection and provides one way to create a finite view onto an infinite collection.

The whole numbers are a pretty useful sequence to have around, so let's defn them for future use:

```
(defn whole-numbers [] (iterate inc 1))
-> #'user/whole-numbers
```

When called with a single argument, repeat returns a lazy, infinite sequence:

`(repeat x)`

Try repeating some elements at the REPL. Don't forget to wrap the result in a take:

```
(take 20 (repeat 1))
-> (1 1 1 1 1 1 1 1 1 1 1 1 1 1 1 1 1 1 1 1)
```

The cycle function takes a collection and cycles it infinitely:

`(cycle coll)`

Try cycling some collections at the REPL:

```
(take 10 (cycle (range 3)))
-> (0 1 2 0 1 2 0 1 2 0)
```

The interleave function takes multiple collections and produces a new collection that interleaves values from each collection until one of the collections is exhausted.

`(interleave & colls)`

When one of the collections is exhausted, the interleave stops. So, you can mix finite and infinite collections:

```
(interleave (whole-numbers) ["A" "B" "C" "D" "E"])
-> (1 "A" 2 "B" 3 "C" 4 "D" 5 "E")
```

Closely related to interleave is interpose, which returns a sequence with each of the elements of the input collection segregated by a separator:

```
(interpose separator coll)
```

You can use interpose to build delimited strings:

```
(interpose "," ["apples" "bananas" "grapes"])
-> ("apples" "," "bananas" "," "grapes")
```

interpose works nicely with (apply str ...) to produce output strings:

```
(apply str (interpose \, ["apples" "bananas" "grapes"]))
-> "apples,bananas,grapes"
```

The (apply str ...) idiom is common enough that Clojure wraps it as clojure.string/join:

```
(join separator sequence)
```

Use clojure.string/join to comma-delimit a list of words:

```
(use '[clojure.string :only (join)])
(join \, ["apples" "bananas" "grapes"])
-> "apples,bananas,grapes"
```

For each collection type in Clojure, there is a function that takes an arbitrary number of arguments and creates a collection of that type:

```
(list & elements)
```

```
(vector & elements)
```

```
(hash-set & elements)
```

```
(hash-map key-1 val-1 ...)
```

hash-set has a cousin set that works a little differently: set expects a collection as its first argument:

```
(set [1 2 3])
-> #{1 2 3}
```

hash-set takes a variable list of arguments:

```
(hash-set 1 2 3)
-> #{1 2 3}
```

vector also has a cousin, vec, that takes a single collection argument instead of a variable argument list:

```
(vec (range 3))
-> [0 1 2]
```

Now that you have the basics of creating sequences, you can use other Clojure functions to filter and transform them.

Filtering Sequences

Clojure provides a number of functions that filter a sequence, returning a subsequence of the original sequence. The most basic of these is filter:

```
(filter pred coll)
```

filter takes a predicate and a collection and returns a sequence of objects for which the filter returns true (when interpreted in a boolean context). You can filter the whole-numbers from the previous section to get the odd numbers or the even numbers:

```
(take 10 (filter even? (whole-numbers)))
-> (2 4 6 8 10 12 14 16 18 20)

(take 10 (filter odd? (whole-numbers)))
-> (1 3 5 7 9 11 13 15 17 19)
```

You can take from a sequence while a predicate remains true with take-while:

```
(take-while pred coll)
```

For example, to take all the characters in a string up to the first vowel, use this:

```
(take-while (complement #{\a\e\i\o\u}) "the-quick-brown-fox")
-> (\t \h)
```

There are a couple of interesting things happening here:

- Sets also act as functions. So, you can read #{\a\e\i\o\u} either as "the set of vowels" or as "the function that tests to see whether its argument is vowel."

- complement reverses the behavior of another function. The previous complemented function tests to see whether its argument is *not* a vowel.

The opposite of take-while is drop-while:

```
(drop-while pred coll)
```

drop-while drops elements from the beginning of a sequence while a predicate is true and then returns the rest. You could drop-while to drop all leading non-vowels from a string:

```
(drop-while (complement #{\a\e\i\o\u}) "the-quick-brown-fox")
-> (\e \- \q \u \i \c \k \- \b \r \o \w \n \- \f \o \x)
```

split-at and split-with will split a collection into two collections:

```
(split-at index coll)
```

```
(split-with pred coll)
```

split-at takes an index, and split-with takes a predicate:

```
(split-at 5 (range 10))
->[(0 1 2 3 4) (5 6 7 8 9)]

(split-with #(<= % 10) (range 0 20 2))
->[(0 2 4 6 8 10) (12 14 16 18)]
```

All the take-, split-, and drop- functions return lazy sequences, of course.

Sequence Predicates

Filter functions take a predicate and return a sequence. Closely related are the sequence predicates. A sequence predicate asks how some other predicate applies to every item in a sequence. For example, the every? predicate asks whether some other predicate is true for every element of a sequence.

```
(every? pred coll)
```

```
(every? odd? [1 3 5])
-> true

(every? odd? [1 3 5 8])
-> false
```

A lower bar is set by some:

```
(some pred coll)
```

some returns the first nonfalse value for its predicate or returns nil if no element matched:

```
(some even? [1 2 3])
-> true

(some even? [1 3 5])
-> nil
```

Notice that some does not end with a question mark. some is not a predicate, although it is often used like one. some returns the *actual value* of the first match instead of true. The distinction is invisible when you pair some with even?, since even? is itself a predicate. To see a non-true match, try using some with identity to find the first non-nil value in a sequence:

```
(some identity [nil false 1 nil 2])
-> 1
```

The behavior of the other predicates is obvious from their names:

`(not-every? pred coll)`

`(not-any? pred coll)`

Not every whole number is even:

```
(not-every? even? (whole-numbers))
-> true
```

But it would be a lie to claim that not any whole number is even:

```
(not-any? even? (whole-numbers))
-> false
```

Note that we picked questions to which we already knew the answer. In general, you have to be careful when applying predicates to infinite collections. They might run forever.

Transforming Sequences

Transformation functions transform the values in the sequence. The simplest transformation is map:

`(map f coll)`

map takes a source collection coll and a function f, and it returns a new sequence by invoking f on each element in the coll. You could use map to wrap every element in a collection with an HTML tag.

```
(map #(format "<p>%s</p>" %) ["the" "quick" "brown" "fox"])
-> ("<p>the</p>" "<p>quick</p>" "<p>brown</p>" "<p>fox</p>")
```

map can also take more than one collection argument. f must then be a function of multiple arguments. map will call f with one argument from each collection, stopping whenever the smallest collection is exhausted:

```
(map #(format "<%s>%s</%s>" %1 %2 %1)
["h1" "h2" "h3" "h1"] ["the" "quick" "brown" "fox"])
-> ("<h1>the</h1>" "<h2>quick</h2>" "<h3>brown</h3>"
"<h1>fox</h1>")
```

Another common transformation is reduce:

```
(reduce f coll)
```

f is a function of two arguments. reduce applies f on the first two elements in coll and then applies f to the result and the third element, and so on. reduce is useful for functions that "total up" a sequence in some way. You can use reduce to add items:

```
(reduce + (range 1 11))
-> 55
```

or to multiply them:

```
(reduce * (range 1 11))
-> 3628800
```

You can sort a collection with sort or sort-by:

```
(sort comp? coll)
```

```
(sort-by a-fn comp? coll)
```

sort sorts a collection by the natural order of its elements, where sort-by sorts a sequence by the result of calling a-fn on each element:

```
(sort [42 1 7 11])
-> (1 7 11 42)
```

```
(sort-by #(.toString %) [42 1 7 11])
-> (1 11 42 7)
```

If you do not want to sort by natural order, you can specify an optional comparison function comp for either sort or sort-by:

```
(sort > [42 1 7 11])
-> (42 11 7 1)
```

```
(sort-by :grade > [{:grade 83} {:grade 90} {:grade 77}])
-> ({:grade 90} {:grade 83} {:grade 77})
```

The granddaddy of all filters and transformations is the *list comprehension*. A list comprehension creates a list based on an existing list, using set notation. In other words, a comprehension states the properties that the result list must satisfy. In general, a list comprehension will consist of the following:

- Input list(s)
- Placeholder variables[2] for elements in the input lists

---

2. "Variables" in the mathematical sense, not the imperative programming sense. You can't vary them. I humbly apologize for this overloading of the English language.

- Predicates on the elements
- An output form that produces output from the elements of the input lists that satisfy the predicates

Of course, Clojure generalizes the notion of list comprehension to *sequence* comprehension. Clojure comprehensions use the for macro.[3]

```
(for [binding-form coll-expr filter-expr? ...] expr)
```

for takes a vector of binding-form/coll-exprs, plus an optional filter-expr, and then yields a sequence of exprs.

List comprehension is more general than functions such as map and filter and can in fact emulate most of the filtering and transformation functions described earlier.

You can rewrite the previous map example as a list comprehension:

```
(for [word ["the" "quick" "brown" "fox"]]
  (format "<p>%s</p>" word))
-> ("<p>the</p>" "<p>quick</p>" "<p>brown</p>" "<p>fox</p>")
```

This reads almost like English: "For [each] word in [a sequence of words] format [according to format instructions]."

Comprehensions can emulate filter using a :when clause. You can pass even? to :when to filter the even numbers:

```
(take 10 (for [n (whole-numbers) :when (even? n)] n))
-> (2 4 6 8 10 12 14 16 18 20)
```

A :while clause continues the evaluation only while its expression holds true:

```
(for [n (whole-numbers) :while (even? n)] n)
-> ()
```

The real power of for comes when you work with more than one binding expression. For example, you can express all possible positions on a chessboard in algebraic notation by binding both rank and file:

```
(for [file "ABCDEFGH" rank (range 1 9)] (format "%c%d" file rank))
-> ("A1" "A2" ... elided ... "H7" ""H8")
```

Clojure iterates over the rightmost binding expression in a sequence comprehension first and then works its way left. Because rank is listed to the right of file in the binding form, rank iterates faster. If you want files to iterate faster, you can reverse the binding order and list rank first:

---

3. The list comprehension for has nothing to do with the for loop found in imperative languages.

```
(for [rank (range 1 9) file "ABCDEFGH"] (format "%c%d" file rank))
-> ("A1" "B1" ... elided ... "G8" "H8")
```

In many languages, transformations, filters, and comprehensions do their work immediately. Do not assume this in Clojure. Most sequence functions do not traverse elements until you actually try to use them.

3.3 Lazy and Infinite Sequences

Most Clojure sequences are *lazy*; in other words, elements are not calculated until they are needed. Using lazy sequences has many benefits:

- You can postpone expensive computations that may not in fact be needed.
- You can work with huge data sets that do not fit into memory.
- You can delay I/O until it is absolutely needed.

Consider the code and following expression:

src/examples/primes.clj

```
(ns examples.primes)
;; Taken from clojure.contrib.lazy-seqs
; primes cannot be written efficiently as a function, because
; it needs to look back on the whole sequence. contrast with
; fibs and powers-of-2 which only need a fixed buffer of 1 or 2
; previous values.
(def primes
  (concat
   [2 3 5 7]
   (lazy-seq
    (let [primes-from
          (fn primes-from [n [f & r]]
            (if (some #(zero? (rem n %))
                      (take-while #(<= (* % %) n) primes))
              (recur (+ n f) r)
              (lazy-seq (cons n (primes-from (+ n f) r)))))
          wheel (cycle [2 4 2 4 6 2 6 4 2 4 6 6 2 6  4  2
                        6 4 6 8 4 2 4 2 4 8 6 4 6 2  4  6
                        2 6 6 4 2 4 6 2 6 4 2 4 2 10 2 10])]
      (primes-from 11 wheel)))))

(use 'examples.primes)
(def ordinals-and-primes (map vector (iterate inc 1) primes))
-> #'user/ordinals-and-primes
```

ordinals-and-primes includes pairs like [5, 11] (eleven is the fifth prime number). Both ordinals and primes are infinite, but ordinals-and-primes fits into memory just fine, because it is lazy. Just take what you need from it:

```
(take 5 (drop 1000 ordinals-and-primes))
-> ([1001 7927] [1002 7933] [1003 7937] [1004 7949] [1005 7951])
```

When should you prefer lazy sequences? Most of the time. Most sequence functions return lazy sequences, so you pay only for what you use. More important, lazy sequences do not require any special effort on your part. In the previous example, iterate, primes, and map return lazy sequences, so ordinals-and-primes gets laziness "for free."

Lazy sequences are critical to functional programming in Clojure. Section 4.2, *How to Be Lazy*, on page 90 explores creating and using lazy sequences in much greater detail.

Forcing Sequences

When you are viewing a large sequence from the REPL, you may want to use take to prevent the REPL from evaluating the entire sequence. In other contexts, you may have the opposite problem. You have created a lazy sequence, and you want to force the sequence to evaluate fully. The problem usually arises when the code generating the sequence has side effects. Consider the following sequence, which embeds side effects via println:

```
(def x (for [i (range 1 3)] (do (println i) i)))
-> #'user/x
```

Newcomers to Clojure are surprised that the previous code prints nothing. Since the definition of x does not actually use the elements, Clojure does not evaluate the comprehension to get them. You can force evaluation with doall:

`(doall coll)`

doall forces Clojure to walk the elements of a sequence and returns the elements as a result:

```
(doall x)
| 1
| 2
-> (1 2)
```

You can also use dorun:

`(dorun coll)`

dorun walks the elements of a sequence without keeping past elements in memory. As a result, dorun can walk collections too large to fit in memory.

```
(def x (for [i (range 1 3)] (do (println i) i)))
-> #'user/x
```

```
(dorun x)
| 1
| 2
-> nil
```

The nil return value is a telltale reminder that dorun does not hold a reference to the entire sequence. The dorun and doall functions help you deal with side effects, while most of the rest of Clojure discourages side effects. You should use these functions rarely.

3.4 Clojure Makes Java Seq-able

The seq abstraction of first/rest applies to anything that there can be more than one of. In the Java world, that includes the following:

- The Collections API
- Regular expressions
- File system traversal
- XML processing
- Relational database results

Clojure wraps these Java APIs, making the sequence library available for almost everything you do.

Seq-ing Java Collections

If you try to apply the sequence functions to Java collections, you will find that they behave as sequences. Collections that can act as sequences are called *seq-able*. For example, arrays are seq-able:

```
; String.getBytes returns a byte array
(first (.getBytes "hello"))
-> 104

(rest (.getBytes "hello"))
-> (101 108 108 111)

(cons (int \h) (.getBytes "ello"))
-> (104 101 108 108 111)
```

Hashtables and Maps are also seq-able:

```
; System.getProperties returns a Hashtable
(first (System/getProperties))
-> #<Entry java.runtime.name=Java(TM) SE Runtime Environment>

(rest (System/getProperties))
-> (#<Entry sun.boot.library.path=/System/Library/... etc. ...
```

Remember that the sequence wrappers are immutable, even when the underlying Java collection is mutable. So, you cannot update the system properties by consing a new item onto (System/getProperties). cons will return a new sequence; the existing properties are unchanged.

Since strings are sequences of characters, they also are seq-able:

```
(first "Hello")
-> \H

(rest "Hello")
-> (\e \l \l \o)

(cons \H "ello")
-> (\H \e \l \l \o)
```

Clojure will automatically wrap collections in sequences, but it will not automatically rewrap them back to their original type. With most collection types this behavior is intuitive, but with strings you will often want to convert the result to a string. Consider reversing a string. Clojure provides reverse:

```
; probably not what you want
(reverse "hello")
-> (\o \l \l \e \h)
```

To convert a sequence back to a string, use (apply str seq):

```
(apply str (reverse "hello"))
-> "olleh"
```

The Java collections are seq-able, but for most scenarios they do not offer advantages over Clojure's built-in collections. Prefer the Java collections only in interop scenarios where you are working with legacy Java APIs.

Seq-ing Regular Expressions

Clojure's regular expressions use the java.util.regex library under the hood. At the lowest level, this exposes the mutable nature of Java's Matcher. You can use re-matcher to create a Matcher for a regular expression and a string and then loop on re-find to iterate over the matches.

```
(re-matcher regexp string)
```

src/examples/sequences.clj
```
; don't do this!
(let [m (re-matcher #"\w+" "the quick brown fox")]
  (loop [match (re-find m)]
    (when match
      (println match)
      (recur (re-find m)))))
```

```
| the
| quick
| brown
| fox
-> nil
```

Much better is to use the higher-level re-seq.

`(re-seq regexp string)`

re-seq exposes an immutable seq over the matches. This gives you the power of all of Clojure's sequence functions. Try these expressions at the REPL:

```
(re-seq #"\w+" "the quick brown fox")
-> ("the" "quick" "brown" "fox")

(sort (re-seq #"\w+" "the quick brown fox"))
-> ("brown" "fox" "quick" "the")

(drop 2 (re-seq #"\w+" "the quick brown fox"))
-> ("brown" "fox")

(map #(.toUpperCase %) (re-seq #"\w+" "the quick brown fox"))
-> ("THE" "QUICK" "BROWN" "FOX")
```

re-seq is a great example of how good abstractions reduce code bloat. Regular expression matches are not a special kind of thing, requiring special methods to deal with them. They are sequences, just like everything else. Thanks to the large number of sequence functions, you get more functionality *for free* than you would likely end up with after a misguided foray into writing regexp-specific functions.

Seq-ing the File System

You can seq over the file system. For starters, you can call java.io.File directly:

```
(import '(java.io File))
(.listFiles (File. "."))
-> [Ljava.io.File;@1f70f15e
```

The [Ljava.io.File… is Java's toString() representation for an array of Files. Sequence functions would call seq on this automatically, but the REPL doesn't.

So, seq it yourself:

```
(seq (.listFiles (File. ".")) )
-> (#<./concurrency> #<./sequences> ...)
```

If the default print format for files does not suit you, you could map them to a string form with getName:

```
; overkill
(map #(.getName %) (seq (.listFiles (File. "."))))
-> ("concurrency" "sequences" ...)
```

Once you decide to use a function like map, calling seq is redundant. Sequence library functions call seq for you, so you don't have to. The previous code simplifies to this:

```
(map #(.getName %) (.listFiles (File. ".")))
-> ("concurrency" "sequences" ...)
```

Often, you want to recursively traverse the entire directory tree. Clojure provides a depth-first walk via file-seq. If you file-seq from the sample code directory for this book, you will see a lot of files:

```
(count (file-seq (File. ".")))
-> 104 ; the final number will be larger!
```

What if you want to see only the files that have been changed recently? Write a predicate recently-modified? that checks to see whether File was touched in the last half hour:

src/examples/sequences.clj
```
(defn minutes-to-millis [mins] (* mins 1000 60))

(defn recently-modified? [file]
  (> (.lastModified file)
     (- (System/currentTimeMillis) (minutes-to-millis 30))))
```

Give it a try: [4]

```
(filter recently-modified? (file-seq (File. ".")))
-> (./sequences ./sequences/sequences.clj)
```

Seq-ing a Stream

You can seq over the lines of any Java Reader using line-seq. To get a Reader, you can use Clojure's clojure.java.io library. The clojure.java.io library provides a reader function that returns a reader on a stream, file, URL, or URI.

```
(use '[clojure.java.io :only (reader)])
; leaves reader open...
(take 2 (line-seq (reader "src/examples/utils.clj")))
-> ("(ns examples.utils" "  (:import [java.io BufferedReader InputStreamReader]))")
```

Since readers can represent nonmemory resources that need to be closed, you should wrap reader creation in a with-open. Create an expression that uses

---

4.   Your results will vary from those shown here.

the sequence function count to count the number of lines in a file and uses with-open to correctly close the reader:

```
(with-open [rdr (reader "src/examples/utils.clj")]
  (count (line-seq rdr)))
-> 64
```

To make the example more useful, add a filter to count only nonblank lines:

```
(with-open [rdr (reader "src/examples/utils.clj")]
  (count (filter #(re-find #"\S" %) (line-seq rdr))))
-> 55
```

Using seqs both on the file system and on the contents of individual files, you can quickly create interesting utilities. Create a program that defines these three predicates:

- non-blank? detects nonblank lines.
- non-svn? detects files that are not Subversion metadata.
- clojure-source? detects Clojure source code files.

Then, create a clojure-loc function that counts the lines of Clojure code in a directory tree, using a combination of sequence functions along the way: reduce, for, count, and filter.

src/examples/sequences.clj
```
(use '[clojure.java.io :only (reader)])
(defn non-blank? [line] (if (re-find #"\S" line) true false))

(defn non-svn? [file] (not (.contains (.toString file) ".svn")))

(defn clojure-source? [file] (.endsWith (.toString file) ".clj"))

(defn clojure-loc [base-file]
  (reduce
   +
   (for [file (file-seq base-file)
         :when (and (clojure-source? file) (non-svn? file))]
     (with-open [rdr (reader file)]
       (count (filter non-blank? (line-seq rdr)))))))
```

Now let's use clojure-loc to find out how much Clojure code is in Clojure itself:

```
(clojure-loc (java.io.File. "/home/abedra/src/opensource/clojure/clojure"))
-> 38716
```

The clojure-loc function is very task-specific, but because it is built out of sequence functions and simple predicates, you can easily tweak it to very different tasks.

Seq-ing XML

Clojure can seq over XML data. The examples that follow use this XML:

```
data/sequences/compositions.xml
<compositions>
  <composition composer="J. S. Bach">
    <name>The Art of the Fugue</name>
  </composition>
  <composition composer="F. Chopin">
    <name>Fantaisie-Impromptu Op. 66</name>
  </composition>
  <composition composer="W. A. Mozart">
    <name>Requiem</name>
  </composition>
</compositions>
```

The function clojure.xml/parse parses an XML file/stream/URI, returning the tree of data as a Clojure map, with nested vectors for descendants:

```
(use '[clojure.xml :only (parse)])
(parse (java.io.File. "data/sequences/compositions.xml"))
-> {:tag :compositions,
:attrs nil,
:content [{:tag :composition, ... etc. ...
```

You can manipulate this map directly, or you can use the xml-seq function to view the tree as a seq:

```
(xml-seq root)
```

The following example uses a list comprehension over an xml-seq to extract just the composers:

```
src/examples/sequences.clj
(for [x (xml-seq
          (parse (java.io.File. "data/sequences/compositions.xml")))
      :when (= :composition (:tag x))]
  (:composer (:attrs x)))

-> ("J. S. Bach" "F. Chopin" "W. A. Mozart")
```

3.5 Calling Structure-Specific Functions

Clojure's sequence functions allow you to write very general code. Sometimes you will want to be more specific and take advantage of the characteristics of a specific data structure. Clojure includes functions that specifically target lists, vectors, maps, structs, and sets.

We will take a quick tour of some of these structure-specific functions next. For a complete list of structure-specific functions in Clojure, see the Data Structures section of the Clojure website.[5]

Functions on Lists

Clojure supports the traditional names peek and pop for retrieving the first element of a list and the remainder, respectively:

```
(peek coll)
```

```
(pop coll)
```

Give a simple list a peek and pop:

```
(peek '(1 2 3))
-> 1

(pop '(1 2 3))
-> (2 3)
```

peek is the same as first, but pop is *not* the same as rest. pop will throw an exception if the sequence is empty:

```
(rest ())
-> ()

(pop ())
-> java.lang.IllegalStateException: Can't pop empty list
```

Functions on Vectors

Vectors also support peek and pop, but they deal with the element at the end of the vector:

```
(peek [1 2 3])
-> 3

(pop [1 2 3])
-> [1 2]
```

get returns the value at an index or returns nil if the index is outside the vector:

```
(get [:a :b :c] 1)
-> :b

(get [:a :b :c] 5)
-> nil
```

---

5. http://clojure.org/data_structures

Vectors are themselves functions. They take an index argument and return a value, or they throw an exception if the index is out of bounds:

```
([:a :b :c] 1)
-> :b

([:a :b :c] 5)
-> java.lang.ArrayIndexOutOfBoundsException: 5
```

assoc associates a new value with a particular index:

```
(assoc [0 1 2 3 4] 2 :two)
-> [0 1 :two 3 4]
```

subvec returns a subvector of a vector:

```
(subvec avec start end?)
```

If end is not specified, it defaults to the end of the vector:

```
(subvec [1 2 3 4 5] 3)
-> [4 5]

(subvec [1 2 3 4 5] 1 3)
-> [2 3]
```

Of course, you could simulate subvec with a combination of drop and take:

```
(take 2 (drop 1 [1 2 3 4 5]))
-> (2 3)
```

The difference is that take and drop are general and can work with any sequence. On the other hand, subvec is *much* faster for vectors. Whenever a structure-specific function like subvec duplicates functionality already available in the sequence library, it is probably there for performance. The documentation string for functions like subvec includes performance characteristics.

Functions on Maps

Clojure provides several functions for reading the keys and values in a map. keys returns a sequence of the keys, and vals returns a sequence of the values:

```
(keys map)
```

```
(vals map)
```

Try taking keys and values from a simple map:

```
(keys {:sundance "spaniel", :darwin "beagle"})
-> (:sundance :darwin)
```

```
(vals {:sundance "spaniel", :darwin "beagle"})
-> ("spaniel" "beagle")
```

get returns the value for a key or returns nil.

`(get map key value-if-not-found?)`

Use your REPL to test that get behaves as expected for keys both present and missing:

```
(get {:sundance "spaniel", :darwin "beagle"} :darwin)
-> "beagle"

(get {:sundance "spaniel", :darwin "beagle"} :snoopy)
-> nil
```

There is an approach even simpler than get. Maps are functions of their keys. So, you can leave out the get entirely, putting the map in function position at the beginning of a form:

```
({:sundance "spaniel", :darwin "beagle"} :darwin)
-> "beagle"

({:sundance "spaniel", :darwin "beagle"} :snoopy)
-> nil
```

Keywords are also functions. They take a collection as an argument and look themselves up in the collection. Since :darwin and :sundance are keywords, the earlier forms can be written with their elements in reverse order.

```
(:darwin {:sundance "spaniel", :darwin "beagle"} )
-> "beagle"

(:snoopy {:sundance "spaniel", :darwin "beagle"} )
-> nil
```

If you look up a key in a map and get nil back, you cannot tell whether the key was missing from the map or present with a value of nil. The contains? function solves this problem by testing for the mere presence of a key.

`(contains? map key)`

Create a map where nil is a legal value:

```
(def score {:stu nil :joey 100})
```

:stu is present, but if you see the nil value, you might not think so:

```
(:stu score)
-> nil
```

If you use contains?, you can verify that :stu is in the game, although presumably not doing very well:

```
(contains? score :stu)
-> true
```

Another approach is to call get, passing in an optional third argument that will be returned if the key is not found:

```
(get score :stu :score-not-found)
-> nil

(get score :aaron :score-not-found)
-> :score-not-found
```

The default return value of :score-not-found makes it possible to distinguish that :aaron is not in the map, while :stu is present with a value of nil.

If nil is a legal value in map, use contains? or the three-argument form of get to test the presence of a key.

Clojure also provides several functions for building new maps:

- assoc returns a map with a key/value pair added.
- dissoc returns a map with a key removed.
- select-keys returns a map, keeping only the keys passed in.
- merge combines maps. If multiple maps contain a key, the rightmost map wins.

To test these functions, create some song data:

src/examples/sequences.clj
```
(def song {:name "Agnus Dei"
           :artist "Krzysztof Penderecki"
           :album "Polish Requiem"
           :genre "Classical"})
```

Next, create various modified versions of the song collection:

```
(assoc song :kind "MPEG Audio File")
-> {:name "Agnus Dei", :album "Polish Requiem",
:kind "MPEG Audio File", :genre "Classical",
:artist "Krzysztof Penderecki"}

(dissoc song :genre)
-> {:name "Agnus Dei", :album "Polish Requiem",
:artist "Krzysztof Penderecki"}

(select-keys song [:name :artist])
-> {:name "Agnus Dei", :artist "Krzysztof Penderecki"}
```

```
(merge song {:size 8118166, :time 507245})
-> {:name "Agnus Dei", :album "Polish Requiem",
:genre "Classical", :size 8118166,
:artist "Krzysztof Penderecki", :time 507245}
```

Remember that song itself never changes. Each of the functions shown previously returns a new collection.

The most interesting map construction function is merge-with.

(merge-with merge-fn & maps)

merge-with is like merge, except that when two or more maps have the same key, you can specify your own function for combining the values under the key. Use merge-with and concat to build a sequence of values under each key:

```
(merge-with
  concat
  {:rubble ["Barney"], :flintstone ["Fred"]}
  {:rubble ["Betty"], :flintstone ["Wilma"]}
  {:rubble ["Bam-Bam"], :flintstone ["Pebbles"]})
  -> {:rubble ("Barney" "Betty" "Bam-Bam"),
      :flintstone ("Fred" "Wilma" "Pebbles")}
```

Starting with three distinct collections of family members keyed by last name, the previous code combines them into one collection keyed by last name.

Functions on Sets

In addition to the set functions in the clojure namespace, Clojure provides a group of functions in the clojure.set namespace. To use these functions with unqualified names, call (use 'clojure.set) from the REPL. For the following examples, you will also need the following vars:

src/examples/sequences.clj
```
(def languages #{"java" "c" "d" "clojure"})
(def beverages #{"java" "chai" "pop"})
```

The first group of clojure.set functions performs operations from set theory:

- union returns the set of all elements present in either input set.
- intersection returns the set of all elements present in *both* input sets.
- difference returns the set of all elements present in the first input set, minus those in the second.
- select returns the set of all elements matching a predicate.

Write an expression that finds the union of all languages and beverages:

```
(union languages beverages)
-> #{"java" "c" "d" "clojure" "chai" "pop"}
```

Next, try the languages that are not also beverages:

```
(difference languages beverages)
-> #{"c" "d" "clojure"}
```

If you enjoy terrible puns, you will like the fact that some things are both languages *and* beverages:

```
(intersection languages beverages)
-> #{"java"}
```

A surprising number of languages cannot afford a name larger than a single character:

```
(select #(= 1 (.length %)) languages)
-> #{"c" "d"}
```

Set union and difference are part of set theory, but they are also part of *relational algebra*, which is the basis for query languages such as SQL. The relational algebra consists of six primitive operators: set union and set difference (described earlier), plus rename, selection, projection, and cross product.

You can understand the relational primitives by following the analogy with relational databases (see the following table).

Relational Algebra	Database	Clojure Type System
Relation	Table	Anything set-like
Tuple	Row	Anything map-like

The following examples work against an in-memory database of musical compositions. Load the database before continuing:

src/examples/sequences.clj
```
(def compositions
  #{{:name "The Art of the Fugue" :composer "J. S. Bach"}
    {:name "Musical Offering" :composer "J. S. Bach"}
    {:name "Requiem" :composer "Giuseppe Verdi"}
    {:name "Requiem" :composer "W. A. Mozart"}})
(def composers
  #{{:composer "J. S. Bach" :country "Germany"}
    {:composer "W. A. Mozart" :country "Austria"}
    {:composer "Giuseppe Verdi" :country "Italy"}})
(def nations
  #{{:nation "Germany" :language "German"}
    {:nation "Austria" :language "German"}
    {:nation "Italy" :language "Italian"}})
```

The rename function renames keys (*database columns*), based on a map from original names to new names.

```
(rename relation rename-map)
```

Rename the compositions to use a title key instead of name:

```
(rename compositions {:name :title})
-> #{{:title "Requiem", :composer "Giuseppe Verdi"}
{:title "Musical Offering", :composer "J.S. Bach"}
{:title "Requiem", :composer "W. A. Mozart"}
{:title "The Art of the Fugue", :composer "J.S. Bach"}}
```

The select function returns maps for which a predicate is true and is analogous to the WHERE portion of a SQL SELECT:

```
(select pred relation)
```

Write a select expression that finds all the compositions whose title is "Requiem":

```
(select #(= (:name %) "Requiem") compositions)
-> #{{:name "Requiem", :composer "W. A. Mozart"}
{:name "Requiem", :composer "Giuseppe Verdi"}}
```

The project function returns only the parts of maps that match a set of keys.

```
(project relation keys)
```

project is similar to a SQL SELECT that specifies a subset of columns. Write a projection that returns only the name of the compositions:

```
(project compositions [:name])
-> #{{:name "Musical Offering"}
{:name "Requiem"}
{:name "The Art of the Fugue"}}
```

The final relational primitive, which is a cross product, is the foundation for the various kinds of joins in relational databases. The cross product returns every possible combination of rows in the different tables. You can do this easily enough in Clojure with a list comprehension:

```
(for [m compositions c composers] (concat m c))
-> ... 4 x 3 = 12 rows ...
```

Although the cross product is theoretically interesting, you will typically want some subset of the full cross product. For example, you might want to join sets based on shared keys:

```
(join relation-1 relation-2 keymap?)
```

You can join the composition names and composers on the shared key :composer:

```
(join compositions composers)
-> #{{:name "Requiem", :country "Austria",
:composer "W. A. Mozart"}
```

```
{:name "Musical Offering", :country "Germany",
:composer "J. S. Bach"}
{:name "Requiem", :country "Italy",
:composer "Giuseppe Verdi"}
{:name "The Art of the Fugue", :country "Germany",
:composer "J. S. Bach"}}
```

If the key names in the two relations do not match, you can pass a keymap that maps the key names in relation-1 to their corresponding keys in relation-2. For example, you can join composers, which uses :country, to nations, which uses :nation. For example:

```
(join composers nations {:country :nation})
-> #{{:language "German", :nation "Austria",
:composer "W. A. Mozart", :country "Austria"}
{:language "German", :nation "Germany",
:composer "J. S. Bach", :country "Germany"}
{:language "Italian", :nation "Italy",
:composer "Giuseppe Verdi", :country "Italy"}}
```

You can combine the relational primitives. Perhaps you want to know the set of all countries that are home to the composer of a requiem. You can use select to find all the requiems, join them with their composers, and project to narrow the results to just the country names:

```
(project
(join
(select #(= (:name %) "Requiem") compositions)
composers)
[:country])
-> #{{:country "Italy"} {:country "Austria"}}
```

The analogy between Clojure's relational algebra and a relational database is instructive. Remember, though, that Clojure's relational algebra is a general-purpose tool. You can use it on any kind of set-relational data. And while you're using it, you have the entire power of Clojure and Java at your disposal.

3.6 Wrapping Up

Clojure unifies all kinds of collections under a single abstraction, the sequence. After more than a decade dominated by object-oriented programming, Clojure's sequence library is the "Revenge of the Verbs."

Clojure's sequences are implemented using functional programming techniques: immutable data, recursive definition, and lazy realization. In the next chapter, you will see how to use these techniques directly, further expanding the power of Clojure.

CHAPTER 4

Functional Programming

Functional programming (FP) is a big topic, not to be learned in twenty-one days[1] or in a single chapter of a book. Nevertheless, you can reach a first level of effectiveness using lazy and recursive techniques in Clojure fairly quickly, and that is what we'll accomplish this chapter.

Here's how we'll do that:

- In Section 4.1, *Functional Programming Concepts*, on page 85, you'll get a quick overview of FP terms and concepts. This section also introduces the "Six Rules of Clojure FP" that we will refer to throughout the chapter.

- In Section 4.2, *How to Be Lazy*, on page 90, you'll experience the power of lazy sequences. You will create several implementations of the Fibonacci numbers, starting with a terrible approach and improving it to an elegant, lazy solution.

- As cool as lazy sequences are, you rarely need to work with them directly. In Section 4.3, *Lazier Than Lazy*, on page 98, you'll see how to rethink problems so that they can be solved directly using the sequence library described in Chapter 3, *Unifying Data with Sequences*, on page 55.

- And in Section 4.4, *Recursion Revisited*, on page 103, we'll explore some advanced issues. Some programmers will never need the techniques discussed here. If you are new to FP, it is OK to skip this section.

4.1 Functional Programming Concepts

Functional programming leads to code that is easier to write, read, test, and reuse. Here's how it works.

---

1. http://norvig.com/21-days.html

Pure Functions

Programs are built out of *pure functions*. A pure function has no *side effects*; that is, it does not depend on anything but its arguments, and its only influence on the outside world is through its return value.

Mathematical functions are pure functions. Two plus two is four, no matter where and when you ask. Also, asking doesn't *do* anything other than return the answer.

Program output is decidedly *impure*. For example, when you println, you change the outside world by pushing data onto an output stream. Also, the results of println depend on state outside the function: the standard output stream might be redirected, closed, or broken.

If you start writing pure functions, you will quickly realize that pure functions and *immutable* data go hand in hand. Consider the following mystery function:

```
(defn mystery [input]
  (if input data-1 data-2))
```

If mystery is a pure function, then regardless of what it does, data-1 and data-2 have to be immutable! Otherwise, changes to the data would cause the function to return different values for the same input.

A single piece of mutable data can ruin the game, rendering an entire call chain of functions impure. So, once you make a commitment to writing pure functions, you end up using immutable data in large sections of your application.

Persistent Data Structures

Immutable data is critical to Clojure's approach to both FP and state. On the FP side, pure functions cannot have side effects, such as updating the state of a mutable object. On the state side, Clojure's reference types require immutable data structures to implement their concurrency guarantees.

The fly in the ointment is performance. When all data is immutable, "update" translates into "create a copy of the original data, plus my changes." This will use up memory quickly! Imagine that you have an address book that takes up 5MB of memory. Then, you make five small updates. With a mutable address book, you are still consuming about 5MB of memory. But if you have to copy the whole address book for each update, then an immutable version would balloon to 25MB!

Clojure's data structures do not take this naive "copy everything" approach. Instead, all Clojure data structures are *persistent*. In this context, persistent means that the data structures preserve old copies of themselves by efficiently *sharing structure* between older and newer versions.

Structural sharing is easiest to visualize with a list. Consider list a with two elements:

```
(def a '(1 2))
-> #'user/a
```

Then, from a you can create a b with an additional element added:

```
(def b (cons 0 a))
-> #'user/b
```

b is able to reuse all of a's structure, rather than having its own private copy:

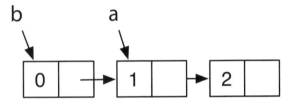

All of Clojure's data structures share structure where possible. For structures other than simple lists, the mechanics are more complex, of course. If you are interested in the details, check out the following articles:

- "Ideal Hash Trees"[2] by Phil Bagwell
- "Understanding Clojure's PersistentVector Implementation"[3] by Karl Krukow

Laziness and Recursion

Functional programs make heavy use of *recursion* and *laziness*. A recursion occurs when a function calls itself, either directly or indirectly. With laziness, an expression's evaluation is postponed until it is actually needed. Evaluating a lazy expression is called *realizing* the expression.

In Clojure, functions and expressions are not lazy. However, sequences *are* generally lazy. Because so much Clojure programming is sequence manipulation, you get many of the benefits of a fully lazy language. In particular, you can build complex expressions using lazy sequences and then pay only for the elements you actually need.

---

2. http://lampwww.epfl.ch/papers/idealhashtrees.pdf
3. http://tinyurl.com/clojure-persistent-vector

Lazy techniques imply pure functions. You never have to worry about when to call a pure function, since it always returns the same thing. Impure functions, on the other hand, do not play well with lazy techniques. As a programmer, you must explicitly control when an impure function is called, because if you call it at some other time, it may behave differently!

Referential Transparency

Laziness depends on the ability to replace a function call with its result at any time. Functions that have this ability are called *referentially transparent*, because calls to such functions can be replaced without affecting the behavior of the program. In addition to laziness, referentially transparent functions can also benefit from the following:

- *Memoization*, automatic caching of results
- Automatic *parallelization*, moving function evaluation to another processor or machine

Pure functions are referentially transparent *by definition*. Most other functions are *not* referentially transparent, and those that are must be proven safe by code review.

Benefits of FP

Well, that is a lot of terminology, and we promised it would make your code easier to write, read, test, and compose. Here's how.

You'll find functional code easier to *write* because the relevant information is right in front of you, in a function's argument list. You do not have to worry about global scope, session scope, application scope, or thread scope. Functional code is easier to *read* for exactly the same reason.

Code that is easier to read and write is going to be easier to test, but functional code brings an additional benefit for testing. As projects get large, it often takes a lot of effort to set up the right environment to execute a test. This is much less of a problem with functional code, because there *is no relevant environment* beyond the function's arguments.

Functional code improves *reuse*. To reuse code, you must be able to do the following:

- Find and understand a piece of useful code.
- Compose the reusable code with other code.

The readability of functional code helps you find and understand the functions you need, but the benefit for *composing* code is even more compelling.

Composability is a hard problem. For years programmers have used *encapsulation* to try to create composable code. Encapsulation creates a firewall, providing access to data only through a public API.

Encapsulation helps, but it is nowhere near enough. Even with encapsulated objects, there are far too many surprising interactions when you try to compose entire systems. The problem is those darn side effects. *Impure functions* violate encapsulation, because they let the outside world reach in (invisibly!) and change the behavior of your code. Pure functions, on the other hand, are truly encapsulated and composable. Put them anywhere you want in a system, and they will always behave in the same way.

The Six Rules

Although the benefits of FP are compelling, FP is a wholesale change from the imperative programming style that dominates much of the programming world today. Plus, Clojure takes a unique approach to FP that strikes a balance between academic purity and the reality of running well on the JVM. That means there is a lot to learn all at once. But fear not. If you are new to FP, the following "Six Rules of Clojure FP" will help you on your initial steps toward FP mastery, Clojure-style:

1. Avoid direct recursion. The JVM cannot optimize recursive calls, and Clojure programs that recurse will blow their stack.

2. Use recur when you are producing scalar values or small, fixed sequences. Clojure *will* optimize calls that use an explicit recur.

3. When producing large or variable-sized sequences, always be lazy. (Do *not* recur.) Then, your callers can consume just the part of the sequence they actually need.

4. Be careful not to realize more of a lazy sequence than you need.

5. Know the sequence library. You can often write code without using recur or the lazy APIs at all.

6. Subdivide. Divide even simple-seeming problems into smaller pieces, and you will often find solutions in the sequence library that lead to more general, reusable code.

Rules 5 and 6 are particularly important. If you are new to FP, you can translate these two rules to this: "Ignore this chapter and just use the techniques in Chapter 3, *Unifying Data with Sequences*, on page 55 until you hit a wall."

Like most rules, the six rules are guidelines, not absolutes. As you become comfortable with FP, you will find reasons to break them.

Now, let's get started writing functional code.

4.2 How to Be Lazy

Functional programs make great use of *recursive definitions*. A recursive definition consists of two parts:

- A *basis*, which explicitly enumerates some members of the sequence

- An *induction*, which provides rules for combining members of the sequence to produce additional members

Our challenge in this section is converting a recursive definition into working code. You might do this in several ways:

- A simple recursion, using a function that calls itself in some way to implement the induction step.

- A tail recursion, using a function only calling itself at the tail end of its execution. Tail recursion enables an important optimization.

- A lazy sequence that eliminates actual recursion and calculates a value later, when it is needed.

Choosing the right approach is important. Implementing a recursive definition poorly can lead to code that performs terribly, consumes all available stack and fails, consumes all available heap and fails, or does all of these. In Clojure, being lazy is often the right approach.

We will explore all of these approaches by applying them to the Fibonacci numbers. Named for the Italian mathematician Leonardo (Fibonacci) of Pisa (c.1170–c.1250), the Fibonacci numbers were actually known to Indian mathematicians as far back as 200 BC. The Fibonacci numbers have many interesting properties, and they crop up again and again in algorithms, data structures, and even biology.[4] The Fibonaccis have a very simple recursive definition:

- Basis: F_0, the zeroth Fibonacci number, is zero. F_1, the first Fibonacci number, is one.

- Induction: For $n > 1$, F_n equals $F_{n-1}+F_{n-2}$.

---

4. http://en.wikipedia.org/wiki/Fibonacci_number

Using this definition, the first ten Fibonacci numbers are as follows:

```
(0 1 1 2 3 5 8 13 21 34)
```

Let's begin by implementing the Fibonaccis using a simple recursion. The following Clojure function will return the *nth* Fibonacci number:

src/examples/functional.clj

```
Line 1 ; bad idea
     2 (defn stack-consuming-fibo [n]
     3   (cond
     4     (= n 0) 0
     5     (= n 1) 1
     6     :else (+ (stack-consuming-fibo (- n 1))
     7              (stack-consuming-fibo (- n 2)))))
```

Lines 4 and 5 define the basis, and line 6 defines the induction. The implementation is recursive because stack-consuming-fibo calls itself on lines 6 and 7.

Test that stack-consuming-fibo works correctly for small values of n:

```
(stack-consuming-fibo 9)
-> 34
```

Good so far, but there is a problem calculating larger Fibonacci numbers such as $F_{1000000}$:

```
(stack-consuming-fibo 1000000)
-> StackOverflowError clojure.lang.Numbers.minus (Numbers.java:1837)
```

Because of the recursion, each call to stack-consuming-fibo for $n > 1$ begets two more calls to stack-consuming-fibo. At the JVM level, these calls are translated into method calls, each of which allocates a data structure called a *stack frame*.[5]

The stack-consuming-fibo creates a depth of stack frames proportional to n, which quickly exhausts the JVM stack and causes the StackOverflowError shown earlier. (It also creates a total number of stack frames that is exponential in n, so its performance is terrible even when the stack does not overflow.)

Clojure function calls are designated as *stack-consuming* because they allocate stack frames that use up stack space. In Clojure, you should almost always avoid stack-consuming recursion as shown in stack-consuming-fibo.

---

5. For more on how the JVM manages its stack, see "Runtime Data Areas" at http://tinyurl.com/jvm-spec-toc.

Tail Recursion

Functional programs can solve the stack-usage problem with *tail recursion*. A tail-recursive function is still defined recursively, but the recursion must come at the tail, that is, at an expression that is a return value of the function. Languages can then perform *tail-call optimization* (TCO), converting tail recursions into iterations that do not consume the stack.

The stack-consuming-fibo definition of Fibonacci is not tail-recursive, because it calls add (+) *after* both calls to stack-consuming-fibo. To make fibo tail-recursive, you must create a function whose arguments carry enough information to move the induction forward, without any extra "after" work (like an addition) that would push the recursion out of the tail position. For fibo, such a function needs to know two Fibonacci numbers, plus an ordinal n that can count down to zero as new Fibonaccis are calculated. You can write tail-fibo thusly:

```
src/examples/functional.clj
Line 1 (defn tail-fibo [n]
     2   (letfn [(fib
     3            [current next n]
     4            (if (zero? n)
     5              current
     6              (fib next (+ current next) (dec n))))]
     7     (fib 0N 1N n)))
```

Line 2 introduces the letfn macro:

```
(letfn fnspecs & body)  ; fnspecs ==> [(fname [params*] exprs)+]
```

letfn is like let but is dedicated to letting local functions. Each function declared in a letfn can call itself or any other function in the same letfn block. Line 3 declares that fib has three arguments: the current Fibonacci, the next Fibonacci, and the number n of steps remaining.

Line 5 returns current when there are no steps remaining, and line 6 continues the calculation, decrementing the remaining steps by one. Finally, line 7 kicks off the recursion with the basis values 0 and 1, plus the ordinal n of the Fibonacci we are looking for.

tail-fibo works for small values of n:

```
(tail-fibo 9)
-> 34N
```

But even though it is tail-recursive, it still fails for large n:

```
(tail-fibo 1000000)
-> StackOverflowError java.lang.Integer.numberOfLeadingZeros (Integer.java:1054)
```

The problem here is the JVM. While functional languages such as Haskell can perform TCO, the JVM was not designed for functional languages. No language that runs directly on the JVM can perform automatic TCO.[6]

The absence of TCO is unfortunate but not a showstopper for functional programs. Clojure provides several pragmatic workarounds: explicit self-recursion with recur, lazy sequences, and explicit mutual recursion with trampoline.

Self-recursion with recur

One special case of recursion that *can* be optimized away on the JVM is a self-recursion. Fortunately, the tail-fibo is an example: it calls itself directly, not through some series of intermediate functions.

In Clojure, you can convert a function that tail-calls itself into an explicit self-recursion with recur. Using this approach, convert tail-fibo into recur-fibo:

src/examples/functional.clj

```
Line 1 ; better but not great
   2 (defn recur-fibo [n]
   3   (letfn [(fib
   4             [current next n]
   5             (if (zero? n)
   6               current
   7               (recur next (+ current next) (dec n))))]
   8     (fib 0N 1N n)))
```

The critical difference between tail-fibo and recur-fibo is on line 7, where recur replaces the call to fib.

The recur-fibo will not consume stack as it calculates Fibonacci numbers and can calculate F_n for large n if you have the patience:

```
(recur-fibo 9)
-> 34N
```

```
(recur-fibo 1000000)
-> 195 ... 208,982 other digits ... 875N
```

The complete value of $F_{1000000}$ is included in the sample code at output/f-1000000.

The recur-fibo calculates one Fibonacci number. But what if you want several? Calling recur-fibo multiple times would be wasteful, since none of the work from

---

6. On today's JVMs, languages can provide automatic TCO for *some* kinds of recursion but not for *all*. Since there is no general solution, Clojure forces you to be explicit. When and if general TCO becomes widely supported on the JVM, Clojure will support it as well.

any call to recur-fibo is ever cached for the next call. But how many values should be cached? Which ones? These choices should be made by the *caller* of the function, not the implementer.

Ideally you would define sequences with an API that makes *no reference* to the specific range that a particular client cares about and then let clients pull the range they want with take and drop. This is exactly what lazy sequences provide.

Lazy Sequences

Lazy sequences are constructed using the macro lazy-seq:

`(lazy-seq & body)`

A lazy-seq will invoke its body only when needed, that is, when seq is called directly or indirectly. lazy-seq will then cache the result for subsequent calls. You can use lazy-seq to define a lazy Fibonacci series as follows:

```
src/examples/functional.clj
Line 1 (defn lazy-seq-fibo
     2   ([]
     3     (concat [0 1] (lazy-seq-fibo 0N 1N)))
     4   ([a b]
     5     (let [n (+ a b)]
     6       (lazy-seq
     7        (cons n (lazy-seq-fibo b n)))))))
```

On line 3, the zero-argument body returns the concatenation of the basis values [0 1] and then calls the two-argument body to calculate the rest of the values. On line 5, the two-argument body calculates the next value n in the series, and on line 7 it conses n onto the rest of the values.

The key is line 6, which makes its body lazy. Without this, the recursive call to lazy-seq-fibo on line 7 would happen immediately, and lazy-seq-fibo would recurse until it blew the stack. This illustrates the general pattern: wrap the recursive part of a function body with lazy-seq to replace recursion with laziness.

lazy-seq-fibo works for small values:

```
(take 10 (lazy-seq-fibo))
-> (0 1 1N 2N 3N 5N 8N 13N 21N 34N)
```

lazy-seq-fibo also works for large values. Use (rem ... 1000) to print only the last three digits of the one millionth Fibonacci number:

```
(rem (nth (lazy-seq-fibo) 1000000) 1000)
-> 875N
```

The lazy-seq-fibo approach follows rule 3, using laziness to implement an infinite sequence. But as is often the case, you do not need to explicitly call lazy-seq yourself. By rule 5, you can reuse existing sequence library functions that return lazy sequences. Consider this use of iterate:

```
(take 5 (iterate (fn [[a b]] [b (+ a b)]) [0 1]))
-> ([0 1] [1 1] [1 2] [2 3] [3 5])
```

The iterate begins with the first pair of Fibonacci numbers: [0 1]. By working pairwise, it then calculates the Fibonaccis by carrying along just enough information (two values) to calculate the next value.

The Fibonaccis are simply the first value of each pair. They can be extracted by calling map first over the entire sequence, leading to the following definition of fibo suggested by Christophe Grand:

src/examples/functional.clj
```
(defn fibo []
  (map first (iterate (fn [[a b]] [b (+ a b)]) [0N 1N])))
```

fibo returns a lazy sequence because it builds on map and iterate, which also return lazy sequences. fibo is also *simple*. fibo is the shortest implementation we have seen so far. But if you are accustomed to writing imperative, looping code, correctly *choosing* fibo over other approaches may not seem simple at all! Learning to think recursively, lazily, and within the JVM's limitations on recursion—all at the same time—can be intimidating. Let the rules help you. The Fibonacci numbers are infinite: rule 3 correctly predicts that the right approach in Clojure will be a lazy sequence, and rule 5 lets the existing sequence functions do most of the work.

Lazy definitions consume *some* stack and heap. But they do not consume resources proportional to the size of an entire (possibly infinite!) sequence. Instead, *you choose* how many resources to consume when you traverse the sequence. If you want the one millionth Fibonacci number, you can get it from fibo, without having to consume stack or heap space for all the previous values.

There is no such thing as a free lunch. But with lazy sequences, you can have an infinite menu and pay only for the menu items you are eating at a given moment. When writing Clojure programs, you should prefer lazy sequences over loop/recur for any sequence that varies in size and for any large sequence.

Coming to Realization

Lazy sequences consume significant resources only as they are *realized*, that is, as a portion of the sequence is actually instantiated in memory. Clojure works hard to be lazy and avoid realizing sequences until it is absolutely necessary. For example, take returns a lazy sequence and does no realization at all. You can see this by creating a var to hold, say, the first billion Fibonacci numbers:

```
(def lots-o-fibs (take 1000000000 (fibo)))
-> #'user/lots-o-fibs
```

The creation of lots-o-fibs returns almost immediately, because it does *almost nothing*. If you ever call a function that needs to *actually use* some values in lots-o-fibs, Clojure will calculate them. Even then, it will do only what is necessary. For example, the following will return the 100th Fibonacci number from lots-o-fibs, without calculating the millions of other numbers that lots-o-fibs promises to provide:

```
(nth lots-o-fibs 100)
-> 354224848179261915075N
```

Most sequence functions return lazy sequences. If you are not sure whether a function returns a lazy sequence, the function's documentation string typically will tell you the answer:

```
(doc take)
-------------------------
clojure.core/take
([n coll])
Returns a lazy seq of the first n items in coll, or all items if
there are fewer than n.
```

The REPL, however, is *not lazy*. The printer used by the REPL will, by default, print the entirety of a collection. That is why we stuffed the first billion Fibonaccis into lots-o-fibs, instead of evaluating them at the REPL. Don't enter the following at the REPL:

```
; don't do this
(take 1000000000 (fibo))
```

If you enter the previous expression, the printer will attempt to print a billion Fibonacci numbers, realizing the entire collection as it goes. You will probably get bored and exit the REPL before Clojure runs out of memory.

As a convenience for working with lazy sequences, you can configure how many items the printer will print by setting the value of *print-length*:

```
(set! *print-length* 10)
-> 10
```

For collections with more than ten items, the printer will now print only the first ten followed by an ellipsis. So, you can safely print a billion fibos:

```
(take 1000000000 (fibo))
-> (0N 1N 1N 2N 3N 5N 8N 13N 21N 34N ...)
```

Or even all the fibos:

```
(fibo)
-> (0N 1N 1N 2N 3N 5N 8N 13N 21N 34N ...)
```

Lazy sequences are wonderful. They do only what is needed, and for the most part you don't have to worry about them. If you ever want to force a sequence to be fully realized, you can use either doall or dorun, discussed in *Forcing Sequences*, on page 70.

Losing Your Head

There is one last thing to consider when working with lazy sequences. Lazy sequences let you define a large (possibly infinite) sequence and then work with a small part of that sequence in memory at a given moment. This clever ploy will fail if you (or some API) unintentionally hold a reference to the part of the sequence you no longer care about.

The most common way this can happen is if you accidentally hold the head (first item) of a sequence. In the examples in the previous sections, each variant of the Fibonacci numbers was defined as a function returning a sequence, not the sequence itself.

You could define the sequence directly as a top-level var:

src/examples/functional.clj
```
; holds the head (avoid!)
(def head-fibo (lazy-cat [0N 1N] (map + head-fibo (rest head-fibo))))
```

This definition uses lazy-cat, which is like concat except that the arguments are evaluated only when needed. This is a very pretty definition in that it defines the recursion by mapping a sum over (each element of the Fibonaccis) and (each element of the *rest* of the Fibonaccis).

head-fibo works great for small Fibonacci numbers:

```
(take 10 head-fibo)
-> (0N 1N 1N 2N 3N 5N 8N 13N 21N 34N)
```

but not so well for huge ones:

```
(nth head-fibo 1000000)
-> java.lang.OutOfMemoryError: GC overhead limit exceeded
```

The problem is that the top-level var head-fibo *holds the head* of the collection. This prevents the garbage collector from reclaiming elements of the sequence after you have moved past those elements. So, any part of the Fibonacci sequence that you actually use gets cached for the life of the value referenced by head-fibo, which is likely to be the life of the program.

Unless you want to cache a sequence as you traverse it, you must be careful not to keep a reference to the head of the sequence. As the head-fibo example demonstrates, you should normally expose lazy sequences as a function that *returns* the sequence, not as a var that *contains* the sequence. If a caller of your function wants an explicit cache, the caller can always create its own var. With lazy sequences, losing your head is often a good idea.

4.3 Lazier Than Lazy

Clojure's lazy sequences are a great form of laziness at the language level. As a programmer, you can be *even lazier* by finding solutions that do not require explicit sequence manipulation at all. You can often combine existing sequence functions to solve a problem, without having to get your hands dirty at the level of recur or lazy sequences.

As an example of this, you will implement several solutions to the following problem.[7] You are given a sequence of coin toss results, where heads is :h and tails is :t:

```
[:h :t :t :h :h :h]
```

How many times in the sequence does heads come up twice in a row? In the previous example, the answer is two. Toss 3 and toss 4 are both heads, and toss 4 and toss 5 are both heads.

The sequence of coin tosses might be very large, but it will be finite. Since you are looking for a scalar answer (a count), by rule 2 it is acceptable to use recur:

```
src/examples/functional.clj
Line 1 (defn count-heads-pairs [coll]
     2    (loop [cnt 0 coll coll]
     3      (if (empty? coll)
     4        cnt
     5        (recur (if (= :h (first coll) (second coll))
     6                 (inc cnt)
     7                 cnt)
     8               (rest coll)))))
```

---

7. Hat tip to Jeff Brown, who posed this problem over breakfast at a No Fluff, Just Stuff symposium.

Since the purpose of the function is to count something, the loop introduces a cnt binding, initially zero on line 2. The loop also introduces its own binding for the coll so that we can shrink the coll each time through the recur. Line 3 provides the basis for the recurrence. If a sequence of coin tosses is empty, it certainly has zero runs of two heads in a row.

Line 5 is the meat of the function, incrementing the cnt by one if the first and second items of coll are both heads (:h).

Try a few inputs to see that count-heads-pairs works as advertised:

```
(count-heads-pairs [:h :h :h :t :h])
-> 2

(count-heads-pairs [:h :t :h :t :h])
-> 0
```

Although count-heads-pairs works, it fails as code prose. The key notion of "two in a rowness" is completely obscured by the boilerplate for loop/recur. To fix this, you will need to use rules 5 and 6, subdividing the problem to take advantage of Clojure's sequence library.

The first problem you will encounter is that almost all the sequence functions do something to each element in a sequence in turn. This doesn't help us at all, since we want to look at each element in the context of its immediate neighbors. So, let's transform the sequence. When you see this:

```
[:h :t :t :h :h :h]
```

you should mentally translate that into a sequence of every adjacent pair:

```
[[:h :t] [:t :t] [:t :h] [:h :h] [:h :h]]
```

Write a function named by-pairs that performs this transformation. Because the output of by-pairs varies based on the size of its input, by rule 3 you should build this sequence lazily:

```
src/examples/functional.clj
Line 1  ; overly complex, better approaches follow...
     2  (defn by-pairs [coll]
     3    (let [take-pair (fn [c]
     4                      (when (next c) (take 2 c)))]
     5      (lazy-seq
     6        (when-let [pair (seq (take-pair coll))]
     7          (cons pair (by-pairs (rest coll)))))))
```

Line 3 defines a function that takes the first pair of elements from the collection. Line 5 ensures that the recursion is evaluated lazily.

Line 6 is a conditional: if the next pair does not actually contain two elements, we must be (almost) at the end of the list, and we implicitly terminate. If we do get two elements, then on line 7 we continue building the sequence by consing our pair onto the pairs to be had from the rest of the collection.

Check that by-pairs works:

```
(by-pairs [:h :t  :t :h :h :h])
-> ((:h :t) (:t :t) (:t :h) (:h :h) (:h :h))
```

Now that you can think of the coin tosses as a sequence *of pairs* of results, it is easy to describe count-heads-pairs in English:

"Count the pairs of results that are all heads."

This English description translates directly into existing sequence library functions: "Count" is count, of course, and "that are all heads" suggests a filter:

src/examples/functional.clj
```
(defn count-heads-pairs [coll]
  (count (filter (fn [pair] (every? #(= :h %) pair))
                 (by-pairs coll))))
```

This is much more expressive than the recur-based implementation, and it makes clear that we are counting all the adjacent pairs of heads. But we can make things even simpler. Clojure already has a more general version of by-pairs named partition:

(**partition** size step? coll)

partition breaks a collection into chunks of size size. So, you could break a heads/tails vector into a sequence of pairs:

```
(partition 2 [:h :t  :t :h :h :h])
-> ((:h :t) (:t :h) (:h :h))
```

That isn't quite the same as by-pairs, which yields overlapping pairs. But partition can do overlaps too. The optional step argument determines how far partition moves down the collection before starting its next chunk. If not specified, step is the same as size. To make partition work like by-pairs, set size to 2 and set step to 1:

```
(partition 2 1 [:h :t  :t :h :h :h])
-> ((:h :t) (:t :t) (:t :h) (:h :h) (:h :h))

(by-pairs [:h :t  :t :h :h :h])
-> ((:h :t) (:t :t) (:t :h) (:h :h) (:h :h))
```

> ## Faces of def
>
> Throughout the book you will use various def forms to create vars, such as defn, defmacro, and defmulti. These forms are all eventually wrappers around the def special form.
>
> defonce ensures that a var exists and sets the root binding for the var *only if it is not already set*:
>
> ```
> (defonce a-symbol initial-value?)
> ```
>
> defn- works just like defn but yields a *private* function that is accessible only in the namespace where it was defined.
>
> ```
> (defn- name & args-as-for-defn)
> ```
>
> Many other def forms also have dash-suffixed variants that are private.

Another possible area of improvement is the count/filter idiom used to count the pairs that are both heads. This combination comes up often enough that it is worth encapsulating in a count-if function:

src/examples/functional.clj
```
(def ^{:doc "Count items matching a filter"}
  count-if (comp count filter))
```

comp is used to *compose* two or more functions:

```
(comp f & fs)
```

The composed function is a new function that applies the rightmost function to its arguments, the next-rightmost function to that result, and so on. So, count-if will first filter and then count the results of the filter:

```
(count-if odd? [1 2 3 4 5])
-> 3
```

Finally, you can use count-if and partition to create a count-runs function that is more general than count-heads-pairs:

src/examples/functional.clj
```
(defn count-runs
  "Count runs of length n where pred is true in coll."
  [n pred coll]
  (count-if #(every? pred %) (partition n 1 coll)))
```

count-runs is a winning combination: both simpler and more general than the previous versions of count-heads-pairs. You can use it to count pairs of heads:

```
(count-runs 2 #(= % :h) [:h :t :t :h :h :h])
-> 2
```

But you can just as easily use it to count pairs of tails:

```
(count-runs 2 #(= % :t) [:h :t :t :h :h :h])
-> 1
```

Or, instead of pairs, how about runs of three heads in a row?

```
(count-runs 3 #(= % :h) [:h :t :t :h :h :h])
-> 1
```

If you still want to have a function named count-heads-pairs, you can implement it in terms of count-runs:

src/examples/functional.clj

```
(def ^{:doc "Count runs of length two that are both heads"}
  count-heads-pairs (partial count-runs 2 #(= % :h)))
```

This version of count-heads-pairs builds a new function using partial:

```
(partial f & partial-args)
```

partial performs a *partial application* of a function. You specify a function f and part of the argument list when you perform the partial. You specify the remainder of the argument list later, when you call the function created by partial. So, the following:

```
(partial count-runs 1 #(= % :h))
```

is a more expressive way of saying this:

```
(fn [coll] (count-runs 1 #(= % :h) coll))
```

Partial application is similar but not identical to *currying*.

Currying and Partial Application

When you *curry* a function, you get a new function that takes one argument and returns the original function with that one argument fixed. (Curry is named for Haskell Curry, an American logician best known for his work in combinatory logic.) If Clojure had a curry, it might be implemented like this:

```
; almost a curry
(defn faux-curry [& args] (apply partial partial args))
```

One use of curry is partial application. Here is partial application in Clojure:

```
(def add-3 (partial + 3))
(add-3 7)
-> 10
```

And here is partial application using our faux-curry:

```
(def add-3 ((faux-curry +) 3))
(add-3 7)
-> 10
```

If all you want is partial application, currying is just an intermediate step. Our faux-curry is not a real curry. A real curry would return a result, not a function of no arguments, once all the arguments were fixed. You can see the difference here, using the function true?, which takes only one argument:

```
; faux curry
((faux-curry true?) (= 1 1))
-> #<... mangled function name ...>

; if the curry were real
((curry true?) (= 1 1))
-> true
```

Since Clojure functions can have variable-length argument lists, Clojure cannot know when all the arguments are fixed. But you, the programmer, do know when you are done adding arguments. Once you have curried as many arguments as you want, just invoke the function. That amounts to adding an extra set of parentheses around the earlier expression:

```
(((faux-curry true?) (= 1 1)))
-> true
```

The absence of curry from Clojure is not a major problem, since partial is available and that is what people generally want out of curry anyway. In fact, many programmers use the terms *currying* and *partial application* interchangeably.

You have seen a lot of new forms in this section. Do not let all the details obscure the key idea: by combining existing functions from the sequence library, you were able to create a solution that was both simpler and more general than the direct approach. And, you did not have to worry about laziness or recursion at all. Instead, you worked at a higher level of abstraction and let Clojure deal with laziness and recursion for you.

4.4 Recursion Revisited

Clojure works very hard to balance the power of functional programming with the reality of the Java Virtual Machine. One example of this is the well-motivated choice of explicit TCO through loop/recur.

But blending the best of two worlds always runs the risk of unpleasant compromises, and it certainly makes sense to ask the question "Does Clojure contain hidden design compromises that, while not obvious on day one, will bite me later?"

This question is *never* fully answerable for any language, but let's consider it by exploring some more complex recursions. First we will look at *mutual recursion*.

A mutual recursion occurs when the recursion bounces between two or more functions. Instead of A calls A calls A, you have A calls B calls A again. As a simple example, you could define my-odd? and my-even? using mutual recursion:

```
src/examples/functional.clj
(declare my-odd? my-even?)

(defn my-odd? [n]
  (if (= n 0)
    false
    (my-even? (dec n))))

(defn my-even? [n]
  (if (= n 0)
    true
    (my-odd? (dec n))))
```

Because my-odd? and my-even? each call the other, you need to create both vars before actually defining the functions. You could do this with def, but the declare macro lets you create both vars (with no initial binding) in a single line of code.

Verify that my-odd? and my-even? work for small values:

```
(map my-even? (range 10))
-> (true false true false true false true false true false)

(map my-odd? (range 10))
-> (false true false true false true false true false true)
```

my-odd? and my-even? consume stack frames proportional to the size of their argument, so they will fail with large numbers.

```
(my-even? (* 1000 1000 1000))
-> StackOverflowError clojure.lang.Numbers$LongOps.equiv (Numbers.java:490)
```

This is very similar to the problem that motivated the introduction of recur. But you cannot use recur to fix it, because recur works with self-recursion, not mutual recursion. Of course, odd/even can be implemented more efficiently *without* recursion anyway. Clojure's implementation uses bit-and (bitwise and) to implement odd? and even?:

```
; from core.clj
(defn even? [n] (zero? (bit-and n 1)))
(defn odd? [n] (not (even? n)))
```

We picked odd/even for its simplicity. Other recursive problems are not so simple and do not have an elegant nonrecursive solution. We will examine four approaches that you can use to solve such problems:

- Converting to self-recursion
- Trampolining a mutual recursion
- Replacing recursion with laziness
- Shortcutting recursion with memoization

Converting to Self-recursion

Mutual recursion is often a nice way to model separate but related concepts. For example, oddness and evenness are separate concepts but clearly related to one another.

You can convert a mutual recursion to a self-recursion by coming up with a single abstraction that deals with multiple concepts simultaneously. For example, you can think of oddness and evenness in terms of a single concept: *parity*. Define a parity function that uses recur and returns 0 for even numbers and 1 for odd numbers:

src/examples/functional.clj
```
(defn parity [n]
  (loop [n n par 0]
    (if (= n 0)
      par
      (recur (dec n) (- 1 par)))))
```

Test that parity works for small values:

```
(map parity (range 10))
-> (0 1 0 1 0 1 0 1 0 1)
```

At this point, you can trivially implement my-odd? and my-even? in terms of parity:

src/examples/functional.clj
```
(defn my-even? [n] (= 0 (parity n)))
(defn my-odd? [n] (= 1 (parity n)))
```

Parity is a straightforward concept. Unfortunately, many mutual recursions will not simplify down into an elegant self-recursion. If you try to convert a mutual recursion into a self-recursion and you find the resulting code to be full of conditional expressions that obfuscate the definition, then do not use this approach.

Trampolining Mutual Recursion

A *trampoline* is a technique for optimizing mutual recursion. A trampoline is like an after-the-fact recur, imposed by the *caller* of a function instead of the *implementer*. Since the caller can call more than one function inside a trampoline, trampolines can optimize mutual recursion.

Clojure's trampoline function invokes one of your mutually recursive functions:

```
(trampoline f & partial-args)
```

If the return value is not a function, then a trampoline works just like calling the function directly. Try trampolining a few simple Clojure functions:

```
(trampoline list)
-> ()
(trampoline + 1 2)
-> 3
```

If the return value *is* a function, then trampoline assumes you want to call it recursively and calls it for you. trampoline manages its own recur, so it will keep calling your function until it stops returning functions.

Back in *Tail Recursion*, on page 92, you implemented a tail-fibo function. You saw how the function consumed stack space and replaced the tail recursion with a recur. Now you have another option. You can take the code of tail-fibo and prepare it for trampolining by wrapping the recursive return case inside a function.

This requires adding only a single character, the #, to introduce an anonymous function:

src/examples/trampoline.clj

```
Line 1 ; Example only. Don't write code like this.
   -  (defn trampoline-fibo [n]
   -    (let [fib (fn fib [f-2 f-1 current]
   -                (let [f (+ f-2 f-1)]
   5                  (if (= n current)
   -                    f
   -                    #(fib f-1 f (inc current)))))]
   -      (cond
   -        (= n 0) 0
   10       (= n 1) 1
   -        :else (fib 0N 1 2))))
```

The only difference between this and the original version of tail-fibo is the initial # on line 7. Try bouncing trampoline-fibo on a trampoline:

```
(trampoline trampoline-fibo 9)
-> 34N
```

Since trampoline does a recur for you, it can handle large inputs just fine, without throwing a StackOverflowError:

```
(rem (trampoline trampoline-fibo 1000000) 1000)
-> 875N
```

We have ported tail-fibo to use trampoline in order to compare and contrast trampoline and recur. For self-recursions like trampoline-fibo, trampoline offers no advantage, and you should prefer recur. But with mutual recursion, trampoline comes into its own.

Consider the mutually recursive definition of my-odd? and my-even?, which we presented at the beginning of Section 4.4, *Recursion Revisited*, on page 103. You can convert these broken, stack-consuming implementations to use trampoline using the same approach you used to convert tail-fibo: simply prepend a # to any recursive tail calls:

src/examples/trampoline.clj
```
Line 1  (declare my-odd? my-even?)

      - (defn my-odd? [n]
      -   (if (= n 0)
      5     false
      -     #(my-even? (dec n))))

      - (defn my-even? [n]
      -   (if (= n 0)
     10     true
      -     #(my-odd? (dec n))))
```

The only difference from the original implementation is the # wrappers on lines 6 and 11. With this change in place, you can trampoline large values of n without blowing the stack:

```
(trampoline my-even? 1000000)
-> true
```

A trampoline is a special-purpose solution to a specific problem. It requires doctoring your original functions to return a different type to indicate recursion. If one of the other techniques presented here provides a more elegant implementation for a particular recursion, that is great. If not, you will be happy to have trampoline in your box of tools.

Replacing Recursion with Laziness

Of all the techniques for eliminating or optimizing recursion discussed in this chapter, laziness is the one you will probably use most often.

For our example, we will implement the replace function developed by Eugene Wallingford to demonstrate mutual recursion. (See http://www.cs.uni.edu/~wallingf/patterns/recursion.html.)

replace works with an *s-list* data structure, which is a list that can contain both symbols and lists of symbols. replace takes an s-list, an oldsym, and a newsym and replaces all occurrences of oldsym with newsym. For example, this call to replace replaces all occurrences of b with a:

```
(replace '((a b) (((b g r) (f r)) c (d e)) b) 'b 'a)
-> ((a a) (((a g r) (f r)) c (d e)) a)
```

The following is a fairly literal translation of the Scheme implementation from Wallingford's paper. We have converted from Scheme functions to Clojure functions, changed the name to replace-symbol to avoid collision with Clojure's replace, and shortened names to better fit the printed page, but we otherwise have preserved the structure of the original:

```
src/examples/wallingford.clj
; overly-literal port, do not use
(declare replace-symbol replace-symbol-expression)
(defn replace-symbol [coll oldsym newsym]
  (if (empty? coll)
    ()
    (cons (replace-symbol-expression
            (first coll) oldsym newsym)
          (replace-symbol
            (rest coll) oldsym newsym))))
(defn replace-symbol-expression [symbol-expr oldsym newsym]
  (if (symbol? symbol-expr)
    (if (= symbol-expr oldsym)
      newsym
      symbol-expr)
    (replace-symbol symbol-expr oldsym newsym)))
```

The two functions replace-symbol and replace-symbol-expression are mutually recursive, so a deeply nested structure could blow the stack. To demonstrate the problem, create a deeply-nested function that builds deeply nested lists containing a single bottom element:

```
src/examples/replace_symbol.clj
(defn deeply-nested [n]
  (loop [n n
         result '(bottom)]
```

```
  (if (= n 0)
    result
    (recur (dec n) (list result)))))
```

Try deeply-nested for a few small values of n:

```
(deeply-nested 5)
-> ((((((bottom))))))

(deeply-nested 25)
-> ((((((((((((((((((((((((((bottom))))))))))))))))))))))))))
```

Clojure provides a *print-level* that controls how deeply the Clojure printer will go into a nested data structure. Set the *print-level* to a modest value so that the printer doesn't go crazy trying to print a deeply nested structure. You will see that when nesting deeper, the printer simply prints a # and stops:

```
(set! *print-level* 25)
-> 25

(deeply-nested 5)
-> ((((((bottom))))))

(deeply-nested 25)
-> (((((((((((((((((((((((((#))))))))))))))))))))))))))
```

Now, try to use replace-symbol to change bottom to deepest for different levels of nesting. You will see that large levels blow the stack. Depending on your JVM implementation, you may need a larger value than the 10000 shown here:

```
(replace-symbol (deeply-nested 5) 'bottom 'deepest)
-> ((((((deepest))))))

(replace-symbol (deeply-nested 10000) 'bottom 'deepest)
-> java.lang.StackOverflowError
```

All of the recursive calls to replace-symbol are inside a cons. To break the recursion, all you have to do is wrap the recursion with lazy-seq. *It's really that simple.* You can break a sequence-generating recursion by wrapping it with a lazy-seq. Here's the improved version. Since the transition to laziness was so simple, we could not resist the temptation to make the function more Clojurish in another way as well:

```
src/examples/replace_symbol.clj
Line 1 (defn- coll-or-scalar [x & _] (if (coll? x) :collection :scalar))
     2 (defmulti replace-symbol coll-or-scalar)
     3 (defmethod replace-symbol :collection [coll oldsym newsym]
     4   (lazy-seq
     5     (when (seq coll)
     6       (cons (replace-symbol (first coll) oldsym newsym)
```

```
7              (replace-symbol (rest coll) oldsym newsym)))))
8 (defmethod replace-symbol :scalar [obj oldsym newsym]
9   (if (= obj oldsym) newsym obj))
```

On line 4, the lazy-seq breaks the recursion, preventing stack overflow on deeply nested structures. The other improvement is on line 2. Rather than have two different functions to deal with symbols and lists, there is a single multimethod replace-symbol with one method for lists and another for symbols. (Multimethods are covered in detail in Chapter 8, *Multimethods*, on page 187.) This gets rid of an if form and improves readability.

Make sure the improved replace-symbol can handle deep nesting:

```
(replace-symbol (deeply-nested 10000) 'bottom 'deepest)
-> (((((((((((((((((((((((((#)))))))))))))))))))))))))
```

Laziness is a powerful ally. You can often write recursive and even mutually recursive functions and then break the recursion with laziness.

Shortcutting Recursion with Memoization

To demonstrate a more complex mutual recursion, we will look at the Hofstadter Female and Male sequences. The first Hofstadter sequences were described in *Gödel, Escher, Bach: An Eternal Golden Braid* [Hof99]. The Female and Male sequences are defined as follows:[8]

$F(0) = 1; M(0) = 0$

$F(n) = n - M(F(n-1)), n > 0$

$M(n) = n - F(M(n-1)), n > 0$

This suggests a straightforward definition in Clojure:

src/examples/male_female.clj
```
; do not use these directly
(declare m f)
(defn m [n]
  (if (zero? n)
    0
    (- n (f (m (dec n)))))))
(defn f [n]
  (if (zero? n)
    1
    (- n (m (f (dec n)))))))
```

The Clojure definition is easy to read and closely parallels the mathematical definition. However, it performs *terribly* for large values of n. Each value in

---

8.   http://en.wikipedia.org/wiki/Hofstadter_sequence

the sequence requires calculating two other values from scratch, which in turn requires calculating two other values from scratch. On one of our MacBook Pro computers,[9] it takes more than half a minute to calculate (m 250):

```
(time (m 250))
"Elapsed time: 38443.902083 msecs"
-> 155
```

Is it possible to preserve the clean, mutually recursive definition *and* have decent performance? Yes, with a little help from *memoization*. Memoization trades space for time by caching the results of past calculations. When you call a memoized function, it first checks your input against a map of previous inputs and their outputs. If it finds the input in the map, it can return the output immediately, without having to perform the calculation again.

Rebind m and f to memoized versions of themselves, using Clojure's memoize function:

src/examples/memoized_male_female.clj
```
(def m (memoize m))
(def f (memoize f))
```

Now Clojure needs to calculate *F* and *M* only once for each *n*. The speedup is enormous. Calculating (m 250) is thousands of times faster:

```
(time (m 250))
"Elapsed time: 5.190739 msecs"
-> 155
```

And, of course, once the memoization cache is built, "calculation" of a cached value is almost instantaneous:

```
(time (m 250))
"Elapsed time: 0.065877 msecs"
-> 155
```

Memoization alone is not enough, however. Memoization shortcuts the recursion only if the memoization cache is already populated. If you start with an empty cache and ask for m or f of a large number, you will blow the stack before the cache can be built:

```
(m 10000)
-> java.lang.StackOverflowError
```

The final trick is to guarantee that the cache is built from the ground up by exposing *sequences*, instead of *functions*. Create m-seq and f-seq by mapping m and f over the whole numbers:

---

9.   3.06 GHz Intel Core 2 Duo, 4 GB 667 MHz DDR2 SDRAM, Ubuntu 10.10, SSD

src/examples/male_female_seq.clj

```
(def m-seq (map m (iterate inc 0)))
(def f-seq (map f (iterate inc 0)))
```

Now callers can get *M(n)* or *F(n)* by taking the nth value from a sequence:

```
(nth m-seq 250)
-> 155
```

The approach is quite fast, even for larger values of n:

```
(time (nth m-seq 10000))
"Elapsed time: 0.735 msecs"
-> 6180
```

The approach we have used here is as follows:

- Define a mutually recursive function in a natural way.
- Use memoization in order to shortcut recursion for values that have already been calculated.
- Expose a sequence so that dependent values are cached before they are needed.

This approach *is* heap-consuming, in that it does cache all previously seen values. If this is a problem, you can in some situations eliminate it by selecting a more complex caching policy.

4.5 Wrapping Up

In this chapter you've seen how Clojure's support for FP strikes a well-motivated balance between academic purity and effectiveness on the Java Virtual Machine. Clojure provides a wide variety of techniques including self-recursion with recur, mutual recursion with trampoline, lazy sequences, and memoization.

Better still, for a wide variety of everyday programming tasks, you can use the sequence library, without ever having to define your own explicit recursions of lazy sequences. Functions like partition create clean, expressive solutions that are much easier to write.

If Clojure were an exclusively FP language, we would turn our attention next to the challenges of living in a world without mutable state and perhaps begin discussing the state monad. But Clojure leads us in a different direction with its most innovative feature: explicit APIs for managing mutable state. Clojure reference model provides four different semantics to model state and is what we'll tackle in Chapter 5, *State*, on page 113.

State

A *state* is the value of an identity at a point in time.

Quite a lot is packed into the previous sentence. Let's unpack the word *value* first. A value is an immutable, persistent data structure. When you can program entirely with values, life is easy, as we saw in Chapter 4, *Functional Programming*, on page 85.

The flow of time makes things substantially more difficult. Are the New York Yankees the same now as they were last year? In 1927? The roster of the Yankees is an *identity* whose value changes over time.

Updating an identity does not destroy old values. In fact, updating an identity has no impact on existing values whatsoever. The Yankees could trade every player, or disband in a fit of boredom, without in any way altering our ability to think about any past Yankees we happen to care about.

Clojure's reference model clearly separates identities from values. Almost everything in Clojure is a value. For identities, Clojure provides four reference types:

- Refs manage *coordinated, synchronous* changes to shared state.
- Atoms manage *uncoordinated, synchronous* changes to shared state.
- Agents manage *asynchronous* changes to shared state.
- Vars manage *thread-local* state.

Each of these APIs is discussed in this chapter. At the end of the chapter, we will develop a sample application. The Snake game demonstrates how to divide an application model into immutable and mutable components.

Before we start, we will review the intersection of state with concurrency and parallelism, as well as comment on the difficulty with traditional lock-based approaches.

5.1 Concurrency, Parallelism, and Locking

A concurrent program models more than one thing happening simultaneously. A parallel program takes an operation that could be sequential and chooses to break it into separate pieces that can execute concurrently to speed overall execution.

There are many reasons to write concurrent or parallel programs:

- For decades, performance improvements have come from packing more power into cores. Now, and for the near future, performance improvements will come from using more cores. Our hardware is itself more concurrent than ever, and systems must be concurrent to take advantage of this power.

- Expensive computations may need to execute in parallel on multiple cores (or multiple boxes) in order to complete in a timely manner.

- Tasks that are blocked waiting for a resource should stand down and let other tasks use available processors.

- User interfaces need to remain responsive while performing long-running tasks.

- Operations that are logically independent are easier to implement if the platform can recognize and take advantage of their independence.

Concurrency makes it glaringly obvious that more than one observer (e.g., thread) may be looking at your data. This is a big problem for languages that complect[1] value and identity. Such languages treat a piece of data as a bank ledger with only one line. Each new operation erases history, potentially corrupting the work of every other thread on the system.

While concurrency makes the challenges more obvious, it is a mistake to assume that multiple observers come into play only with concurrency. If your program ever has two variables that refer to the same data, those variables are different observers. If your program allows mutability at all, then you must think carefully about state.

Mutable languages tend to tackle the challenge by locking and defensive copying. Continuing the ledger analogy: the bank hires guards (locks) to supervise the activities of anybody using a ledger, and nobody is allowed to modify a ledger while anybody else is using it.

---

1. http://www.infoq.com/presentations/Simple-Made-Easy

When the performance becomes really bad, the bank may even ask ledger readers to make their own private copies of the ledger so they can get out of the way and let transactions continue. These copies must still be supervised by the guards!

As irritating as this model sounds, it gets worse at the level of implementation detail. Choosing what and where to lock is a difficult task. If you get it wrong, all sorts of bad things can happen. *Race conditions* between threads can corrupt data. *Deadlocks* can stop an entire program from functioning at all. *Java Concurrency in Practice* [Goe06] covers these and other problems, plus their solutions, in detail. It is a terrific book, but it is difficult to read it and not ask yourself, "Is there another way?"

Clojure's model for state and identity solves these problems. The bulk of program code is functional. The small parts of the codebase that truly benefit from mutability are distinct and must explicitly select one of four reference models. Using these models, you can split your models into two layers:

- A *functional model* that has no mutable state. Most of your code will normally be in this layer, which is easier to read, easier to test, and easier to parallelize.

- *Reference models* for the parts of the application that you find more convenient to deal with using mutable state (despite its disadvantages).

Let's get started working with state in Clojure, using the most notorious of Clojure's reference models: software transactional memory.

5.2 Refs and Software Transactional Memory

Most objects in Clojure are immutable. When you really want mutable data, you must be explicit about it, such as by creating a mutable *reference* (ref) to an immutable object. You create a ref with this:

```
(ref initial-state)
```

For example, you could create a reference to the current song in your music playlist:

```
(def current-track (ref "Mars, the Bringer of War"))
-> #'user/current-track
```

The ref wraps and protects access to its internal state. To read the contents of the reference, you can call deref:

```
(deref reference)
```

The deref function can be shortened to the @ reader macro. Try using both deref and @ to dereference current-track:

```
(deref current-track)
-> "Mars, the Bringer of War"

@current-track
-> "Mars, the Bringer of War"
```

Notice how in this example the Clojure model fits the real world. A track is an immutable entity. It doesn't change into another track when you are finished listening to it. But the *current* track is a reference to an entity, and it does change.

ref-set

You can change where a reference points with ref-set:

```
(ref-set reference new-value)
```

Call ref-set to listen to a different track:

```
(ref-set current-track "Venus, the Bringer of Peace")
-> java.lang.IllegalStateException: No transaction running
```

Oops. Because refs are mutable, you must protect their updates. In many languages, you would use a *lock* for this purpose. In Clojure, you can use a *transaction*. Transactions are wrapped in a dosync:

```
(dosync & exprs)
```

Wrap your ref-set with a dosync, and all is well.

```
(dosync (ref-set current-track "Venus, the Bringer of Peace"))
-> "Venus, the Bringer of Peace"
```

The current-track reference now refers to a different track.

Transactional Properties

Like database transactions, STM transactions guarantee some important properties:

- Updates are *atomic*. If you update more than one ref in a transaction, the cumulative effect of all the updates will appear as a single instantaneous event to anyone not inside your transaction.

- Updates are *consistent*. Refs can specify validation functions. If any of these functions fail, the entire transaction will fail.

- Updates are *isolated*. Running transactions cannot see partially completed results from other transactions.

Databases provide the additional guarantee that updates are *durable*. Because Clojure's transactions are in-memory transactions, Clojure does not guarantee that updates are durable. If you want a durable transaction in Clojure, you should use a database.

Together, the four transactional properties are called ACID. Databases provide ACID; Clojure's STM provides ACI.

If you change more than one ref in a single transaction, those changes are all coordinated to "happen at the same time" from the perspective of any code outside the transaction. So, you can make sure that updates to current-track and current-composer are *coordinated*:

```
(def current-track (ref "Venus, the Bringer of Peace"))
-> #'user/current-track
(def current-composer (ref "Holst"))
-> #'user/current-composer

(dosync
  (ref-set current-track "Credo")
  (ref-set current-composer "Byrd"))
-> "Byrd"
```

Because the updates are in a transaction, no other thread will ever see an updated track with an out-of-date composer, or vice versa.

alter

The current-track example is deceptively easy, because updates to the ref are totally independent of any previous state. Let's build a more complex example, where transactions need to update existing information. A simple chat application fits the bill. First, create a message record that has a sender and some text:

```
src/examples/chat.clj
(defrecord Message [sender text])
```

Now, you can create messages by instantiating the record:

```
(user.Message. "Aaron" "Hello")
-> #:user.Message{:sender "Aaron", :text "Hello"}
```

Users of the chat application want to see the most recent message first, so a list is a good data structure. Create a messages reference that points to an initially empty list:

```
(def messages (ref ()))
```

Now you need a function to add a new message to the front of messages. You could simply deref to get the list of messages, cons the new message, and then ref-set the updated list back into messages:

```
; bad idea
(defn naive-add-message [msg]
  (dosync (ref-set messages (cons msg @messages))))
```

But there is a better option. Why not perform the read and update in a single step? Clojure's alter will apply an update function to a referenced object within a transaction:

```
(alter ref update-fn & args...)
```

alter returns the new value of the ref within the transaction. When a transaction successfully completes, the ref will take on its last in-transaction value. Using alter instead of ref-set makes the code more readable:

```
(defn add-message [msg]
  (dosync (alter messages conj msg)))
```

Notice that the update function is conj (short for "conjoin"), not cons. This is because conj takes arguments in an order suitable for use with alter:

```
(cons item sequence)
(conj sequence item)
```

The alter function calls its update-fn with the current reference value as its first argument, as conj expects. If you plan to write your own update functions, they should follow the same structure as conj:

```
(your-func thing-that-gets-updated & optional-other-args)
```

Try adding a few messages to see that the code works as expected:

```
(add-message (user.Message. "user 1" "hello"))
-> (#:user.Message{:sender "user 1", :text "hello"})

(add-message (user.Message. "user 2" "howdy"))
-> (#:user.Message{:sender "user 2", :text "howdy"}
    #:user.Message{:sender "user 1", :text "hello"})
```

alter is the workhorse of Clojure's STM and is the primary means of updating refs. But if you know a little about how the STM works, you may be able to optimize your transactions in certain scenarios.

How STM Works: MVCC

Clojure's STM uses a technique called Multiversion Concurrency Control (MVCC), which is also used in several major databases. Here's how MVCC works in Clojure.

Transaction A begins by taking a *point*, which is simply a number that acts as a unique timestamp in the STM world. Transaction A has access to its own *effectively private* copy of any reference it needs, associated with the point. Clojure's persistent data structures (*Persistent Data Structures*, on page 86) make it cheap to provide these effectively private copies.

During Transaction A, operations on a ref work against (and return) the transaction's private copy of the ref's data, called the *in-transaction value*.

If at any point the STM detects that another transaction has already set/altered a ref that Transaction A wants to set/alter, Transaction A will be forced to retry. If you throw an exception out of the dosync block, then Transaction A will abort *without* a retry.

If and when Transaction A commits, its heretofore private writes will become visible to the world, associated with a single point in the transaction timeline.

Sometimes the approach implied by alter is too cautious. What if you *don't care* that another transaction altered a reference out from under you in the middle of your transaction? If in such a situation you would be willing to commit your changes anyway, you can beat alter's performance with commute.

commute

commute is a specialized variant of alter allowing for more concurrency:

```
(commute ref update-fn & args...)
```

Of course, there is a trade-off. Commutes are so named because they must be *commutative*. That is, updates must be able to occur in any order. This gives the STM system freedom to reorder commutes.

To use commute, simply replace alter with commute in your implementation of add-message:

```
(defn add-message-commute [msg]
  (dosync (commute messages conj msg)))
```

commute returns the new value of the ref. However, the last in-transaction value you see from a commute will *not* always match the end-of-transaction value of a ref, because of reordering. If another transaction sneaks in and alters a ref that you are trying to commute, the STM will not restart your transaction. Instead, it will simply run your commute function again, out of order. Your transaction will *never even see* the ref value that your commute function finally ran against.

Since Clojure's STM can reorder commutes behind your back, you can use them only when you do not care about ordering. Literally speaking, this is not true for a chat application. The list of messages most certainly has an order, so if two message adds get reversed, the resulting list will not correctly show the order in which the messages arrived.

Practically speaking, chat message updates are *commutative enough*. STM-based reordering of messages will likely happen on time scales of microseconds or less. For users of a chat application, there are already reorderings on much larger time scales due to network and human latency. (Think about times that you have "spoken out of turn" in an online chat because another speaker's message had not reached you yet.) Since these larger reorderings are unfixable, it is reasonable for a chat application to ignore the smaller reorderings that might bubble up from Clojure's STM.

Prefer alter

Many updates are not commutative. For example, consider a counter that returns an increasing sequence of numbers. You might use such a counter to build unique IDs in a system. The counter can be a simple reference to a number:

`src/examples/concurrency.clj`
```
(def counter (ref 0))
```

You should not use commute to update the counter. commute returns the in-transaction value of the counter at the time of the commute, but reorderings could cause the actual end-of-transaction value to be different. This could lead to more than one caller getting the same counter value. Instead, use alter:

```
(defn next-counter [] (dosync (alter counter inc)))
```

Try calling next-counter a few times to verify that the counter works as expected:

```
(next-counter)
-> 1

(next-counter)
-> 2
```

In general, you should prefer alter over commute. Its semantics are easy to understand and error-proof. commute, on the other hand, requires that you think carefully about transactional semantics. If you use alter when commute would suffice, the worst thing that might happen is performance degradation. But if you use commute when alter is required, you will introduce a subtle bug that is difficult to detect with automated tests.

Adding Validation to Refs

Database transactions maintain consistency through various integrity checks. You can do something similar with Clojure's transactional memory, by specifying a validation function when you create a ref:

```
(ref initial-state options*)
; options include:
;   :validator validate-fn
;   :meta metadata-map
```

The options to ref include an optional validation function that can throw an exception to prevent a transaction from completing. Note that options is *not* a map; it is simply a sequence of key/value pairs spliced into the function call.

Continuing the chat example, add a validation function to the messages reference that guarantees that all messages have non-nil values for :sender and :text:

```
src/examples/chat.clj
(def validate-message-list
  (partial every? #(and (:sender %) (:text %))))


(def messages (ref () :validator validate-message-list))
```

This validation acts like a key constraint on a table in a database transaction. If the constraint fails, the entire transaction rolls back. Try adding an ill-formed message such as a simple string:

```
(add-message "not a valid message")
-> java.lang.IllegalStateException: Invalid reference state

@messages
-> ()
```

Messages that match the constraint are no problem:

```
(add-message (user.Message. "Aaron" "Real Message"))
-> (#:user.Message{:sender "Aaron", :text "Real Message"})
```

Refs are great for coordinated access to shared state, but not all tasks require such coordination. For updating a single piece of isolated data, prefer an atom.

5.3 Use Atoms for Uncoordinated, Synchronous Updates

Atoms are a lighter-weight mechanism than refs. Where multiple ref updates can be coordinated in a transaction, atoms allow updates of a single value, uncoordinated with anything else.

You create atoms with atom, which has a signature very similar to ref:

```
(atom initial-state options?)
; options include:
;    :validator validate-fn
;    :meta metadata-map
```

Returning to our music player example, you could store the current-track in an atom instead of a ref:

```
(def current-track (atom "Venus, the Bringer of Peace"))
-> #'user/current-track
```

You can dereference an atom to get its value, just as you would a ref:

```
(deref current-track)
-> "Venus, the Bringer of Peace"

@current-track
-> "Venus, the Bringer of Peace"
```

Atoms do not participate in transactions and thus do not require a dosync. To set the value of an atom, simply call reset!

```
(reset! an-atom newval)
```

For example, you can set current-track to "Credo":

```
(reset! current-track "Credo")
-> "Credo"
```

What if you want to coordinate an update of both current-track and current-composer with an atom? The short answer is "You can't." That is the difference between refs and atoms. If you need coordinated access, use a ref.

The longer answer is "You can...if you are willing to change the way you model the problem." What if you store the track title and composer in a map and then store the whole map in a single atom?

```
(def current-track (atom {:title "Credo" :composer "Byrd"}))
-> #'user/current-track
```

Now you can update both values in a single reset!

```
(reset! current-track {:title "Spem in Alium" :composer "Tallis"})
-> {:title "Spem in Alium", :composer "Tallis"}
```

Maybe you like to listen to several tracks in a row by the same composer. If so, you want to change the track title but keep the same composer. swap! will do the trick:

```
(swap! an-atom f & args)
```

swap! updates an-atom by calling function f on the current value of an-atom, plus any additional args.

To change just the track title, use swap! with assoc to update only the :title:

```
(swap! current-track assoc :title "Sancte Deus")
-> {:title "Sancte Deus", :composer "Tallis"}
```

swap! returns the new value. Calls to swap! might be retried, if other threads are attempting to modify the same atom. So, the function you pass to swap! should have no side effects.

Both refs and atoms perform synchronous updates. When the update function returns, the value is already changed. If you do not need this level of control and can tolerate updates happening asynchronously at some later time, prefer an agent.

5.4   Use Agents for Asynchronous Updates

Some applications have tasks that can proceed independently with minimal coordination between tasks. Clojure *agents* support this style of task.

Agents have much in common with refs. Like refs, you create an agent by wrapping some piece of initial state:

```
(agent initial-state)
```

Create a counter agent that wraps an initial count of zero:

```
(def counter (agent 0))
-> #'user/counter
```

Once you have an agent, you can send the agent a function to update its state. send queues an update-fn to run later, on a thread in a thread pool:

```
(send agent update-fn & args)
```

Sending to an agent is very much like commuting a ref. Tell the counter to inc:

```
(send counter inc)
-> #<clojure.lang.Agent@23451c74: 0>
```

Notice that the call to send does not return the new value of the agent, returning instead the agent itself. That is because send *does not know* the new value. After send queues the inc to run later, it returns immediately.

Although send does not know the new value of an agent, the REPL *might* know. Depending on whether the agent thread or the REPL thread runs first, you might see a 1 or a 0 after the colon in the previous output.

You can check the current value of an agent with deref/@, just as you would a ref. By the time you get around to checking the counter, the inc will almost certainly have completed on the thread pool, raising the value to 1:

```
@counter
-> 1
```

If the race condition between the REPL and the agent thread bothers you, there is a solution. If you want to be sure that the agent has completed the actions *you sent* to it, you can call await or await-for:

```
(await & agents)
```

```
(await-for timeout-millis & agents)
```

These functions will cause the current thread to block until all actions sent from the current thread or agent have completed. await-for will return nil if the timeout expires and will return a non-nil value otherwise. await has no timeout, so be careful: await is willing to wait forever.

Validating Agents and Handling Errors

Agents have other points in common with refs. They also can take a validation function:

```
(agent initial-state options*)
; options include:
;    :validator validate-fn
;    :meta metadata-map
```

Re-create the counter with a validator that ensures it is a number:

```
(def counter (agent 0 :validator number?))
-> #'user/counter
```

Try to set the agent to a value that is not a number by passing an update function that ignores the current value and simply returns a string:

```
(send counter (fn [_] "boo"))
-> #<clojure.lang.Agent@4de8ce62: 0>
```

Everything looks fine (so far) because send still returns immediately. After the agent tries to update itself on a pooled thread, it will enter an exceptional state. You will discover the error when you try to dereference the agent:

```
@counter
-> java.lang.Exception: Agent has errors
```

To discover the specific error (or errors), call agent-errors, which will return a sequence of errors thrown during agent actions:

```
(agent-errors counter)
-> (#<IllegalStateException ...>)
```

Once an agent has errors, all subsequent attempts to query the agent will return an error. You make the agent usable again by calling clear-agent-errors:

```
(clear-agent-errors agent)
```

which returns the agent to its pre-error state. Clear the counter's errors, and verify that its state is the same as before the error occurred:

```
(clear-agent-errors counter)
-> nil

@counter
-> 0
```

Now that you know the basics of agents, let's use them in conjunction with refs and transactions.

Including Agents in Transactions

Transactions should not have side effects, because Clojure may retry a transaction an arbitrary number of times. However, sometimes you *want* a side effect when a transaction succeeds. Agents provide a solution. If you send an action to an agent from within a transaction, that action will be sent exactly once, if and only if the transaction succeeds.

As an example of where this would be useful, consider an agent that writes to a file when a transaction succeeds. You could combine such an agent with the chat example from *commute*, on page 119, to automatically back up chat messages. First, create a backup-agent that stores the filename to write to:

```
src/examples/concurrency.clj
(def backup-agent (agent "output/messages-backup.clj"))
```

Then, create a modified version of add-message. The new function add-message-with-backup should do two additional things:

- Grab the return value of commute, which is the current database of messages, in a let binding.

- While still inside a transaction, send an action to the backup agent that writes the message database to filename. For simplicity, have the action function return filename so that the agent will use the same filename for the next backup.

```
(defn add-message-with-backup [msg]
  (dosync
    (let [snapshot (commute messages conj msg)]
      (send-off backup-agent (fn [filename]
                               (spit filename snapshot)
                               filename))
      snapshot)))
```

The new function has one other critical difference: it calls send-off instead of send to communicate with the agent. send-off is a variant of send for actions that expect to block, as a file write might do. send-off actions get their own expandable thread pool. Never send a blocking function, or you may unnecessarily prevent other agents from making progress.

Try adding some messages using add-message-with-backup:

```
(add-message-with-backup (user.Message. "John" "Message One"))
-> (#:user.Message{:sender "John", :text "Message One"})

(add-message-with-backup (user.Message. "Jane" "Message Two"))
-> (#:user.Message{:sender "Jane", :text "Message Two"}
    #:user.Message{:sender "John", :text "Message One"})
```

You can check both the in-memory messages as well as the backup file messages-backup to verify that they contain the same structure.

You could enhance the backup strategy in this example in various ways. You could provide the option to back up less often than on every update or back up only information that has changed since the last backup.

Since Clojure's STM provides the ACI properties of ACID and since writing to a file provides the D ("durability"), it is tempting to think that STM plus a backup agent equals a database. This is *not* the case. A Clojure transaction promises only to send/sendoff an action to the agent; it does not actually *perform* the action under the ACI umbrella. So, for example, a transaction could complete, and then someone could unplug the power cord before the agent writes to the database. The moral is simple. If your problem calls for a real database, use a real database.

The Unified Update Model

As you have seen, refs, atoms, and agents all provide functions for updating their state by applying a function to their previous state. This unified model for handling shared state is one of the central concepts of Clojure. The unified model and various ancillary functions are summarized in the following tabler.

Update Mechanism	Ref Function	Atom Function	Agent Function
Function application	alter	swap!	send-off
Function (commutative)	commute	N/A	N/A
Function (nonblocking)	N/A	N/A	send
Simple setter	ref-set	reset!	N/A

The unified update model is by far the most important way to update refs, atoms, and agents. The ancillary functions, on the other hand, are optimizations and options that stem from the semantics peculiar to each API:

- The opportunity for the commute optimization arises when coordinating updates. Since only refs provide coordinated updates, commute makes sense only for refs.

- Updates to refs and atoms take place on the thread they are called on, so they provide no scheduling options. Agents update later, on a thread pool, making blocking/nonblocking a relevant scheduling option.

Clojure's final reference type, the var, is a different beast entirely. They do not participate in the unified update model and are instead used to manage thread-local, private state.

5.5 Managing Per-Thread State with Vars

When you call def or defn, you create a *dynamic var*, often called just a *var*. In all the examples so far in the book, you pass an initial value to def, which becomes the *root binding* for the var. For example, the following code creates a root binding for foo of 10:

```
(def ^:dynamic foo 10)
-> #'user/foo
```

The binding of foo is shared by all threads. You can check the value of foo on your own thread:

```
foo
-> 10
```

You can also verify the value of foo from another thread. Create a new thread, passing it a function that prints foo. Don't forget to start the thread:

```
user=> (.start (Thread. (fn [] (println foo))))
-> nil
| 10
```

In the previous example, the call to start() returns nil, and then the value of foo is printed from a new thread.

Most vars are content to keep their root bindings forever. However, you can create a *thread-local* binding for a var with the binding macro:

(binding [bindings] & body)

Bindings have *dynamic scope*. In other words, a binding is visible anywhere a thread's execution takes it, until the thread exits the scope where the binding began. A binding is not visible to any other threads.

Structurally, a binding looks a lot like a let. Create a thread-local binding for foo and check its value:

```
(binding [foo 42] foo)
-> 42
```

To see the difference between binding and let, create a simple function that prints the value of foo:

```
(defn print-foo [] (println foo))
-> #'user/print-foo
```

Now, try calling print-foo from both a let and a binding:

```
(let [foo "let foo"] (print-foo))
| 10

(binding [foo "bound foo"] (print-foo))
| bound foo
```

As you can see, the let has no effect outside its own form, so the first print-foo prints the root binding 10. The binding, on the other hand, stays in effect down any chain of calls that begins in the binding form, so the second print-foo prints bound foo.

Acting at a Distance

Vars intended for dynamic binding are sometimes called *special* variables. It is good style to name them with leading and trailing asterisks. For example, Clojure uses dynamic binding for thread-wide options such as the standard I/O streams *in*, *out*, and *err*. Dynamic bindings enable *action at a distance*.

When you change a dynamic binding, you can change the behavior of distant functions without changing any function arguments.

One kind of action at a distance is temporarily augmenting the behavior of a function. In some languages this would be classified as aspect-oriented programming; in Clojure it is simply a side effect of dynamic binding. As an example, imagine that you have a function that performs an expensive calculation. To simulate this, write a function named slow-double that sleeps for a tenth of a second and then doubles its input.

```
(defn ^:dynamic slow-double [n]
  (Thread/sleep 100)
  (* n 2))
```

Next, write a function named calls-slow-double that calls slow-double for each item in [1 2 1 2 1 2]:

```
(defn calls-slow-double []
  (map slow-double [1 2 1 2 1 2]))
```

Time a call to calls-slow-double. With six internal calls to slow-double, it should take a little over six tenths of a second. Note that you will have to run through the result with dorun; otherwise, Clojure's map will outsmart you by immediately returning a lazy sequence.

```
(time (dorun (calls-slow-double)))
| "Elapsed time: 601.418 msecs"
-> nil
```

Reading the code, you can tell that calls-slow-double is slow because it does the same work over and over again. One times two is two, no matter how many times you ask.

Calculations such as slow-double are good candidates for *memoization*. When you memoize a function, it keeps a cache mapping past inputs to past outputs. If subsequent calls hit the cache, they will return almost immediately. Thus, you are trading space (the cache) for time (calculating the function again for the same inputs).

Clojure provides memoize, which takes a function and returns a memoization of that function:

```
(memoize function)
```

slow-double is a great candidate for memoization, but it isn't memoized yet, and clients like calls-slow-double already use the slow, unmemoized version. With dynamic binding, this is no problem. Simply create a binding to a memoized version of slow-double, and call calls-slow-double from within the binding.

```
(defn demo-memoize []
  (time
   (dorun
    (binding [slow-double (memoize slow-double)]
     (calls-slow-double)))))
```

With the memoized version of slow-double, calls-slow-double runs three times faster, completing in about two-tenths of a second:

```
(demo-memoize)
"Elapsed time: 203.115 msecs"
```

This example demonstrates the power and the danger of action at a distance. By dynamically rebinding a function such as slow-double, you change the behavior of *other* functions such as calls-slow-double without their knowledge or consent. With lexical binding forms such as let, it is easy to see the entire range of your changes. Dynamic binding is not so simple. It can change the behavior of other forms in other files, far from the point in your source where the binding occurs.

Used occasionally, dynamic binding has great power. But it should not become your primary mechanism for extension or reuse. Functions that use dynamic bindings are not pure functions and can quickly lose the benefits of Clojure's functional style.

Working with Java Callback APIs

Several Java APIs depend on callback event handlers. GUI frameworks such as Swing use event handlers to respond to user input. XML parsers such as SAX depend on the user implementing a callback handler interface.

These callback handlers are written with mutable objects in mind. Also, they tend to be single-threaded. In Clojure, the best way to meet such APIs halfway is to use dynamic bindings. This will involve mutable references that feel almost like variables, but because they are used in a single-threaded setting, they will not present any concurrency problems.

Clojure provides the set! special form for setting a thread-local dynamic binding:

```
(set! var-symbol new-value)
```

set! should be used rarely. In fact, the only place in the entire Clojure core that uses set! is the Clojure implementation of a SAX ContentHandler.

A ContentHandler receives callbacks as a parser encounters various bits of an XML stream. In nontrivial scenarios, the ContentHandler needs to keep track of *where it is* in the XML stream: the current stack of open elements, current character data, and so on.

In Clojure-speak, you can think of a ContentHandler's current position as a mutable pointer to a specific spot in an immutable XML stream. It is unnecessary to use references in a ContentHandler, since everything will happen on a single thread. Instead, Clojure's ContentHandler uses dynamic variables and set!. Here is the relevant detail:

```
; redacted from Clojure's xml.clj to focus on dynamic variable usage
(startElement
 [uri local-name q-name #^Attributes atts]
 ; details omitted
 (set! *stack* (conj *stack* *current*))
 (set! *current* e)
 (set! *state* :element))
nil)
(endElement
 [uri local-name q-name]
 ; details omitted
 (set! *current* (push-content (peek *stack*) *current*))
 (set! *stack* (pop *stack*))
 (set! *state* :between)
nil)
```

A SAX parser calls startElement when it encounters an XML start tag. The callback handler updates three thread-local variables. The *stack* is a stack of all the elements the current element is nested inside. The *current* is the current element, and the *state* keeps track of what kind of content is inside. (This is important primarily when inside character data, which is not shown here.)

endElement reverses the work of startElement by popping the *stack* and placing the top of the *stack* in *current*.

It is worth noting that this style of coding is the industry norm: objects are mutable, and programs are single-threadedly oblivious to the possibility of concurrency. Clojure permits this style as an explicit special case, and you should use it for interop purposes only.

The ContentHandler's use of set! does not leak mutable data out into the rest of Clojure. Clojure uses the ContentHandler implementation to build an immutable Clojure structure.

You have now seen four different models for dealing with state. And since Clojure is built atop Java, you can also use Java's lock-based model. The models, and their use, are summarized in the following table.

Model	Usage	Functions
Refs and STM	Coordinated, synchronous updates	Pure
Atoms	Uncoordinated, synchronous updates	Pure
Agents	Uncoordinated, asynchronous updates	Any
Vars	Thread-local dynamic scopes	Any
Java locks	Coordinated, synchronous updates	Any

Let's put these models to work in designing a small but complete application.

5.6 A Clojure Snake

The Snake game features a player-controlled snake that moves around a game grid hunting for an apple. When your snake eats an apple, it grows longer by a segment, and a new apple appears. If your snake reaches a certain length, you win. But if your snake crosses over its own body, you lose.

Before you start building your own snake, take a minute to try the completed version. From the book's REPL, enter the following:

```
(use 'examples.snake)

(game)
-> [#<Ref clojure.lang.Ref@65694ee6>
#<Ref clojure.lang.Ref@261ae209>
#<Timer javax.swing.Timer@7f0df737>]
```

Select the Snake window, and use the arrow keys to control your snake.

Our design for the snake is going to take advantage of Clojure's functional nature and its support for explicit mutable state by dividing the game into three layers:

- The *functional model* will use pure functions to model as much of the game as possible.

- The *mutable model* will handle the mutable state of the game. The mutable model will use one or more of the reference models discussed in this chapter. Mutable state is much harder to test, so we will keep this part small.

- The *GUI* will use Swing to draw the game and to accept input from the user.

These layers will make the Snake easy to build, test, and maintain.

As you work through this example, add your code to the file reader/snake.clj in the sample code. When you open the file, you will see that it already imports/uses the Swing classes and Clojure libraries you will need:

```
src/reader/snake.clj
(ns reader.snake
  (:import (java.awt Color Dimension)
           (javax.swing JPanel JFrame Timer JOptionPane)
           (java.awt.event ActionListener KeyListener))
  (:use examples.import-static))
(import-static java.awt.event.KeyEvent VK_LEFT VK_RIGHT VK_UP VK_DOWN)
```

Now you are ready to build the functional model.

The Functional Model

First, create a set of constants to describe time, space, and motion:

```
(def width 75)
(def height 50)
(def point-size 10)
(def turn-millis 75)
(def win-length 5)
(def dirs { VK_LEFT  [-1  0]
            VK_RIGHT [ 1  0]
            VK_UP    [ 0 -1]
            VK_DOWN  [ 0  1]})
```

width and height set the size of the game board, and point-size is used to convert a game point into screen pixels. turn-millis is the heartbeat of the game, controlling how many milliseconds pass before each update of the game board. win-length is how many segments your snake needs before you win the game. (Five is a boringly small number suitable for testing.) The dirs maps symbolic constants for the four directions to their vector equivalents. Since Swing already defines the VK_ constants for different directions, we will reuse them here rather than defining our own.

Next, create some basic math functions for the game:

```
(defn add-points [& pts]
  (vec (apply map + pts)))

(defn point-to-screen-rect [pt]
  (map #(* point-size %)
       [(pt 0) (pt 1) 1 1]))
```

The add-points function adds points together. You can use add-points to calculate the new position of a moving game object. For example, you can move an object at [10, 10] left by one:

Other Snake Implementations

There's more than one way to skin a snake. You may enjoy comparing the snake presented here with these other snakes:

- David Van Horn's Snake.[a] written in Typed Scheme, has no mutable state.
- Jeremy Read wrote a Java Snake[b] designed to be "just about as small as you can make it in Java and still be readable."
- Abhishek Reddy wrote a tiny (35-line) Snake[c] in Clojure. The design goal was to be abnormally terse.
- Dale Vaillancourt's Worm Game.[d]
- Mark Volkmann wrote a Clojure Snake[e] designed for readability.

Each of the snake implementations has its own distinctive style. What would *your* style look like?

---

a. http://planet.plt-scheme.org/package-source/dvanhorn/snake.plt/1/0/main.ss
b. http://www.plt1.com/1069/smaller-snake/
c. http://www.plt1.com/1070/even-smaller-snake/
d. http://www.ccs.neu.edu/home/cce/acl2/worm.html includes some verifications using the theorem prover ACL2.
e. http://www.ociweb.com/mark/programming/ClojureSnake.html

```
(add-points [10 10] [-1 0])
-> [9 10]
```

point-to-screen-rect simply converts a point in game space to a rectangle on the screen:

```
(point-to-screen-rect [5 10])
-> (50 100 10 10)
```

Next, let's write a function to create a new apple:

```
(defn create-apple []
  {:location [(rand-int width) (rand-int height)]
   :color (Color. 210 50 90)
   :type :apple})
```

Apples occupy a single point, the :location, which is guaranteed to be on the game board. Snakes are a little bit more complicated:

```
(defn create-snake []
  {:body (list [1 1])
   :dir [1 0]
   :type :snake
   :color (Color. 15 160 70)})
```

Because a snake can occupy multiple points on the board, it has a :body, which is a list of points. Also, snakes are always in motion in some direction expressed by :dir.

Next, create a function to move a snake. This should be a pure function, returning a new snake. Also, it should take a grow option, allowing the snake to grow after eating an apple.

```
(defn move [{:keys [body dir] :as snake} & grow]
  (assoc snake :body (cons (add-points (first body) dir)
                           (if grow body (butlast body)))))
```

move uses a fairly complex binding expression. The {:keys [body dir]} part makes the snake's body and dir available as their own bindings, and the :as snake part binds snake to the entire snake. The function then proceeds as follows:

1. add-points creates a new point, which is the head of the original snake offset by the snake's direction of motion.

2. cons adds the new point to the front of the snake. If the snake is growing, the entire original snake is kept. Otherwise, it keeps all the original snake except the last segment (butlast).

3. assoc returns a new snake, which is a copy of the old snake but with an updated :body.

Test move by moving and growing a snake:

```
(move (create-snake))
-> {:body ([2 1]), ; etc.
```

```
(move (create-snake) :grow)
-> {:body ([2 1] [1 1]), ; etc.
```

Write a win? function to test whether a snake has won the game:

```
(defn win? [{body :body}]
  (>= (count body) win-length))
```

Test win? against different body sizes. Note that win? binds only the :body, so you don't need a "real" snake, just anything with a body:

```
(win? {:body [[1 1]]})
-> false
```

```
(win? {:body [[1 1] [1 2] [1 3] [1 4] [1 5]]})
-> true
```

A snake loses if its head ever comes back into contact with the rest of its body. Write a head-overlaps-body? function to test for this, and use it to define lose?:

```
(defn head-overlaps-body? [{[head & body] :body}]
  (contains? (set body) head))

(def lose? head-overlaps-body?)
```

Test lose? against overlapping and nonoverlapping snake bodies:

```
(lose? {:body [[1 1] [1 2] [1 3]]})
-> false

(lose? {:body [[1 1] [1 2] [1 1]]})
-> true
```

A snake eats an apple if its head occupies the apple's location. Define an eats? function to test this:

```
(defn eats? [{[snake-head] :body} {apple :location}]
  (= snake-head apple))
```

Notice how clean the body of the eats? function is. All the work is done in the bindings: {[snake-head] :body} binds snake-head to the first element of the snake's :body, and {apple :location} binds apple to the apple's :location. Test eats? from the REPL:

```
(eats? {:body [[1 1] [1 2]]} {:location [2 2]})
-> false

(eats? {:body [[2 2] [1 2]]} {:location [2 2]})
-> true
```

Finally, you need some way to turn the snake, updating its :dir:

```
(defn turn [snake newdir]
  (assoc snake :dir newdir))
```

turn returns a new snake, with an updated direction:

```
(turn (create-snake) [0 -1])
-> {:body ([1 1]), :dir [0 -1], ; etc.
```

All of the code you have written so far is part of the functional model of the Snake game. It is easy to understand in part because it has no local variables and no mutable state. As you will see in the next section, the amount of *mutable* state in the game is quite small. (It is even possible to implement the Snake with *no* mutable state, but that is not the purpose of this demo.)

Building a Mutable Model with STM

The mutable state of the Snake game can change in only three ways:

- A game can be reset to its initial state.

- Every turn, the snake updates its position. If it eats an apple, a new apple is placed.

- A snake can turn.

We will implement each of these changes as functions that modify Clojure refs inside a transaction. That way, changes to the position of the snake and the apple will be synchronous and coordinated.

reset-game is trivial:

```
(defn reset-game [snake apple]
  (dosync (ref-set apple (create-apple))
          (ref-set snake (create-snake)))
  nil)
```

You can test reset-game by passing in some refs and then checking that they dereference to a snake and an apple:

```
(def test-snake (ref nil))
(def test-apple (ref nil))

(reset-game test-snake test-apple)
-> nil

@test-snake
-> {:body ([1 1]), :dir [1 0], ; etc.

@test-apple
-> {:location [52 8], ; etc.
```

update-direction is even simpler; it's just a trivial wrapper around the functional turn:

```
(defn update-direction [snake newdir]
  (when newdir (dosync (alter snake turn newdir))))
```

Try turning your test-snake to move in the "up" direction:

```
(update-direction test-snake [0 -1])
-> {:body ([1 1]), :dir [0 -1], ; etc.
```

The most complicated mutating function is update-positions. If the snake eats the apple, a new apple is created, and the snake grows. Otherwise, the snake simply moves:

```
(defn update-positions [snake apple]
  (dosync
    (if (eats? @snake @apple)
      (do (ref-set apple (create-apple))
          (alter snake move :grow))
      (alter snake move)))
  nil)
```

To test update-positions, reset the game:

```
(reset-game test-snake test-apple)
-> nil
```

Then, move the apple into harm's way, under the snake:

```
(dosync (alter test-apple assoc :location [1 1]))
-> {:location [1 1], ; etc.
```

Now, after you update-positions, you should have a bigger, two-segment snake:

```
(update-positions test-snake test-apple)
-> nil
```

```
(:body @test-snake)
-> ([2 1] [1 1])
```

And that is all the mutable state of the Snake world: three functions, about a dozen lines of code.

The Snake GUI

The Snake GUI consists of functions that paint screen objects, respond to user input, and set up the various Swing components. Since snakes and apples are drawn from simple points, the painting functions are simple. The fill-point function fills in a single point:

```
(defn fill-point [g pt color]
  (let [[x y width height] (point-to-screen-rect pt)]
    (.setColor g color)
    (.fillRect g x y width height)))
```

The paint multimethod knows how to paint snakes and apples:

```
Line 1 (defmulti paint (fn [g object & _] (:type object)))
     2
     3 (defmethod paint :apple [g {:keys [location color]}]
     4   (fill-point g location color))
     5
     6 (defmethod paint :snake [g {:keys [body color]}]
     7   (doseq [point body]
     8     (fill-point g point color)))
```

paint takes two required arguments: g is a java.awt.Graphics instance, and object is the object to be painted. The defmulti includes an optional rest argument so that future implementations of paint have the option of taking more arguments. (See Section 8.2, *Defining Multimethods*, on page 189 for an in-depth description of defmulti.) On line 3, the :apple method of paint binds the location and color of the apple and uses them to paint a single point on the screen. On line 6, the :snake method binds the snake's body and color and then uses doseq to paint each point in the body.

The meat of the UI is the game-panel function, which creates a Swing JPanel with handlers for painting the game, updating on each timer tick, and responding to user input:

```
Line 1 (defn game-panel [frame snake apple]
  -    (proxy [JPanel ActionListener KeyListener] []
  -      (paintComponent [g]
  -        (proxy-super paintComponent g)
  5        (paint g @snake)
  -        (paint g @apple))
  -      (actionPerformed [e]
  -        (update-positions snake apple)
  -        (when (lose? @snake)
  10         (reset-game snake apple)
  -          (JOptionPane/showMessageDialog frame "You lose!"))
  -        (when (win? @snake)
  -          (reset-game snake apple)
  -          (JOptionPane/showMessageDialog frame "You win!"))
  15        (.repaint this))
  -      (keyPressed [e]
  -        (update-direction snake (dirs (.getKeyCode e))))
  -      (getPreferredSize []
  -        (Dimension. (* (inc width) point-size)
  -                    (* (inc height) point-size)))
  20      (keyReleased [e])
  -      (keyTyped [e])))
```

game-panel is long but simple. It uses proxy to create a panel with a set of Swing callback methods.

- Swing calls paintComponent (line 3) to draw the panel. paintComponent calls proxy-super to invoke the normal JPanel behavior, and then it paints the snake and the apple.

- Swing will call actionPerformed (line 7) on every timer tick. actionPerformed updates the positions of the snake and the apple. If the game is over, it displays a dialog and resets the game. Finally, it triggers a repaint with (.repaint this).

- Swing calls keyPressed (line 16) in response to keyboard input. keyPressed calls update-direction to change the snake's direction. (If the keyboard input is not an arrow key, the dirs function returns nil and update-direction does nothing.)

- The game panel ignores keyReleased and keyTyped.

The game function creates a new game:

```
Line 1  (defn game []
  -       (let [snake (ref (create-snake))
  -             apple (ref (create-apple))
  -             frame (JFrame. "Snake")
  5             panel (game-panel frame snake apple)
  -             timer (Timer. turn-millis panel)]
  -         (doto panel
  -           (.setFocusable true)
  -           (.addKeyListener panel))
  10        (doto frame
  -           (.add panel)
  -           (.pack)
  -           (.setVisible true))
  -         (.start timer)
  15        [snake, apple, timer]))
```

On line 2, game creates all the necessary game objects: the mutable model objects snake and apple and the UI components frame, panel, and timer. Lines 7 and 10 perform boilerplate initialization of the panel and frame. Line 14 starts the game by kicking off the timer.

Line 15 returns a vector with the snake, apple, and time. This is for convenience when testing at the REPL: you can use these objects to move the snake and apple or to start and stop the game.

Go ahead and play the game again; you have earned it. To start the game, use the snake library at the REPL, and run game. If you have entered the code yourself, you can use the library name you picked (examples.reader in the instructions); otherwise, you can use the completed sample at examples.snake:

```
(use 'examples.snake)
```

```
(game)
-> [#<Ref clojure.lang.Ref@6ea27cbe>
#<Ref clojure.lang.Ref@6dabd6b0>
#<Timer javax.swing.Timer@32f60451>]
```

The game window may appear behind your REPL window. If this happens, use your local operating-system fu to locate the game window.

There are many possible improvements to the Snake game. If the snake reaches the edge of the screen, perhaps it should turn to avoid disappearing from view. Or (tough love) maybe you just lose the game! Make the Snake game your own by improving it to suit your personal style.

Snakes Without Refs

We chose to implement the Snake game's mutable model using refs so that we could coordinate the updates to the snake and the apple. Other approaches are also valid. For example, you could combine the snake and apple state into a single game object. With only one object, coordination is no longer required, and you can use an atom instead.

The file examples/atom-snake.clj demonstrates this approach. Functions like update-positions become part of the functional model and return a new game object with updated state:

```
src/examples/atom_snake.clj
(defn update-positions [{snake :snake, apple :apple, :as game}]
  (if (eats? snake apple)
    (merge game {:apple (create-apple) :snake (move snake :grow)})
    (merge game {:snake (move snake)}))))
```

Notice how destructuring makes it easy to get at the internals of the game: both snake and apple are bound by the argument list.

The actual mutable updates are now all atom swap!s. We found these to be simple enough to leave them in the UI function game-panel, as this excerpt shows:

```
(actionPerformed [e]
  (swap! game update-positions)
  (when (lose? (@game :snake))
    (swap! game reset-game)
    (JOptionPane/showMessageDialog frame "You lose!"))
```

There are other possibilities as well. Chris Houser's fork of the book's sample code[2] demonstrates using an agent that Thread/sleeps instead of a Swing timer, as well as using a new agent per game turn to update the game's state.

5.7 Wrapping Up

Clojure's reference model is the most innovative part of the language. The combination of software transactional memory, agents, atoms, and dynamic

---

2. http://github.com/Chouser/programming-clojure

binding that you have seen in this chapter gives Clojure powerful abstractions for all sorts of stateful systems. It also makes Clojure one of the few languages suited to the coming generation of multicore computer hardware.

Next, we will look at one of Clojure's newer features. Some call it a solution to the "expression problem."[3] We call it a protocol.

---

3. http://en.wikipedia.org/wiki/Expression_problem

CHAPTER 6

Protocols and Datatypes

Abstractions lay at the foundation of reusable code. The Clojure language itself has abstractions for sequences, collections, and callability. Traditionally, these abstractions were described with Java interfaces and implemented using Java classes. In the beginning, Clojure provided proxy and genclass, removing the need to drop all the way to Java to achieve this, but that has changed with the introduction of protocols.

- Protocols provide an alternative to Java interfaces for high-performance polymorphic method dispatch.
- Datatypes provide an alternative to Java classes for creating implementations of abstractions defined with either protocols or interfaces.

Protocols and datatypes provide a high-performance, flexible mechanism for abstraction and concretion that removes the need to write Java interfaces and classes when programming in Clojure. With protocols and datatypes, you can create new abstractions and new types that implement those abstractions and even extend new abstractions to existing types.

In this chapter, we will explore Clojure's approach to abstraction using protocols and datatypes. First, we will implement our own version of Clojure's built-in spit and slurp functions. Then, we will take a short detour to build a CryptoVault, where you will learn about extending some of Java's standard library. Finally, we will put everything together using records and protocols to define musical notes and sequences. After working through these exercises, you will certainly see the power of Clojure's composable abstractions.

6.1 Programming to Abstractions

Clojure's spit and slurp I/O functions are built on two abstractions, reading and writing. This means you can use them with a variety of source and destination types, including files, URLs, and sockets, and they can be extended to support new types by anybody, whether they are existing types or newly defined.

- The slurp function takes an input source, reads the contents, and returns it as a string.
- The spit function takes an output destination and a value, converts the value to a string, and writes it to the output destination.

We will start by writing basic versions of the two functions that can read from and write to files only. We will then refactor the basic versions several times as we explore different approaches to supporting additional datatypes. Working through this will give you a good feel for the usefulness of programming to abstractions in general and the flexibility and power of Clojure's protocols and datatypes in particular.

After writing our versions of spit and slurp, called expectorate and gulp, respectively, that work with several existing datatypes, we will create a new datatype, Crypto-Vault, that can be used with our versions of the functions as well as the originals.

gulp and expectorate

The gulp function is a simplified version of Clojure's slurp function, and expectorate, despite its highfalutin name, is a dumbed-down version of Clojure's spit function. Let's write a basic version of gulp that can read from a java.io.File only.

```
src/examples/gulp.clj
(ns examples.gulp
  (:import (java.io FileInputStream InputStreamReader BufferedReader)))
(defn gulp [src]
  (let [sb (StringBuilder.)]
    (with-open [reader (-> src
                           FileInputStream.
                           InputStreamReader.
                           BufferedReader.)]
      (loop [c (.read reader)]
        (if (neg? c)
          (str sb)
          (do
            (.append sb (char c))
            (recur (.read reader))))))))
```

The gulp function creates a BufferedReader from a given File object and then loops/recurs over it, reading a character at a time and appending each to a StringBuilder until it reaches the end of the input where it returns a string. The basic expectorate function is even smaller:

```
src/examples/expectorate.clj
(ns examples.expectorate
  (:import (java.io FileOutputStream OutputStreamWriter BufferedWriter)))

(defn expectorate [dst content]
  (with-open [writer (-> dst
                         FileOutputStream.
                         OutputStreamWriter.
                         BufferedWriter.)]
    (.write writer (str content))))
```

It creates a BufferedWriter file, converts the value of the content parameter to a string, and writes it out to the BufferedWriter.

But what if we want to support additional types like Sockets, URLs, and basic input and output streams? We need to update gulp and expectorate to be able to make BufferedReaders and BufferedWriters from datatypes other than files. So, let's create two new functions, make-reader and make-writer, that will be responsible for this behavior.

- The make-reader function makes a BufferedReader from an input source.
- The make-writer makes a BufferedWriter from an output destination.

```
(defn make-reader [src]
  (-> src FileInputStream. InputStreamReader. BufferedReader.))

(defn make-writer [dst]
  (-> dst FileOutputStream. OutputStreamWriter. BufferedWriter.))
```

Like our basic gulp and expectorate functions, make-reader and make-writer work only on files, but that will change shortly. Now let's refactor gulp and expectorate to use the new functions:

```
src/examples/protocols.clj
(defn gulp [src]
  (let [sb (StringBuilder.)]
    (with-open [reader (make-reader src)]
      (loop [c (.read reader)]
        (if (neg? c)
          (str sb)
          (do
            (.append sb (char c))
            (recur (.read reader))))))))

(defn expectorate [dst content]
  (with-open [writer (make-writer dst)]
    (.write writer (str content))))
```

We can now add support for additional source and destination types to gulp and expectorate just by updating make-reader and make-writer. One approach to supporting additional types is to use a cond, or condp, statement to process different types appropriately. For example, the following version of make-reader replaces the call to the FileInputStream constructor with a condp statement that creates an InputStream from the given input, whether it is a File, Socket, or URL or already is an InputStream.

```
(defn make-reader [src]
  (-> (condp = (type src)
        java.io.InputStream src
        java.lang.String (FileInputStream. src)
        java.io.File (FileInputStream. src)
        java.net.Socket (.getInputStream src)
        java.net.URL (if (= "file" (.getProtocol src))
                       (-> src .getPath FileInputStream.)
                       (.openStream src)))
      InputStreamReader.
      BufferedReader.))
```

Here's a version of make-writer using the same strategy:

```
(defn make-writer [dst]
  (-> (condp = (type dst)
        java.io.OutputStream dst
        java.io.File (FileOutputStream. dst)
        java.lang.String (FileOutputStream. dst)
        java.net.Socket (.getOutputStream dst)
        java.net.URL (if (= "file" (.getProtocol dst))
                       (-> dst .getPath FileOutputStream.)
                       (throw (IllegalArgumentException.
                                "Can't write to non-file URL"))))
      OutputStreamWriter.
      BufferedWriter.))
```

The problem with this approach is that it is closed: nobody else can come along and add support for new source and destination types without rewriting make-reader and make-writer. What we need is an open solution, one where support for new types can be added after the fact and by different parties. What we need is two abstractions, one for reading and one for writing.

6.2 Interfaces

In Java, the usual mechanism for supporting this form of abstraction is the interface. The interface mechanism provides a means for dispatching calls to an abstract function, specified in an interface definition, to a specific implementation based on the datatype of the first parameter passed in the call. In

Java, the first parameter is implicit; it is the object that implements the interface.

The following are the strengths of interfaces:

- Datatypes can implement multiple interfaces.
- Interfaces provide only specification, not implementation, which allows implementation of multiple interfaces without the problems associated with multiple class inheritance.

The weakness of interfaces is that existing datatypes cannot be extended to implement new interfaces without rewriting them.

We can create Java interfaces in Clojure with the definterface macro. This takes a name and one or more method signatures:

```
(definterface name & sigs)
```

Let's create our abstraction for things-that-can-read-from-and-be-written-to as an interface, which we'll call IOFactory.

```
(definterface IOFactory
  (^java.io.BufferReader make-reader [this])
  (^java.io.BufferedWriter make-writer [this]))
```

This will create an interface called IOFactory that includes two abstract functions, make-reader and make-writer. Any class that implements this interface must include make-reader and make-writer functions that take a single parameter and an instance of the datatype itself and that return a BufferedReader and BufferedWriter, respectively.

Unfortunately, the interfaces that a class supports are determined at design time by the author; once a Java class is defined, it cannot be updated to support new interfaces without rewriting it. Therefore, we can't extend the File, Socket, and URL classes to implement the IOFactory interface.

Like the versions of make-reader and make-writer we based on condp, our interface is closed to extension by parties other than the author. This is part of what is called the *expression problem*.[1] Fortunately, Clojure has a solution to it.[2]

6.3 Protocols

One piece of Clojure's solution to the expression problem is the protocol. Protocols provide a flexible mechanism for abstraction that leverages the best

---

1. http://lambda-the-ultimate.org/node/2232
2. http://www.ibm.com/developerworks/java/library/j-clojure-protocols/?ca=drs-

parts of interfaces by providing only specification, not implementation, and by letting datatypes implement multiple protocols. Additionally, protocols address the key weaknesses of interfaces by allowing nonintrusive extension of existing types to support new protocols.

The following are the strengths of protocols:

- Datatypes can implement multiple protocols.

- Protocols provide only specification, not implementation, which allows implementation of multiple interfaces without the problems associated with multiple-class inheritance.

- Existing datatypes can be extended to implement new interfaces with no modification to the datatypes.

- Protocol method names are namespaced, so there is no risk of name collision when multiple parties choose to extend the same extant type.

The defprotocol macro works just like definterface, but now we are able to extend existing datatypes to implement our new abstraction.

`(defprotocol name & opts+sigs)`

Let's redefine IOFactory as a protocol, instead of an interface.

```
(defprotocol IOFactory
  "A protocol for things that can be read from and written to."
  (make-reader [this] "Creates a BufferedReader.")
  (make-writer [this] "Creates a BufferedWriter."))
```

Notice we can include a document string for the protocol as a whole, as well as for each of its methods. Now let's extend java.io.InputStream and java.io.OutputStream to implement our IOFactory protocol.

We use the extend function to associate an existing type to a protocol and to provide the required function implementations, usually referred to as *methods* in this context. The parameters to extend are the name of the type to extend, the name of the protocol to implement, and a map of method implementations, where the keys are keywordized versions of the method names.

`(extend type & proto+mmaps)`

The make-reader implementation for an InputStream just wraps the value passed to it in a BufferedReader.

`src/examples/protocols.clj`
```
(extend InputStream
  IOFactory
  {:make-reader (fn [src]
```

```
                      (-> src InputStreamReader. BufferedReader.))
    :make-writer (fn [dst]
                      (throw (IllegalArgumentException.
                              "Can't open as an InputStream."))))})
```

Similarly, the implementation of make-writer for an OutputStream wraps its given input in a BufferedWriter. And since you can't write to an InputStream or read from an OutputStream, the respective implementations of make-writer and make-reader throw IllegalArgumentExceptions.

```
(extend OutputStream
  IOFactory
  {:make-reader (fn [src]
                    (throw
                     (IllegalArgumentException.
                      "Can't open as an OutputStream.")))
   :make-writer (fn [dst]
                      (-> dst OutputStreamWriter. BufferedWriter.))})
```

We can extend the java.io.File type to implement our IOFactory protocol with the extend-type macro, which provides a slightly cleaner syntax than extend.

(extend-type type & specs)

It takes the name of the type to extend and one or more specs, which includes a protocol name and its respective method implementations.

```
(extend-type File
  IOFactory
  (make-reader [src]
    (make-reader (FileInputStream. src)))
  (make-writer [dst]
    (make-writer (FileOutputStream. dst))))
```

Notice that we create an InputStream, specifically, a FileInputStream, from our file and then make a recursive call to make-reader, which will be dispatched to the implementation defined earlier for InputStreams. We use the same recursive pattern for the make-writer method, as well as for the methods of the following remaining types.

We can extend the remaining types all at once with the extend-protocol macro:

(extend-protocol protocol & specs)

This takes the name of the protocol followed by one or more type names with their respective method implementations.

```
(extend-protocol IOFactory
  Socket
  (make-reader [src]
    (make-reader (.getInputStream src)))
```

```
    (make-writer [dst]
      (make-writer (.getOutputStream dst)))

    URL
    (make-reader [src]
      (make-reader
       (if (= "file" (.getProtocol src))
         (-> src .getPath FileInputStream.)
         (.openStream src))))

    (make-writer [dst]
      (make-writer
       (if (= "file" (.getProtocol dst))
         (-> dst .getPath FileInputStream.)
         (throw (IllegalArgumentException.
                  "Can't write to non-file URL"))))))
```

Now let's put it all together.

```
(ns examples.io
  (:import (java.io File FileInputStream FileOutputStream
                    InputStream InputStreamReader
                    OutputStream OutputStreamWriter
                    BufferedReader BufferedWriter)
           (java.net Socket URL)))

(defprotocol IOFactory
  "A protocol for things that can be read from and written to."
  (make-reader [this] "Creates a BufferedReader.")
  (make-writer [this] "Creates a BufferedWriter."))

(defn gulp [src]
  (let [sb (StringBuilder.)]
    (with-open [reader (make-reader src)]
      (loop [c (.read reader)]
        (if (neg? c)
          (str sb)
          (do
            (.append sb (char c))
            (recur (.read reader))))))))

(defn expectorate [dst content]
  (with-open [writer (make-writer dst)]
    (.write writer (str content))))

(extend-protocol IOFactory
  InputStream
  (make-reader [src]
    (-> src InputStreamReader. BufferedReader.))
```

```
(make-writer [dst]
  (throw
   (IllegalArgumentException.
    "Can't open as an InputStream.")))

OutputStream
(make-reader [src]
  (throw
   (IllegalArgumentException.
    "Can't open as an OutputStream.")))

(make-writer [dst]
  (-> dst OutputStreamWriter. BufferedWriter.))

File
(make-reader [src]
  (make-reader (FileInputStream. src)))

(make-writer [dst]
  (make-writer (FileOutputStream. dst)))

Socket
(make-reader [src]
  (make-reader (.getInputStream src)))

(make-writer [dst]
  (make-writer (.getOutputStream dst)))

URL
(make-reader [src]
  (make-reader
   (if (= "file" (.getProtocol src))
     (-> src .getPath FileInputStream.)
     (.openStream src))))


(make-writer [dst]
  (make-writer
   (if (= "file" (.getProtocol dst))
     (-> dst .getPath FileInputStream.)
     (throw (IllegalArgumentException.
             "Can't write to non-file URL"))))))
```

6.4 Datatypes

We have shown how to extend existing types to implement new abstractions with protocols, but what if we want to create a new type in Clojure? That is where datatypes come in.

A datatype provides the following:

- A unique class, either named or anonymous
- Structure, either explicitly as fields or implicitly as a closure
- Fields that can have type hints and can be primitive
- Optional implementations of abstract methods specified in protocols or interfaces
- Immutability on by default
- Unification with maps (via records)

We will use the deftype macro to define a new datatype, called CryptoVault, that will implement two protocols, including IOFactory.

Now that gulp and expectorate support several existing Java classes, let's create a new supported type, CryptoVault. You'll create an instance of a CryptoVault by passing in an argument that implements the clojure.java.io.IOFactory protocol (not the one we've defined here), a path to a cryptographic key store, and a password. The contents expectorated into the CryptoVault will be encrypted and written to the IOFactory object and then decrypted when gulped back in.

We'll use deftype to create the new type.

```
(deftype name [& fields] & opts+specs)
```

It takes the name of the type and a vector of fields contained by the type. The naming convention for datatypes is the same as used by Java classes, i.e., PascalCase or CamelCase.

```
user=> (deftype CryptoVault [filename keystore password])
user.CryptoVault
```

Once the type has been defined, we can create an instance of our CryptoVault like so:

```
user=> (def vault (->CryptoVault "vault-file" "keystore" "toomanysecrets"))
#'user/vault
```

And its fields can be accessed using the same prefix-dot syntax used to access fields in Java objects.

```
user=> (.filename vault)
"vault-file"

user=> (.keystore vault)
"keystore"

user=> (.password vault)
"toomanysecrets"
```

Now that we have defined the basic CryptoVault type, let's add behavior with some methods. Datatypes can implement only those methods that have been specified in either a protocol or an interface, so let's first create a Vault protocol.

```
(defprotocol Vault
  (init-vault [vault])
  (vault-output-stream [vault])
  (vault-input-stream [vault]))
```

The protocol includes three functions—init-vault, vault-output-stream, and vault-input-stream—that every Vault must implement.

We can define our new type's methods inline with deftype; we just pass the type name and vector of fields as before, followed by a protocol name and one or more method bodies:

src/examples/cryptovault.clj
```
(ns examples.cryptovault
  (:use [examples.io :only [IOFactory make-reader make-writer]])
  (:require [clojure.java.io :as io])
  (:import (java.security KeyStore KeyStore$SecretKeyEntry
                          KeyStore$PasswordProtection)
           (javax.crypto KeyGenerator Cipher CipherOutputStream
                         CipherInputStream)
           (java.io FileOutputStream)))
(deftype CryptoVault [filename keystore password]
  Vault
  (init-vault [vault]
    ... define method body here ...)

  (vault-output-stream [vault]
    ... define method body here ...)

  (vault-input-stream [vault]
    ... define method body here ...)

  IOFactory
  (make-reader [vault]
    (make-reader (vault-input-stream vault)))
  (make-writer [vault]
    (make-writer (vault-output-stream vault))))
```

Notice that the methods for more than one protocol can be defined inline; we have defined the methods for the Vault and IOFactory protocols together, although the bodies of the Vault methods have been elided and will be described next.

The init-vault method will generate an Advanced Encryption Standard (AES) key, place it in a java.security.KeyStore, write the keystore data to the file specified by the keystore field in the CryptoVault, and then password-protect it.

```
(init-vault [vault]
  (let [password (.toCharArray (.password vault))
        key (.generateKey (KeyGenerator/getInstance "AES"))
        keystore (doto (KeyStore/getInstance "JCEKS")
                    (.load nil password)
                    (.setEntry "vault-key"
                              (KeyStore$SecretKeyEntry. key)
                              (KeyStore$PasswordProtection. password)))]
    (with-open [fos (FileOutputStream. (.keystore vault))]
      (.store keystore fos password))))
```

Both the vault-output-stream and vault-input-stream methods will use a function, vault-key, to load the keystore associated with the CryptoVault and extract the AES key used to encrypt and decrypt the contents of the vault.

```
(defn vault-key [vault]
  (let [password (.toCharArray (.password vault))]
    (with-open [fis (FileInputStream. (.keystore vault))]
      (-> (doto (KeyStore/getInstance "JCEKS")
            (.load fis password))
          (.getKey "vault-key" password)))))
```

The vault-output-stream method uses the vault-key method to initialize an AES cipher object, creates an OutputStream from the Vault's filename, and then uses the cipher and OutputStream to create an instance of a CipherOutputStream.

```
(vault-output-stream [vault]
  (let [cipher (doto (Cipher/getInstance "AES")
                 (.init Cipher/ENCRYPT_MODE (vault-key vault)))]
    (CipherOutputStream. (io/output-stream (.filename vault)) cipher)))
```

The vault-input-stream method works just like vault-output-stream, except it returns a CipherInputStream.

```
(vault-input-stream [vault]
  (let [cipher (doto (Cipher/getInstance "AES")
                 (.init Cipher/DECRYPT_MODE (vault-key vault)))]
    (CipherInputStream. (io/input-stream (.filename vault)) cipher)))
```

To create an instance of a CryptoVault, just pass the location where data should be stored, the keystore filename, and the password protecting the keystore.

```
user=> (def vault (->CryptoVault "vault-file" "keystore" "toomanysecrets"))
#'user/vault
```

If the keystore hasn't been initialized yet, call the init-vault method:

```
user=> (init-vault vault)
nil
```

Then use the CryptoVault like any other source/destination used by gulp and expectorate.

```
user=> (expectorate vault "This is a test of the CryptoVault")
nil
```

```
user=> (gulp vault)
"This is a test of the CryptoVault"
```

We can use the CryptoVault with the built-in spit and slurp functions by extending it to support the clojure.java.io/IOFactory protocol. This version of the IOFactory has four methods, instead of two like ours, and there are default method implementations defined in a map called default-streams-impl. We'll override just two of its methods, make-input-stream and make-output-stream, by assoc'ing our new implementations into this map and passing it to the extend function.

```
(extend CryptoVault
  clojure.java.io/IOFactory
  (assoc clojure.java.io/default-streams-impl
    :make-input-stream (fn [x opts] (vault-input-stream x))
    :make-output-stream (fn [x opts] (vault-output-stream x))))
```

That's it; now we can read and write to a CryptoVault using slurp and spit.

```
user=> (spit vault "This is a test of the CryptoVault using
spit and slurp")
nil
```

```
user=> (slurp vault)
"This is a test of the CryptoVault using spit and slurp"
```

Let's put all the pieces together in a .clj file. Make a src/examples/datatypes subdirectory within your project directory, and create a file called vault.clj.

```
src/examples/cryptovault_complete.clj
(ns examples.cryptovault-complete
  (:require [clojure.java.io :as io]
            [examples.protocols.io :as proto])
  (:import (java.security KeyStore KeyStore$SecretKeyEntry
                          KeyStore$PasswordProtection)
           (javax.crypto Cipher KeyGenerator CipherOutputStream
                         CipherInputStream)
           (java.io FileInputStream FileOutputStream)))
(defprotocol Vault
  (init-vault [vault])
  (vault-output-stream [vault])
  (vault-input-stream [vault]))
(defn vault-key [vault]
  (let [password (.toCharArray (.password vault))]
    (with-open [fis (FileInputStream. (.keystore vault))]
```

```clojure
          (-> (doto (KeyStore/getInstance "JCEKS")
                (.load fis password))
              (.getKey "vault-key" password)))))
(deftype CryptoVault [filename keystore password]
  Vault
  (init-vault [vault]
    (let [password (.toCharArray (.password vault))
          key (.generateKey (KeyGenerator/getInstance "AES"))
          keystore (doto (KeyStore/getInstance "JCEKS")
                     (.load nil password)
                     (.setEntry "vault-key"
                                (KeyStore$SecretKeyEntry. key)
                                (KeyStore$PasswordProtection. password)))]
      (with-open [fos (FileOutputStream. (.keystore vault))]
        (.store keystore fos password))))

  (vault-output-stream [vault]
    (let [cipher (doto (Cipher/getInstance "AES")
                   (.init Cipher/ENCRYPT_MODE (vault-key vault)))]
      (CipherOutputStream. (io/output-stream (.filename vault)) cipher)))

  (vault-input-stream [vault]
    (let [cipher (doto (Cipher/getInstance "AES")
                   (.init Cipher/DECRYPT_MODE (vault-key vault)))]
      (CipherInputStream. (io/input-stream (.filename vault)) cipher)))

  proto/IOFactory
  (make-reader [vault]
    (proto/make-reader (vault-input-stream vault)))
  (make-writer [vault]
    (proto/make-writer (vault-output-stream vault))))

(extend CryptoVault
  clojure.java.io/IOFactory
  (assoc io/default-streams-impl
    :make-input-stream (fn [x opts] (vault-input-stream x))
    :make-output-stream (fn [x opts] (vault-output-stream x))))
```

6.5 Records

Classes in object-oriented programs tend to fall into two distinct categories: those that represent programming artifacts, such as String, Socket, InputStream, and OutputStream, and those that represent application domain information, such as Employee and PurchaseOrder.

Unfortunately, using classes to model application domain information hides it behind a class-specific micro-language of setters and getters. You can no longer take a generic approach to information processing, and you end up with a proliferation of unnecessary specificity and reduced reusability. See Clojure's documentation on datatypes[3] for more information.

For this reason, Clojure has always encouraged the use of maps for modeling such information, and that holds true even with datatypes, which is where records come in. A record is a datatype, like those created with deftype, that also implements PersistentMap and therefore can be used like any other map (mostly); and since records are also proper classes, they support type-based polymorphism through protocols. With records, we have the best of both worlds: maps that can implement protocols.

What could be more natural than using records to play music? So, let's create a record that represents a musical note, with fields for pitch, octave, and duration; then we'll use the JDK's built-in MIDI synthesizer to play sequences of these notes.

Since records are maps, we will be able to change the properties of individual notes using the assoc and update-in functions, and we can create or transform entire sequences of notes using map and reduce. This gives us access to the entirety of Clojure's collection API.

We will create a Note record with the defrecord macro, which behaves just like deftype.

```
(defrecord name [& fields] & opts+specs)
```

A Note record has three fields: pitch, octave, and duration.

```
(defrecord Note [pitch octave duration])
-> user.Note
```

The pitch will be represented by a keyword like :C, :C#, and :Db, which represent the notes C, C (C sharp), and D (D flat), respectively. Each pitch can be played at different octaves; for instance, middle C is in the fourth octave. Duration indicates the note length; a whole note is represented by 1, a half note by 1/2, a quarter note by 1/4, and a 16th note by 1/16. For example, we can represent a D half note in the fourth octave with this Note record:

```
(->Note :D# 4 1/2)
-> #user.Note{:pitch :D#, :octave 4, :duration 1/2}
```

We can treat records like any other datatype, accessing their fields with the dot syntax.

```
(.pitch (->Note :D# 4 1/2))
-> :D#
```

---

3. http://clojure.org/datatypes

But records are also map-like:

```
(map? (->Note :D# 4 1/2))
-> true
```

so we can also access their fields using keywords:

```
(:pitch (->Note :D# 4 1/2))
-> :D#
```

We can create modified records with assoc and update-in.

```
(assoc (->Note :D# 4 1/2) :pitch :Db :duration 1/4)
-> #user.Note{:pitch :Db, :octave 4, :duration 1/4}

(update-in (->Note :D# 4 1/2) [:octave] inc)
-> #user.Note{:pitch :D#, :octave 5, :duration 1/2}
```

Records are open, so we can associate extra fields into a record:

```
(assoc (->Note :D# 4 1/2) :velocity 100)
-> #user.Note{:pitch :D#, :octave 4, :duration 1/2, :velocity 100}
```

We will use the optional :velocity field to represent the force with which a note is played.

When used on a record, both assoc and update-in return a new record, but the dissoc function works a bit differently; it will return a new record if the field being dissociated is optional, like velocity in the previous example, but it will return a plain map if the field is mandated by the defrecord specification, like pitch, octave, or duration.

In other words, if you remove a required field from a record of a given type, it is no longer a record of that type, and it simply becomes a map.

```
(dissoc (->Note :D# 4 1/2) :octave)
-> {:pitch :D#, :duration 1/2}
```

Notice that dissoc returns a map in this case, not a record. One difference between records and maps is that, unlike maps, records are not functions of keywords.

```
((->Note. :D# 4 1/2) :pitch)
-> user.Note cannot be cast to clojure.lang.IFn
```

ClassCastException is thrown because records do not implement the IFn interface like maps do. This is by design and drives a stylistic difference that makes code more readable.

When accessing a collection, you should place the collection first. When accessing a map that is acting (conceptually) as a data record, you should place the keyword first, even if the record is implemented as a plain map. Now that we have our basic Note record, let's add some methods so we can play them with the JDK's built-in MIDI synthesizer. We'll start by creating a MidiNote protocol with three methods:

src/examples/protocols.clj

```
(defprotocol MidiNote
  (to-msec [this tempo])
  (key-number [this])
  (play [this tempo midi-channel]))
```

To play our note with the MIDI synthesizer, we need to translate its pitch and octave into a MIDI key number and its duration into milliseconds. Here we have defined to-msec, key-number, and play, which we will use to create our MidiNote.

- to-msec returns the duration of the note in milliseconds.
- key-number returns the MIDI key number corresponding to this note.
- play plays this note at the given tempo on the given channel.

Now let's extend our Note record to implement the MidiNote protocol.

```
(import 'javax.sound.midi.MidiSystem)
(extend-type Note
  MidiNote
  (to-msec [this tempo]
    (let [duration-to-bpm {1 240, 1/2 120, 1/4 60, 1/8 30, 1/16 15}]
      (* 1000 (/ (duration-to-bpm (:duration this))
                 tempo)))))
```

The to-msec function translates the note's duration from whole note, half note, quarter note, and so on, into milliseconds based on the given tempo, which is represented in beats per minute (bpm).

```
(key-number [this]
  (let [scale {:C 0,   :C# 1,  :Db 1,   :D 2,
               :D# 3,  :Eb 3,  :E 4,    :F 5,
               :F# 6,  :Gb 6,  :G 7,    :G# 8,
               :Ab 8,  :A 9,   :A# 10,  :Bb 10,
               :B 11}]
    (+ (* 12 (inc (:octave this)))
       (scale (:pitch this)))))
```

The key-number function maps the keywords used to represent pitch into a number ranging from 0 to 11 [1] and then uses this number along with the given octave to find the corresponding MIDI key-number.[4]

---

4. Notice more than one pitch maps to 1, 3, 6, 8, and 10.

```
(play [this tempo midi-channel]
  (let [velocity (or (:velocity this) 64)]
    (.noteOn midi-channel (key-number this) velocity)
    (Thread/sleep (to-msec this tempo)))))
```

Finally, the play method takes a note, a tempo, and a MIDI channel; sends a noteOn message to the channel; and then sleeps for the note's duration. The note continues to play even while the current thread is asleep, stopping only when the next note is sent to the channel.

Now we need a function that sets up the MIDI synthesizer and plays a sequence of notes:

```
(defn perform [notes & {:keys [tempo] :or {tempo 120}}]
  (with-open [synth (doto (MidiSystem/getSynthesizer) .open)]
    (let [channel (aget (.getChannels synth) 0)]
      (doseq [note notes]
        (play note tempo channel)))))
```

The perform function takes a sequence of notes and an optional tempo value, opens a MIDI synthesizer, gets a channel from it, and then calls each note's play method.

Now that all the pieces are in place, let's make music using a sequence of Note records:

```
(def close-encounters [(->Note :D 3 1/2)
                       (->Note :E 3 1/2)
                       (->Note :C 3 1/2)
                       (->Note :C 2 1/2)
                       (->Note :G 2 1/2)])
-> #'user/close-encounters
```

In this case, our "music" consists of the five notes used to greet the alien ships in the movie *Close Encounters of the Third Kind*. To play it, just pass the sequence to the perform function:

```
(perform close-encounters)
-> nil
```

We can also generate sequences of notes dynamically with the for macro.

```
(def jaws (for [duration [1/2 1/2 1/4 1/4 1/8 1/8 1/8 1/8]
                pitch [:E :F]]
            (Note. pitch 2 duration)))
-> #'user/jaws

(perform jaws)
-> nil
```

The result is the shark theme from *Jaws*—a sequence of alternating E and F notes progressively speeding up as they move from half notes to quarter notes to eighth notes.

Since notes are records and records are map-like, we can manipulate them with any Clojure function that works on maps. For instance, we can map the update-in function across the *Close Encounters* sequence to raise, or lower, its octave.

```
(perform (map #(update-in % [:octave] inc) close-encounters))
-> nil
```

```
(perform (map #(update-in % [:octave] dec) close-encounters))
-> nil
```

Or we can create a sequence of notes that have progressively larger values of the optional :velocity field:

```
(perform (for [velocity [64 80 90 100 110 120]]
          (assoc (Note. :D 3 1/2) :velocity velocity)))
-> nil
```

This results in a sequence of increasingly more forceful D notes. Manipulating sequences is a particular strength of Clojure, so there are endless possibilities for programmatically creating and manipulating sequences of Note records.

Let's put the MidiNote protocol, the Note record, and the perform function together in a Clojure source file called src/examples/midi.clj so we can use them in the future.

src/examples/midi.clj
```
(ns examples.datatypes.midi
  (:import [javax.sound.midi MidiSystem]))
(defprotocol MidiNote
  (to-msec [this tempo])
  (key-number [this])
  (play [this tempo midi-channel]))

(defn perform [notes & {:keys [tempo] :or {tempo 88}}]
  (with-open [synth (doto (MidiSystem/getSynthesizer).open)]
    (let [channel (aget (.getChannels synth) 0)]
      (doseq [note notes]
        (play note tempo channel)))))

(defrecord Note [pitch octave duration]
  MidiNote
  (to-msec [this tempo]
    (let [duration-to-bpm {1 240, 1/2 120, 1/4 60, 1/8 30, 1/16 15}]
      (* 1000 (/ (duration-to-bpm (:duration this))
                 tempo))))
```

```clojure
(key-number [this]
  (let [scale {:C 0,  :C# 1, :Db 1,  :D 2,
              :D# 3, :Eb 3, :E 4,   :F 5,
              :F# 6, :Gb 6, :G 7,   :G# 8,
              :Ab 8, :A 9,  :A# 10, :Bb 10,
              :B 11}]
    (+ (* 12 (inc (:octave this)))
       (scale (:pitch this)))))
(play [this tempo midi-channel]
  (let [velocity (or (:velocity this) 64)]
    (.noteOn midi-channel (key-number this) velocity)
    (Thread/sleep (to-msec this tempo)))))
```

6.6 reify

The reify macro lets you create an anonymous instance of a datatype that implements either a protocol or an interface. Note that you get access by closure, not by declaration. This is because there are no declared members.

`(reify & opts+specs)`

reify, like deftype and defrecord, takes the name of one or more protocols, or interfaces, and a series of method bodies. Unlike deftype and defrecord, it doesn't take a name or a vector of fields; datatype instances produced with reify don't have explicit fields, relying instead on closures.

Let's compose some John Cage–style[5] aleatoric music[6] or, better yet, create an aleatoric music generator. We'll use reify to create an instance of a MidiNote that will play a different random note each time its play method is called.

src/examples/generator.clj
```clojure
(import '[examples.datatypes.midi MidiNote])
(let [min-duration 250
      min-velocity 64
      rand-note (reify
  MidiNote
  (to-msec [this tempo] (+ (rand-int 1000) min-duration))
  (key-number [this] (rand-int 100))
  (play [this tempo midi-channel]
    (let [velocity (+ (rand-int 100) min-velocity)]
      (.noteOn midi-channel (key-number this) velocity)
      (Thread/sleep (to-msec this tempo)))))]
  (perform (repeat 15 rand-note)))
```

---

5. http://en.wikipedia.org/wiki/John_Cage
6. http://en.wikipedia.org/wiki/Aleatoric_music

The first thing we need to do is import (not use or require) our MidiNote protocol from the examples.midi namespace. Next we bind two values, min-duration and min-velocity, that we will use in the MidiNote method implementations. Then we use reify to create an instance of an anonymous type, which implements the MidiNote protocol, that will select a random note, duration, and velocity each time its play method is called. Finally, we use the repeat function to create a sequence of fifteen notes, consisting of a single instance of rand-note, and perform it. *Voila*, you now have a virtual John Cage!

6.7 Wrapping Up

We covered a lot of ground in this chapter, from the general use of abstraction in programming to some (but not all) of the specific abstraction mechanisms Clojure provides. We explored creating concrete abstractions using protocols in Clojure and had some fun in the process!

But there's still more. Clojure's macro implementation is easy to learn and use correctly for common tasks and yet powerful enough for the harder macro-related tasks. In the next chapter, you will see how Clojure is bringing macros to mainstream programming.

CHAPTER 7

Macros

Macros give Clojure great power. With most programming techniques, you build features *within* the language. When you write macros, it is more accurate to say that you are "adding features to" the language. This is a powerful and dangerous ability, so you should follow the rules in Section 7.1, *When to Use Macros*, on page 165, at least until you have enough experience to decide for yourself when to bend the rules. Section 7.2, *Writing a Control Flow Macro*, on page 166 jump-starts that experience, walking you through adding a new feature to Clojure.

While powerful, macros are not always simple. Clojure works to make macros as simple as is feasible by including conveniences to solve many common problems that occur when writing macros. Section 7.3, *Making Macros Simpler*, on page 172 explains these problems and shows how Clojure mitigates them.

Macros are so different from other programming idioms that you may struggle to know when to use them. There is no better guide than the shared experience of the community, so Section 7.4, *Taxonomy of Macros*, on page 177 introduces a taxonomy of Clojure macros, based on the macros in Clojure and contrib libraries.

7.1 When to Use Macros

Macro Club has two rules, plus one exception.

The first rule of Macro Club is Don't Write Macros. Macros are complex, and they require you to think carefully about the interplay of macro expansion time and compile time. If you can write it as a function, think twice before using a macro.

The second rule of Macro Club is Write Macros If That Is the Only Way to Encapsulate a Pattern. All programming languages provide some way to encapsulate patterns, but without macros these mechanisms are incomplete. In most languages, you sense that incompleteness whenever you say, "My life would be easier if only my language had feature X." In Clojure, you just implement feature X using a macro.

The exception to the rule is that *you can write any macro that makes life easier for your callers when compared with an equivalent function.* But to understand this exception, you need some practice writing macros and comparing them to functions. So, let's get started with an example.

7.2 Writing a Control Flow Macro

Clojure provides the if special form as part of the language:

```
(if (= 1 1) (println "yep, math still works today"))
| yep, math still works today
```

Some languages have an unless, which is (almost) the opposite of if. unless performs a test and then executes its body only if the test is logically false.

Clojure doesn't have unless, but it does have an equivalent macro called when-not. For the sake of having a simple example to start with, let's pretend that when-not doesn't exist and create an implementation of unless. To follow the rules of Macro Club, begin by trying to write unless as a function:

src/examples/macros.clj
```
; This is doomed to fail...
(defn unless [expr form]
  (if expr nil form))
```

Check that unless correctly evaluates its form when its test expr is false:

```
(unless false (println "this should print"))
| this should print
```

Things appear fine so far. But let's be diligent and test the true case too:

```
(unless true (println "this should not print"))
| this should not print
```

Clearly something has gone wrong. The problem is that Clojure evaluates all the arguments before passing them to a function, so the println is called before unless *ever sees it.* In fact, both calls to unless earlier call println too soon, before entering the unless function. To see this, add a println inside unless:

```
(defn unless [expr form]
  (println "About to test...")
  (if expr nil form))
```

Now you can clearly see that function arguments are always evaluated before passing them to unless:

```
(unless false (println "this should print"))
| this should print
| About to test...

(unless true (println "this should not print"))
| this should not print
| About to test...
```

Macros solve this problem, because they do not evaluate their arguments immediately. Instead, you get to choose when (and if!) the arguments to a macro are evaluated.

When Clojure encounters a macro, it processes it in two steps. First, it expands (executes) the macro and substitutes the result back into the program. This is called *macro expansion time*. Then, it continues with the normal *compile time*.

To write unless, you need to write Clojure code to perform the following translation at macro expansion time:

```
(unless expr form) -> (if expr nil form)
```

Then, you need to tell Clojure that your code is a macro by using defmacro, which looks almost like defn:

```
(defmacro name doc-string? attr-map? [params*] body)
```

Because Clojure code is just Clojure data, you already have all the tools you need to write unless. Write the unless macro using list to build the if expression:

```
(defmacro unless [expr form]
  (list 'if expr nil form))
```

The body of unless executes at macro expansion time, producing an if form for compilation. If you enter this expression at the REPL:

```
(unless false (println "this should print"))
```

then Clojure will (invisibly to you) expand the unless form into the following:

```
(if false nil (println "this should print"))
```

Then, Clojure compiles and executes the expanded if form. Verify that unless works correctly for both true and false:

```
(unless false (println "this should print"))
| this should print
-> nil
```

```
(unless true (println "this should not print"))
-> nil
```

Congratulations, you have written your first macro. unless may seem pretty simple, but consider this: what you have just done is *impossible* in most languages. In languages without macros, special forms get in the way.

Special Forms, Design Patterns, and Macros

Clojure has no special syntax for code. Code is composed of data structures. This is true for normal functions but also for special forms and macros.

Consider a language with more syntactic variety, such as Java.[1] In Java, the most flexible mechanism for writing code is the instance method. Imagine that you are writing a Java program. If you discover a recurring pattern in some instance methods, you have the entire Java language at your disposal to encapsulate that recurring pattern.

Good so far. But Java also has lots of "special forms" (although they are not normally called by that name). Unlike Clojure special forms, which are just Clojure data, each Java special form has its own syntax. For example, if is a special form in Java. If you discover a recurring pattern of usage involving if, there is *no way to encapsulate* that pattern. You cannot create an unless, so you are stuck simulating unless with an idiomatic usage of if:

```
if (!something) ...
```

This may seem like a relatively minor problem. Java programmers can certainly learn to mentally make the translation from if (!foo) to unless (foo). But the problem is not just with if: *every distinct syntactic form* in the language inhibits your ability to encapsulate recurring patterns involving that form.

As another example, Java new is a special form. Polymorphism is not available for new, so you must simulate polymorphism, for example with an idiomatic usage of a class method:

```
Widget w = WidgetFactory.makeWidget(...)
```

---

1. We are not trying to beat up on Java in particular; it is just easier to talk about a specific language, and Java is well known.

This idiom is a little bulkier. It introduces a whole new class, WidgetFactory. This class is meaningless in the problem domain and exists only to work around the constructor special form. Unlike the unless idiom, the "polymorphic instantiation" idiom is complicated enough that there is more than one way to implement a solution. Thus, the idiom should more properly be called a *design pattern*.

Wikipedia defines a design pattern[2] to be a "general reusable solution to a commonly occurring problem in software design." It goes on to state that a "design pattern is not a finished design that can be transformed *directly* (emphasis added) into code."

That is where macros fit in. Macros provide a layer of *indirection* so that you can *automate the common parts of any recurring pattern*. Macros and code-as-data work together, enabling you to reprogram your language on the fly to encapsulate patterns.

Of course, this argument does not go entirely in one direction. Many people would argue that having a bunch of special syntactic forms makes a programming language easier to learn or read. We do not agree, but even if we did, we would be willing to trade syntactic variety for a powerful macro system. Once you get used to code as data, the ability to automate design patterns is a huge payoff.

Expanding Macros

When you created the unless macro, you quoted the symbol if:

```
(defmacro unless [expr form]
  (list 'if expr nil form))
```

But you did not quote any other symbols. To understand why, you need to think carefully about what happens at macro expansion time:

- By quoting 'if, you prevent Clojure from directly evaluating if at macro expansion time. Instead, evaluation strips off the quote, leaving if to be compiled.

- You do not want to quote expr and form, because they are macro arguments. Clojure will substitute them without evaluation at macro expansion time.

- You do not need to quote nil, since nil evaluates to itself.

---

2. http://en.wikipedia.org/wiki/Design_pattern_(computer_science)

Thinking about what needs to be quoted can get complicated quickly. Fortunately, you do not have to do this work in your head. Clojure includes diagnostic functions so that you can test macro expansions at the REPL.

The function macroexpand-1 will show you what happens at macro expansion time:

`(macroexpand-1 form)`

Use macroexpand-1 to prove that unless expands to a sensible if expression:

```
(macroexpand-1 '(unless false (println "this should print")))
-> (if false nil (println "this should print"))
```

Macros are complicated beasts, and we cannot overstate the importance of testing them with macroexpand-1. Let's go back and try some incorrect versions of unless. Here is one that incorrectly quotes the expr:

```
(defmacro bad-unless [expr form]
  (list 'if 'expr nil form))
```

When you expand bad-unless, you will see that it generates the symbol expr, instead of the actual test expression:

```
(macroexpand-1 '(bad-unless false (println "this should print")))
-> (if expr nil (println "this should print"))
```

If you try to actually use the bad-unless macro, Clojure will complain that it cannot resolve the symbol expr:

```
(bad-unless false (println "this should print"))
-> java.lang.Exception: Unable to resolve symbol: expr in this context
```

Sometimes macros expand into other macros. When this happens, Clojure will continue to expand all macros, until only normal code remains. For example, the .. macro expands recursively, producing a dot operator call, wrapped in another .. to handle any arguments that remain. You can see this with the following macro expansion:

```
(macroexpand-1 '(.. arm getHand getFinger))
-> (clojure.core/.. (. arm getHand) getFinger)
```

If you want to see .. expanded all the way, use macroexpand:

`(macroexpand form)`

If you macroexpand a call to .., it will recursively expand until only dot operators remain:

```
(macroexpand '(.. arm getHand getFinger))
-> (. (. arm getHand) getFinger)
```

(It is not a problem that arm, getHand, and getFinger do not exist. You are only expanding them, not attempting to compile and execute them.)

Another recursive macro is and. If you call and with more than two arguments, it will expand to include another call to and, with one less argument:

```
(macroexpand '(and 1 2 3))
-> (let* [and__3585__auto__ 1]
     (if and__3585__auto__ (clojure.core/and 2 3)
     and__3585__auto__))
```

This time, macroexpand does *not* expand all the way. macroexpand works only against the top level of the form you give it. Since the expansion of and creates a new and nested inside the form, macroexpand does not expand it.

when and when-not

Your unless macro could be improved slightly to execute multiple forms, avoiding this error:

```
(unless false (println "this") (println "and also this"))
-> java.lang.IllegalArgumentException: \
Wrong number of args passed to: macros$unless
```

Think about how you would write the improved unless. You would need to capture a variable argument list and stick a do in front of it so that every form executes. Clojure provides exactly this behavior in its when and when-not macros:

```
(when test & body)
```

```
(when-not test & body)
```

when-not is the improved unless you are looking for:

```
(when-not false (println "this") (println "and also this"))
| this
| and also this
-> nil
```

Given your practice writing unless, you should now have no trouble reading the source for when-not:

```
; from Clojure core
(defmacro when-not [test & body]
  (list 'if test nil (cons 'do body)))
```

And, of course, you can use macroexpand-1 to see how when-not works:

```
(macroexpand-1 '(when-not false (print "1") (print "2")))
-> (if false nil (do (print "1") (print "2")))
```

when is the opposite of when-not and executes its forms only when its test is true. Note that when differs from if in two ways:

- if allows an else clause, and when does not. This reflects English usage, because nobody says "when … else."

- Since when does not have to use its second argument as an else clause, it is free to take a variable argument list and execute all the arguments inside a do.

You don't really need an unless macro. Just use Clojure's when-not. Always check to see whether somebody else has written the macro you need.

7.3 Making Macros Simpler

The unless macro is a great simple example, but most macros are more complex. In this section, we will build a set of increasingly complex macros, introducing Clojure features as we go. For your reference, the features introduced in this section are summarized in the following table.

Form	Description
foo#	Auto-gensym: Inside a syntax-quoted section, create a unique name prefixed with foo.
(gensym prefix?)	Create a unique name, with optional prefix.
(macroexpand form)	Expand form with macroexpand-1 repeatedly until the returned form is no longer a macro.
(macroexpand-1 form)	Show how Clojure will expand form.
(list-frag? ~@form list-frag?)	Splicing unquote: Use inside a syntax quote to splice an unquoted list into a template.
`form	Syntax quote: Quote form, but allow internal unquoting so that form acts a template. Symbols inside form are resolved to help prevent inadvertent symbol capture.
~form	Unquote: Use inside a syntax quote to substitute an unquoted value.

First let's build a replica of Clojure's .. macro. We'll call it chain, since it chains a series of method calls. Here are some sample expansions of chain:

Macro Call	Expansion
(chain arm getHand)	(. arm getHand)
(chain arm getHand getFinger)	(. (. arm getHand) getFinger)

Begin by implementing the simple case where the chain calls only one method. The macro needs only to make a simple list:

src/examples/macros/chain_1.clj
```
; chain reimplements Clojure's .. macro
(defmacro chain [x form]
  (list '. x form))
```

chain needs to support any number of arguments, so the rest of the implementation should define a recursion. The list manipulation becomes more complex, since you need to build two lists and concat them together:

src/examples/macros/chain_2.clj
```
(defmacro chain
  ([x form] (list '. x form))
  ([x form & more] (concat (list 'chain (list '. x form)) more)))
```

Test chain using macroexpand to make sure it generates the correct expansions:

```
(macroexpand '(chain arm getHand))
-> (. arm getHand)

(macroexpand '(chain arm getHand getFinger))
-> (. (. arm getHand) getFinger)
```

The chain macro works fine as written, but it is difficult to read the expression that handles more than one argument:

```
(concat (list 'chain (list '. x form)) more)))
```

The definition of chain oscillates between macro code and the body to be generated. The intermingling of the two makes the entire thing hard to read. And this is just a baby of a form, only one line in length. As macro forms grow more complex, assembly functions such as list and concat quickly obscure the meaning of the macro.

One solution to this kind of problem is a templating language. If macros were created from templates, you could take a "fill-in-the-blanks" approach to creating them. The definition of chain might look like this:

```
; hypothetical templating language
(defmacro chain
  ([x form] (. ${x} ${form}))
  ([x form & more] (chain (. ${x} ${form}) ${more})))
```

In this hypothetical templating language, the ${} lets you substitute arguments into the macro expansion.

Notice how much easier the definition is to read and how it clearly shows what the expansion will look like.

Syntax Quote, Unquote, and Splicing Unquote

Clojure macros support templating without introducing a separate language. The *syntax quote* character, which is a backquote (`), works almost like normal quoting. But inside a syntax-quoted list, the *unquote character* (~, a tilde) turns quoting off again. The overall effect is templates that look like this:

```
src/examples/macros/chain_3.clj
(defmacro chain [x form]
  `(. ~x ~form))
```

Test that this new version of chain can correctly generate a single method call:

```
(macroexpand '(chain arm getHand))
-> (. arm getHand)
```

Unfortunately, the syntax quote/unquote approach will not quite work for the multiple-argument variant of chain:

```
src/examples/macros/chain_4.clj
; Does not quite work
(defmacro chain
  ([x form] `(. ~x ~form))
  ([x form & more] `(chain (. ~x ~form) ~more)))
```

When you expand this chain, the parentheses aren't quite right:

```
(macroexpand '(chain arm getHand getFinger))
-> (. (. arm getHand) (getFinger))
```

The last argument to chain is a list of more arguments. When you drop more into the macro "template," it has parentheses because it is a list. But you don't want these parentheses; you want more to be *spliced* into the list. This comes up often enough that there is a reader macro for it: *splicing unquote* (~@). Rewrite chain using splicing unquote to splice in more:

```
src/examples/macros/chain_5.clj
(defmacro chain
  ([x form] `(. ~x ~form))
  ([x form & more] `(chain (. ~x ~form) ~@more)))
```

Now, the expansion should be spot on:

```
(macroexpand '(chain arm getHand getFinger))
-> (. (. arm getHand) getFinger)
```

Many macros follow the pattern of chain, aka Clojure ..:

1. Begin the macro body with a syntax quote (`) to treat the entire thing as a template.

2. Insert individual arguments with an unquote (~).

3. Splice in more arguments with splicing unquote (~@).

The macros we have built so far have been simple enough to avoid creating any bindings with let or binding. Let's create such a macro next.

Creating Names in a Macro

Clojure has a time macro that times an expression, writing the elapsed time to the console:

```
(time (str "a" "b"))
| "Elapsed time: 0.06 msecs"
-> "ab"
```

Let's build a variant of time called bench, designed to collect data across many runs. Instead of writing to the console, bench will return a map that includes both the return value of the original expression and the elapsed time.

The best way to begin writing a macro is to write its desired expansion by hand. bench should expand like this:

```
; (bench (str "a" "b"))
; should expand to
(let [start (System/nanoTime)
      result (str "a" "b")]
  {:result result :elapsed (- (System/nanoTime) start)})

-> {:elapsed 61000, :result "ab"}
```

The let binds start to the start time and then executes the expression to be benched, binding it to result. Finally, the form returns a map including the result and the elapsed time since start.

With the expansion in hand, you can now work backward and write the macro to generate the expansion. Using the technique from the previous section, try writing bench using syntax quoting and unquoting:

src/examples/macros/bench_1.clj
```
; This won't work
(defmacro bench [expr]
  `(let [start (System/nanoTime)
         result ~expr]
     {:result result :elapsed (- (System/nanoTime) start)}))
```

If you try to call this version of bench, Clojure will complain:

```
(bench (str "a" "b"))
-> java.lang.Exception: Can't let qualified name: examples.macros/start
```

Clojure is accusing you of trying to let a qualified name, which is illegal. Calling macroexpand-1 confirms the problem:

```
(macroexpand-1 '(bench (str "a" "b")))
-> (clojure.core/let [examples.macros/start (System/nanoTime)
     examples.macros/result (str "a" "b")]
   {:elapsed (clojure.core/- (System/nanoTime) examples.macros/start)
    :result examples.macros/result})
```

When a syntax-quoted form encounters a symbol, it resolves the symbol to a fully qualified name. At the moment, this seems like an irritant, because you *want* to create local names, specifically start and result. But Clojure's approach protects you from a nasty macro bug called *symbol capture*.

What would happen if macro expansion *did* allow the unqualified symbols start and result and then bench was later used in a scope where those names were already bound to something else? The macro would *capture* the names and bind them to different values, with bizarre results. If bench captured its symbols, it would appear to work fine most of the time. Adding one and two would give you three:

```
(let [a 1 b 2]
  (bench (+ a b)))

->   {:result 3, :elapsed 39000}
```

...until the unlucky day that you picked a local name like start, which collided with a name inside bench:

```
(let [start 1 end 2]
  (bench (+ start end)))

->   {:result 1228277342451783002, :elapsed 39000}
```

bench captures the symbol start and binds it to (System/nanoTime). All of a sudden, one plus two seems to equal 1228277342451783002.

Clojure's insistence on resolving names in macros helps protect you from symbol capture, but you still don't have a working bench. You need some way to introduce local names, ideally *unique* ones that cannot collide with any names used by the caller.

Clojure provides a reader form for creating unique local names. Inside a syntax-quoted form, you can append an octothorpe (#) to an unqualified name, and Clojure will create an autogenerated symbol, or *auto-gensym*: a symbol based on the name plus an underscore and a unique ID. Try it at the REPL:

```
`foo#
foo__1004
```

With automatically generated symbols at your disposal, it is easy to implement
bench correctly:

```
(defmacro bench [expr]
  `(let [start# (System/nanoTime)
         result# ~expr]
     {:result result# :elapsed (- (System/nanoTime) start#)}))
```

Test it at the REPL:

```
(bench (str "a" "b"))
-> {:elapsed 63000, :result "ab"}
```

Clojure makes it easy to generate unique names, but if you are determined,
you can still force symbol capture. The sample code for the book includes an
evil-bench that shows a combination of syntax quoting, quoting, and unquoting
that leads to symbol capture. Don't use symbol capture unless you have a
thorough understanding of macros.

7.4 Taxonomy of Macros

Now that you have written several macros, we can restate the rules of Macro
Club with more supporting detail.

The first rule of Macro Club is Don't Write Macros. Macros are complex. If
none of the macros in Clojure seems complex to you, my company is hiring.[3]

The second rule of Macro Club is Write Macros If That Is the Only Way to
Encapsulate a Pattern. As you have seen, the patterns that resist encapsula-
tion tend to arise around special forms, which are irregularities in a language.
So, the second rule can also be called the Special Form Rule.

Special forms have special powers that you, the programmer, do not have:

- Special forms provide the most basic flow control structures, such as if
  and recur. All flow control macros must eventually call a special form.
- Special forms provide direct access to Java. Whenever you call Java from
  Clojure, you are going through at least one special form, such as the dot
  or new.
- Names are created and bound through special forms, whether defining a
  var with def, creating a lexical binding with let, or creating a dynamic
  binding with binding.

---

3. http://thinkrelevance.com

As powerful as they are, special forms are not functions. They cannot do some things that functions can do. You cannot apply a special form, store a special form in a var, or use a special form as a filter with the sequence library. In short, special forms are not first-class citizens of the language.

The specialness of special forms could be a major problem and lead to repetitive, unmaintainable patterns in your code. But macros neatly solve the problem, because you can use macros to generate special forms. In a practical sense, *all language features are first-class features at macro expansion time.*

Macros that generate special forms are often the most difficult to write but also the most rewarding. As if by magic, such macros seem to *add new features to the language.*

The exception to the Macro Club rules is caller convenience: *you can write any macro that makes life easier for your callers when compared with an equivalent function.* Because macros do not evaluate their arguments, callers can pass raw code to a macro, instead of wrapping the code in an anonymous function. Or, callers can pass unescaped names, instead of quoted symbols or strings.

We have reviewed the macros in Clojure and contrib libraries, and almost all of them follow the rules of Macro Club. Also, they fit into one or more of the categories shown in the following table, which shows the taxonomy of Clojure macros.

Justification	Category	Examples
Special form	Conditional evaluation	when, when-not, and, or, comment
Special form	Defining vars	defn, defmacro, defmulti, defstruct, declare
Special form	Java interop	.., doto, import-static
Caller convenience	Postponing evaluation	lazy-cat, lazy-seq, delay
Caller convenience	Wrapping evaluation	with-open, dosync, with-out-str, time, assert
Caller convenience	Avoiding a lambda	*(Same as for "Wrapping evaluation")*

Let's examine each of the categories in turn.

Conditional Evaluation

Because macros do not immediately evaluate their arguments, they can be used to create custom control structures. You have already seen this with the unless example in Section 7.2, *Writing a Control Flow Macro*, on page 166.

Macros that do conditional evaluation tend to be fairly simple to read and write. They follow a common form: evaluate some argument (the condition); then, based on that evaluation, pick which other arguments to evaluate, if any. A good example is Clojure's and:

```
Line 1  (defmacro and
   2     ([] true)
   3     ([x] x)
   4     ([x & rest]
   5        `(let [and# ~x]
   6           (if and# (and ~@rest) and#)))))
```

and is defined recursively. The zero- and one-argument bodies set up the base cases:

- For no arguments, return true.
- For one argument, return that argument.

For two or more arguments, and uses the first argument as its condition, evaluating it on line 5. Then, if the condition is true, and proceeds to evaluate the remaining arguments by recursively anding the rest (line 6).

and must be a macro in order to short-circuit evaluation after the first nontrue value is encountered. Unsurprisingly, and has a close cousin macro, or. Their signatures are the same:

```
(and & exprs)
```

```
(or & exprs)
```

The difference is that and stops on the first logical false, while or stops on the first logical true:

```
(and 1 0 nil false)
-> nil
```

```
(or 1 0 nil false)
-> 1
```

The all-time short-circuit evaluation champion is the comment macro:

```
(comment & exprs)
```

comment never evaluates *any* of its arguments and is sometimes used at the end of a source code file to demonstrate the usage of an API.

For example, the Clojure inspector library ends with the following comment, demonstrating the use of the inspector:

```
(comment

(load-file "src/inspector.clj")
(refer 'inspector)
(inspect-tree {:a 1 :b 2 :c [1 2 3 {:d 4 :e 5 :f [6 7 8]}]})
(inspect-table [[1 2 3][4 5 6][7 8 9][10 11 12]])

)
```

Notice the lack of indentation. This would be nonstandard in most Clojure code but is useful in comment, whose purpose is to draw attention to its body.

Creating Vars

Clojure vars are created by the def special form. Anything else that creates a var must eventually call def. So, for example, defn, defmacro, and defmulti are all themselves macros.

To demonstrate writing macros that create vars, we will look at two macros that are also part of Clojure: defstruct and declare.

Clojure provides a low-level function for creating structs called create-struct:

(**create-struct** & key-symbols)

Use create-struct to create a person struct:

```
(def person (create-struct :first-name :last-name))
-> #'user/person
```

create-struct works, but it is visually noisy. Given that you often want to immediately def a new struct, you will typically call defstruct, which combines def and create-struct in a single operation:

(**defstruct** name & key-symbols)

defstruct is a simple macro, and it is already part of Clojure:

```
(defmacro defstruct
  [name & keys]
  `(def ~name (create-struct ~@keys)))
```

This macro looks so simple that you may be tempted to try to write it as a function. You won't be able to, because def is a special form. You must generate def at macro time; you cannot make "dynamic" calls to def at runtime.

defstruct makes a single line easier to read, but some macros can also condense many lines down into a single form. Consider the problem of forward declarations. You are writing a program that needs forward references to vars a, b, c, and d. You can call def with no arguments to define the var names without an initial binding:

```
(def a)
(def b)
(def c)
(def d)
```

But this is tedious and wastes a lot of vertical space. The declare macro takes a variable list of names and defs each name for you:

(declare & names**)**

Now you can declare all the names in a single compact form:

```
(declare a b c d)
-> #'user/d
```

The implementation of declare is built into Clojure:

```
(defmacro declare
  [& names] `(do ~@(map #(list 'def %) names)))
```

Let's analyze declare from the inside out. The anonymous function #(list 'def %) is responsible for generating a single def. Test this form alone at the REPL:

```
(#(list 'def %) 'a)
-> (def a)
```

The map invokes the inner function once for each symbol passed in. Again, you can test this form at the REPL:

```
(map #(list 'def %) '[a b c d])
-> ((def a) (def b) (def c) (def d))
```

Finally, the leading do makes the entire expansion into a single legal Clojure form:

```
`(do ~@(map #(list 'def %) '[a b c d]))
-> (do (def a) (def b) (def c) (def d))
```

Substituting '[a b c d] in the previous form is the manual equivalent of testing the entire macro with macroexpand-1:

```
(macroexpand-1 '(declare a b c d))
-> (do (def a) (def b) (def c) (def d))
```

Many of the most interesting parts of Clojure are macros that expand into special forms involving def. We have explored a few here, but you can read the source of any of them. Most of them live at src/clj/clojure/core.clj in the Clojure source distribution.

Java Interop

Clojure programs call into Java via the . (dot), new, and set! special forms. However, idiomatic Clojure code often uses macros such as .. (threaded member access) and doto to simplify forms that call Java.

You (or anyone else) can extend how Clojure calls Java by writing a macro. Consider the following scenario. You are writing code that uses several of the constants in java.lang.Math:

```
Math/PI
-> 3.141592653589793
(Math/pow 10 3)
-> 1000.0
```

In a longer segment of code, the Math/ prefix would quickly become distracting, so it would be nice if you could say simply PI and pow. Clojure doesn't provide any direct way to do this, but you could define a bunch of vars by hand:

```
(def PI Math/PI)
-> #'user/PI
(defn pow [b e] (Math/pow b e))
-> #'user/pow
```

Stuart Sierra automated the boilerplate with the import-static macro:

```
(examples.import-static/import-static class & members)
```

import-static imports static members of a Java class as names in the local namespace. Use import-static to import the members you want from Math.

```
(use '[examples.import-static :only (import-static)])
(import-static java.lang.Math PI pow)
-> nil

PI
-> 3.141592653589793

(pow 10 3)
-> 1000.0
```

Postponing Evaluation

Most sequences in Clojure are lazy. When you are building a lazy sequence, you often want to combine several forms whose evaluation is postponed until the sequence is forced. Since evaluation is not immediate, a macro is required.

You have already seen such a macro in Section 3.3, *Lazy and Infinite Sequences*, on page 69: lazy-seq. Another example is delay:

```
(delay & exprs)
```

When you create a delay, it holds on to its exprs and does nothing with them until it is forced to. Try creating a delay that simulates a long calculation by sleeping:

```
(def slow-calc (delay (Thread/sleep 5000) "done!"))
-> #'user/slow-calc
```

To actually execute the delay, you must force it:

(force x)

Try forcing your slow-calc a few times:

```
(force slow-calc)
-> "done!"
(force slow-calc)
-> "done!"
```

The first time you force a delay, it executes its expressions and caches the result. Subsequent forces simply return the cached value.

The macros that implement lazy and delayed evaluation all call Java code in clojure.jar. In your own code, you should not call such Java APIs directly. Treat the lazy/delayed evaluation macros as the public API, and treat the Java classes as implementation detail that is subject to change.

Wrapping Evaluation

Many macros wrap the evaluation of a set of forms, adding some special semantics before and/or after the forms are evaluated. You have already seen several examples of this kind of macro:

- time starts a timer, evaluates forms, and then reports how long they took to execute.

- let and binding establish bindings, evaluate some forms, and then tear down the bindings.

- with-open takes an open file (or other resource), executes some forms, and then makes sure the resource is closed in a finally block.

- dosync executes forms within a transaction.

Another example of a wrapper macro is with-out-str:

(with-out-str & exprs)

with-out-str temporarily binds *out* to a new StringWriter, evaluates its exprs, and then returns the string written to *out*. with-out-str makes it easy to use print and println to build strings on the fly:

```
(with-out-str (print "hello, ") (print "world"))
-> "hello, world"
```

The implementation of with-out-str has a simple structure that can act as a template for writing similar macros:

```
Line 1 (defmacro with-out-str
   2   [& body]
   3   `(let [s# (new java.io.StringWriter)]
   4      (binding [*out* s#]
   5        ~@body
   6        (str s#))))
```

Wrapper macros usually take a variable number of arguments (line 2), which are the forms to be evaluated. They then proceed in three steps:

1. *Setup*: Create some special context for evaluation, introducing bindings with let (line 3) and bindings (line 4) as necessary.

2. *Evaluation*: Evaluate the forms (line 5). Since there are typically a variable number of forms, insert them via a splicing unquote: ~@.

3. *Teardown*: Reset the execution context to normal and return a value as appropriate (line 6)

When writing a wrapper macro, always ask yourself whether you need a finally block to implement the teardown step correctly. For with-out-str, the answer is no, because both let and binding take care of their own cleanup. If, however, you are setting some global or thread-local state via a Java API, you will need a finally block to reset this state.

This talk of mutable state leads to another observation. Any code whose behavior changes when executed inside a wrapper macro is obviously *not* a pure function. print and println behave differently based on the value of *out* and so are not pure functions. Macros that set a binding, such as with-out-str, do so to alter the behavior of an impure function somewhere.

Not all wrappers change the behavior of the functions they wrap. You've already seen time, which times a function's execution. Another example is assert:

`(assert expr)`

assert tests an expression and raises an exception if it is not logically true:

```
(assert (= 1 1))
-> nil

(assert (= 1 2))
-> java.lang.Exception: Assert failed: (= 1 2)
```

Macros like assert and time violate the first rule of Macro Club in order to avoid unnecessary lambdas.

Avoiding Lambdas

For historical reasons, anonymous functions are often called *lambdas*. Sometimes a macro can be replaced by a function call, with the arguments wrapped in a lambda. For example, the bench macro from *Syntax Quote, Unquote, and Splicing Unquote*, on page 174 does not need to be a macro. You can write it as a function:

```
(defn bench-fn [f]
  (let [start (System/nanoTime)
        result (f)]
    {:result result :elapsed (- (System/nanoTime) start)}))
```

However, if you want to call bench-fn, you must pass it a function that wraps the form you want to execute. The following code shows the difference:

```
; macro
(bench (+ 1 2))
-> {:elapsed 44000, :result 3}

; function
(bench-fn (fn [] (+ 1 2)))
-> {:elapsed 53000, :result 3}
```

For things like bench, macros and anonymous functions are near substitutes. Both prevent immediate execution of a form. However, the anonymous function approach requires more work on the part of the caller, so it is OK to break the first rule and write a macro instead of a function.

Another reason to prefer a macro for bench is that bench-fn is not a perfect substitute; it adds the overhead of an anonymous function call at runtime. Since bench's purpose is to time things, you should avoid this overhead.

7.5 Wrapping Up

Clojure macros let you automate patterns in your code. Because they transform source code at macro expansion time, you can use macros to abstract away *any* kind of pattern in your code. You are not limited to working within Clojure. With macros, you can *extend* Clojure into your problem domain.

CHAPTER 8

Multimethods

Clojure multimethods provide a flexible way to associate a function with a set of inputs. This is similar to Java polymorphism but more general. When you call a Java method, Java selects a specific implementation to execute by examining the *type* of a *single object*. When you call a Clojure multimethod, Clojure selects a specific implementation to execute by examining the result of *any function you choose*, applied to *all* the function's arguments.

In this chapter, you will develop a thirst for multimethods by first living without them. Then you will build an increasingly complex series of multimethod implementations, first using multimethods to simulate polymorphism and then using multimethods to implement various ad hoc taxonomies.

Multimethods in Clojure are used much less often than polymorphism in object-oriented languages. But where they are used, they are often the key feature in the code. Section 8.5, *When Should I Use Multimethods?*, on page 198 explores how multimethods are used in several open source Clojure projects and offers guidelines for when to use them in your own programs.

If you are reading the book in chapter order, then once you have completed this chapter, you will have seen all the key features of the Clojure language.

8.1 Living Without Multimethods

The best way to appreciate multimethods is to spend a few minutes living without them, so let's do that. Clojure can already print anything with print/println. But pretend for a moment that these functions do not exist and that you need to build a generic print mechanism. To get started, create a my-print function that can print a string to the standard output stream *out*:

```
src/examples/life_without_multi.clj
(defn my-print [ob]
  (.write *out* ob))
```

Next, create a my-println that simply calls my-print and then adds a line feed:

```
src/examples/life_without_multi.clj
(defn my-println [ob]
  (my-print ob)
  (.write *out* "\n"))
```

The line feed makes my-println's output easier to read when testing at the REPL. For the remainder of this section, you will make changes to my-print and test them by calling my-println. Test that my-println works with strings:

```
(my-println "hello")
| hello
-> nil
```

That is nice, but my-println does not work quite so well with nonstrings such as nil:

```
(my-println nil)
-> java.lang.NullPointerException
```

That's not a big deal, though. Just use cond to add special-case handling for nil:

```
src/examples/life_without_multi.clj
(defn my-print [ob]
  (cond
    (nil? ob) (.write *out* "nil")
    (string? ob) (.write *out* ob)))
```

With the conditional in place, you can print nil with no trouble:

```
(my-println nil)
| nil
-> nil
```

Of course, there are still all kinds of types that my-println cannot deal with. If you try to print a vector, neither of the cond clauses will match, and the program will print nothing at all:

```
(my-println [1 2 3])
-> nil
```

By now you know the drill. Just add another cond clause for the vector case. The implementation here is a little more complex, so you might want to separate the actual printing into a helper function, such as my-print-vector:

```
src/examples/life_without_multi.clj
(require '[clojure.string :as str])
(defn my-print-vector [ob]
  (.write *out*"[")
  (.write *out* (str/join " " ob))
  (.write *out* "]"))

(defn my-print [ob]
  (cond
    (vector? ob) (my-print-vector ob)
    (nil? ob) (.write *out* "nil")
    (string? ob) (.write *out* ob)))
```

Make sure that you can now print a vector:

```
(my-println [1 2 3])
| [1 2 3]
-> nil
```

my-println now supports three types: strings, vectors, and nil. And you have a road map for new types: just add new clauses to the cond in my-println. But it is a crummy road map, because it conflates two things: the decision process for selecting an implementation and the specific implementation detail.

You can improve the situation somewhat by pulling out helper functions like my-print-vector. However, then you have to make two separate changes every time you want to a add new feature to my-println:

- Create a new type-specific helper function.
- Modify the existing my-println to add a new cond invoking the feature-specific helper.

What you really want is a way to add new features to the system by adding new code in a single place, without having to modify any existing code. Clojure offers this by way of protocols, covered in Section 6.3, *Protocols*, on page 147, and multimethods.

8.2 Defining Multimethods

To define a multimethod, use defmulti:

```
(defmulti name dispatch-fn)
```

name is the name of the new multimethod, and Clojure will invoke dispatch-fn against the method arguments to select one particular method (implementation) of the multimethod.

Consider my-print from the previous section. It takes a single argument, the thing to be printed, and you want to select a specific implementation based on the type of that argument. So, dispatch-fn needs to be a function of one argument that returns the type of that argument. Clojure has a built-in function matching this description, namely, class. Use class to create a multimethod called my-print:

src/examples/multimethods.clj
```
(defmulti my-print class)
```

At this point, you have provided a description of how the multimethod will select a specific method but no actual specific methods. Unsurprisingly, attempts to call my-print will fail:

```
(my-println "foo")
-> java.lang.IllegalArgumentException: \
No method for dispatch value
```

To add a specific method implementation to my-println, use defmethod:

```
(defmethod name dispatch-val & fn-tail)
```

name is the name of the multimethod to which an implementation belongs. Clojure matches the result of defmulti's dispatch function with dispatch-val to select a method, and fn-tail contains arguments and body forms just like a normal function.

Create a my-print implementation that matches on strings:

src/examples/multimethods.clj
```
(defmethod my-print String [s]
  (.write *out* s))
```

Now, call my-println with a string argument:

```
(my-println "stu")
| stu
-> nil
```

Next, create a my-print that matches on nil:

src/examples/multimethods.clj
```
(defmethod my-print nil [s]
  (.write *out* "nil"))
```

Notice that you have solved the problem raised in the previous section. Instead of being joined in a big cond, each implementation of my-println is separate. Methods of a multimethod can live anywhere in your source, and you can add new ones any time, without having to touch the original code.

Dispatch Is Inheritance-Aware

Multimethod dispatch knows about Java inheritance. To see this, create a my-print that handles Number by printing a number's toString representation:

src/examples/multimethods.clj
```
(defmethod my-print Number [n]
  (.write *out* (.toString n)))
```

Test the Number implementation with an integer:

```
(my-println 42)
| 42
-> nil
```

42 is an Integer, not a Number. Multimethod dispatch is smart enough to know that an integer is a number and match anyway. Internally, dispatch uses the isa? function:

```
(isa? child parent)
```

isa? knows about Java inheritance, so it knows that an Integer is a Number:

```
(isa? Integer Number)
-> true
```

isa? is not limited to inheritance. Its behavior can be extended dynamically at runtime, as you will see later in Section 8.4, *Creating Ad Hoc Taxonomies*, on page 194.

Multimethod Defaults

It would be nice if my-print could have a fallback representation that you could use for any type you have not specifically defined. You can use :default as a dispatch value to handle any methods that do not match anything more specific. Using :default, create a my-println that prints the Java toString value of objects, wrapped in #<>:

src/examples/multimethods.clj
```
(defmethod my-print :default [s]
  (.write *out* "#<")
  (.write *out* (.toString s))
  (.write *out* ">"))
```

Now test that my-println prints random things, using the default method:

```
(my-println (java.sql.Date. 0))
-> #<1969-12-31>

(my-println (java.util.Random.))
-> #<java.util.Random@1c398896>
```

In the unlikely event that :default already has some specific meaning in your domain, you can create a multimethod using this alternate signature:

```
(defmulti name dispatch-fn :default default-value)
```

The default-value lets you specify your own default. Maybe you would like to call it :everything-else:

src/examples/multimethods/default.clj
```
(defmulti my-print class :default :everything-else)
(defmethod my-print String [s]
  (.write *out* s))
(defmethod my-print :everything-else [_]
  (.write *out* "Not implemented yet..."))
```

Any dispatch value that does not otherwise match will now match against :everything-else.

Dispatching a multimethod on the type of the first argument, as you have done with my-print, is by far the most common kind of dispatch. In many object-oriented languages, in fact, it is the *only* kind of dynamic dispatch, and it goes by the name *polymorphism*.

Clojure's dispatch is much more general. Let's add a few complexities to my-print and move beyond what is possible with plain ol' polymorphism.

8.3 Moving Beyond Simple Dispatch

Clojure's print function prints various "sequencey" things as lists. If you wanted my-print to do something similar, you could add a method that dispatched on a collection interface high in the Java inheritance hierarchy, such as Collection:

src/examples/multimethods.clj
```
(require '[clojure.string :as str])
(defmethod my-print java.util.Collection [c]
  (.write *out* "(")
  (.write *out* (str/join " " c))
  (.write *out* ")"))
```

Now, try various sequences to see that they get a nice print representation:

```
(my-println (take 6 (cycle [1 2 3])))
| (1 2 3 1 2 3)
-> nil

(my-println [1 2 3])
| (1 2 3)
-> nil
```

Perfectionist that you are, you cannot stand that vectors print with rounded braces, unlike their literal square-brace syntax. So, add yet another my-print method, this time to handle vectors. Vectors all implement an IPersistentVector, so this should work:

src/examples/multimethods.clj

```
(defmethod my-print clojure.lang.IPersistentVector [c]
  (.write *out* "[")
  (.write *out* (str/join " " c))
  (.write *out* "]"))
```

But it doesn't work. Instead, printing vectors now throws an exception:

```
(my-println [1 2 3])
-> java.lang.IllegalArgumentException: Multiple methods match
dispatch value: class clojure.lang.LazilyPersistentVector ->
interface clojure.lang.IPersistentVector and
interface java.util.Collection,
and neither is preferred
```

The problem is that two dispatch values now match for vectors: Collection and IPersistentVector. Many languages constrain method dispatch to make sure these conflicts never happen, such as by forbidding multiple inheritance. Clojure takes a different approach. You can create conflicts, and you can resolve them with prefer-method:

```
(prefer-method multi-name loved-dispatch dissed-dispatch)
```

When you call prefer-method for a multimethod, you tell it to prefer the loved-dispatch value over the dissed-dispatch value whenever there is a conflict. Since you want the vector version of my-print to trump the collection version, tell the multimethod what you want:

src/examples/multimethods.clj

```
(prefer-method
 my-print clojure.lang.IPersistentVector java.util.Collection)
```

Now, you should be able to route both vectors and other sequences to the correct method implementation:

```
(my-println (take 6 (cycle [1 2 3])))
| (1 2 3 1 2 3)
-> nil

(my-println [1 2 3])
| [1 2 3]
-> nil
```

Many languages create complex rules, or arbitrary limitations, in order to resolve ambiguities in their systems for dispatching functions. Clojure allows a much simpler approach: just don't worry about it! If there is an ambiguity, use prefer-method to resolve it.

8.4 Creating Ad Hoc Taxonomies

Multimethods let you create ad hoc taxonomies, which can be helpful when you discover type relationships that are not explicitly declared as such.

For example, consider a financial application that deals with checking and savings accounts. Define a Clojure struct for an account, using a tag to distinguish the two. Place the code in the namespace examples.multimethods.account. To do this, you will need to create a file named examples/multimethods/account.clj on your classpath[1] and then enter the following code:

src/examples/multimethods/account.clj

```
(ns examples.multimethods.account)

(defstruct account :id :tag :balance)
```

Now, you are going to create two different checking accounts, tagged as ::Checking and ::Savings. The capital names are a Clojure convention to show the keywords are acting as types. The doubled :: causes the keywords to resolve in the current namespace. To see the namespace resolution happen, compare entering :Checking and ::Checking at the REPL:

```
:Checking
-> :Checking

::Checking
-> :user/Checking
```

Placing keywords in a namespace helps prevent name collisions with other people's code. When you want to use ::Savings or ::Checking from another namespace, you will need to fully qualify them:

```
(struct account 1 ::examples.multimethods.account/Savings 100M)
-> {:id 1, :tag :examples.multimethods.account/Savings, :balance 100M}
```

Full names get tedious quickly, so you can use alias to specify a shorter alias for a long namespace name:

```
(alias short-name-symbol namespace-symbol)
```

Use alias to create the short name acc:

---

1. Note that the example code for the book includes a completed version of this example, already on the classpath. To work through the example yourself, simply move or rename the completed example to get it out of the way.

```
(alias 'acc 'examples.multimethods.account)
-> nil
```

Now that the acc alias is available, create two top-level test objects, a savings account and a checking account:

```
(def test-savings (struct account 1 ::acc/Savings 100M))
-> #'user/test-savings

(def test-checking (struct account 2 ::acc/Checking 250M))
-> #'user/test-checking
```

Note that the trailing M creates a BigDecimal literal and does not mean you have millions of dollars.

The interest rate for checking accounts is 0 and for savings accounts is 5 percent. Create a multimethod interest-rate that dispatches based on :tag, like so:

src/examples/multimethods/account.clj
```
(defmulti interest-rate :tag)
(defmethod interest-rate ::acc/Checking [_] 0M)
(defmethod interest-rate ::acc/Savings [_] 0.05M)
```

Check your test-savings and test-checking to make sure that interest-rate works as expected.

```
(interest-rate test-savings)
-> 0.05M

(interest-rate test-checking)
-> 0M
```

Accounts have an annual service charge, with rules as follows:

- Normal checking accounts pay a $25 service charge.
- Normal savings accounts pay a $10 service charge.
- Premium accounts have no fee.
- Checking accounts with a balance of $5,000 or more are premium.
- Savings accounts with a balance of $1,000 or more are premium.

In a realistic example, the rules would be more complex. Premium status would be driven by average balance over time, and there would probably be other ways to qualify. But the previous rules are complex enough to demonstrate the point.

You could implement service-charge with a bunch of conditional logic, but premium feels like a type, even though there is no explicit premium tag on an account. Create an account-level multimethod that returns ::Premium or ::Basic:

```
src/examples/multimethods/account.clj
(defmulti account-level :tag)
(defmethod account-level ::acc/Checking [acct]
  (if (>= (:balance acct) 5000) ::acc/Premium ::acc/Basic))
(defmethod account-level ::acc/Savings [acct]
  (if (>= (:balance acct) 1000) ::acc/Premium ::acc/Basic))
```

Test account-level to make sure that checking and savings accounts require different balance levels to reach ::Premium status:

```
(account-level (struct account 1 ::acc/Savings 2000M))
-> :examples.multimethods.account/Premium

(account-level (struct account 1 ::acc/Checking 2000M))
-> :examples.multimethods.account/Basic
```

Now you might be tempted to implement service-charge using account-level as a dispatch function:

```
src/examples/multimethods/service_charge_1.clj
; bad approach
(defmulti service-charge account-level)
(defmethod service-charge ::Basic [acct]
  (if (= (:tag acct) ::Checking) 25 10))
(defmethod service-charge ::Premium [_] 0)
```

The conditional logic in service-charge for ::Basic is exactly the kind of type-driven conditional that multimethods should help us avoid. The problem here is that you are already dispatching by account-level, and now you need to be dispatching by :tag as well. No problem—you can dispatch on *both*. Write a service-charge whose dispatch function calls both account-level and :tag, returning the results in a vector:

```
src/examples/multimethods/service_charge_2.clj
(defmulti service-charge (fn [acct] [(account-level acct) (:tag acct)]))
(defmethod service-charge [::acc/Basic ::acc/Checking]   [_] 25)
(defmethod service-charge [::acc/Basic ::acc/Savings]    [_] 10)
(defmethod service-charge [::acc/Premium ::acc/Checking] [_] 0)
(defmethod service-charge [::acc/Premium ::acc/Savings]  [_] 0)
```

This version of service-charge dispatches against two different taxonomies: the :tag intrinsic to an account and the externally defined account-level. Try a few accounts to verify that service-charge works as expected:

```
(service-charge {:tag ::acc/Checking :balance 1000})
-> 25

(service-charge {:tag ::acc/Savings :balance 1000})
-> 0
```

Notice that the previous tests did not even bother to create a "real" account for testing. Structs like account are simply maps that are optimized for storing particular fields, but nothing is stopping you from using a plain old map if you find it more convenient.

Adding Inheritance to Ad Hoc Types

There is one further improvement you can make to service-charge. Since all premium accounts have the same service charge, it feels redundant to have to define two separate service-charge methods for ::Savings and ::Checking accounts. It would be nice to have a parent type ::Account so you could define a multi-method that matches ::Premium for any kind of ::Account. Clojure lets you define arbitrary parent-child relationships with derive:

```
(derive child parent)
```

Using derive, you can specify that both ::Savings and ::Checking are kinds of ::Account:

```
src/examples/multimethods/service_charge_3.clj
(derive ::acc/Savings ::acc/Account)
(derive ::acc/Checking ::acc/Account)
```

When you start to use derive, isa? comes into its own. In addition to understanding Java inheritance, isa? knows all about derived relationships:

```
(isa? ::acc/Savings ::acc/Account)
-> true
```

Now that Clojure knows that Savings and Checking are Accounts, you can define a service-charge using a single method to handle ::Premium:

```
src/examples/multimethods/service_charge_3.clj
(defmulti service-charge (fn [acct] [(account-level acct) (:tag acct)]))
(defmethod service-charge [::acc/Basic ::acc/Checking]  [_] 25)
(defmethod service-charge [::acc/Basic ::acc/Savings]   [_] 10)
(defmethod service-charge [::acc/Premium ::acc/Account] [_] 0)
```

At first glance, you may think that derive and isa? simply duplicate functionality that is already available to Clojure via Java inheritance. This is not the case. Java inheritance relationships are forever fixed at the moment you define a class. derived relationships can be created when you need them and can be *applied to existing objects without their knowledge or consent.* So, when you discover a useful relationship between existing objects, you can derive that relationship without touching the original objects' source code and without creating tiresome "wrapper" classes.

If the number of different ways you might define a multimethod has your head spinning, don't worry. In practice, most Clojure code uses multimethods sparingly. Let's take a look at some open source Clojure code to get a better idea of how multimethods are used.

8.5 When Should I Use Multimethods?

Multimethods are extremely flexible, and with that flexibility comes choices. How should you choose when to use multimethods, as opposed to some other technique? We approached this question from two directions, asking the following:

- Where do Clojure projects use multimethods?
- Where do Clojure projects *eschew* multimethods?

The most striking thing is that multimethods are *rare*—about one per 1,000 lines of code. So, don't worry that you are missing something important if you build a Clojure application with few, or no, multimethods. A Clojure program that defines no multimethods is not nearly as odd as an object-oriented program with no polymorphism.

Many multimethods dispatch on class. Dispatch-by-class is the easiest kind of dispatch to understand and implement. We already covered it in detail with the my-print example, so I will say no more about it here.

Clojure multimethods that dispatch on something other than class are fairly rare. We can look directly in Clojure for some examples. The clojure.inspector and clojure.test libraries use unusual dispatch functions.

The Inspector

Clojure's inspector library uses Swing to create simple views of data. You can use it to get a tree view of your system properties:

```
(use '[clojure.inspector :only (inspect inspect-tree)])
(inspect-tree (System/getProperties))
-> #<JFrame ...>
```

inspect-tree returns (and displays) a JFrame with a tree view of anything that is treeish. So, you could also pass a nested map to inspect-tree:

```
(inspect-tree {:clojure {:creator "Rich" :runs-on-jvm true}})
-> #<JFrame ...>
```

Treeish things are made up of nodes that can answer two questions:

- Who are my children?
- Am I a leaf node?

The treeish concepts of "tree," "node," and "leaf" all sound like candidates for classes or interfaces in an object-oriented design. But the inspector does not work this way. Instead, it adds a "treeish" type system in an ad hoc way to existing types, using a dispatch function named collection-tag:

```
; from Clojure's clojure/inspector.clj
(defn collection-tag [x]
  (cond
    (instance? java.util.Map$Entry x) :entry
    (instance? clojure.lang.IPersistentMap x) :map
    (instance? java.util.Map x) :map
    (instance? clojure.lang.Sequential x) :seq
    :else :atom))
```

collection-tag returns one of the keywords :entry, :map, :seq, or :atom. These act as the type system for the treeish world. The collection-tag function is then used to dispatch three different multimethods that select specific implementations based on the treeish type system.

```
(defmulti is-leaf collection-tag)

(defmulti get-child
  (fn [parent index] (collection-tag parent)))

(defmulti get-child-count collection-tag)
; method implementations elided for brevity
```

The treeish type system is added around the existing Java type system. Existing objects do not have to *do* anything to become treeish; the inspector library does it for them. Treeish demonstrates a powerful style of reuse. You can discover new type relationships in existing code and take advantage of these relationships simply, without having to modify the original code.

clojure.test

The clojure.test library in Clojure lets you write several different kinds of assertions using the is macro. You can assert that arbitrary functions are true. For example, 10 is not a string:

```
(use :reload '[clojure.test :only (is)])
(is (string? 10))

FAIL in clojure.lang.PersistentList$EmptyList@1 (NO_SOURCE_FILE:2)
expected: (string? 10)
actual: (not (string? 10))
-> false
```

Although you can use an arbitrary function, is knows about a few specific functions and provides more detailed error messages. For example, you can check that a string is not an instance? of Collection:

```
(is (instance? java.util.Collection "foo"))

FAIL in clojure.lang.PersistentList$EmptyList@1 (NO_SOURCE_FILE:3)
expected: (instance? java.util.Collection "foo")
actual: java.lang.String
-> false
```

is also knows about =. Verify that power does not equal wisdom.

```
(is (= "power" "wisdom"))

FAIL in clojure.lang.PersistentList$EmptyList@1 (NO_SOURCE_FILE:4)
expected: (= "power" "wisdom")
actual: (not (= "power" "wisdom"))
-> false
```

Internally, is uses a multimethod named assert-expr, which dispatches not on the type but on the actual *identity* of its first argument:

```
(defmulti assert-expr (fn [form message] (first form)))
```

Since the first argument is a symbol representing what function to check, this amounts to yet another ad hoc type system. This time, there are three types: =, instance?, and everything else.

The various assert-expr methods add specific error messages associated with different functions you might call from is. Because multimethods are open ended, you can add your own assert-expr methods with improved error messages for other functions you frequently pass to is.

Counterexamples

As you saw in Section 8.4, *Creating Ad Hoc Taxonomies*, on page 194, you can often use multimethods to hoist branches that are based on type out of the main flow of your functions. To find counterexamples where multimethods should not be used, we looked through Clojure's core to find type branches that had *not* been hoisted to multimethods.

A simple example is Clojure's class, which is a null-safe wrapper for the underlying Java getClass. Minus comments and metadata, class is as follows:

```
(defn class [x]
(if (nil? x) x (. x (getClass))))
```

You could write your own version of class as a multimethod by dispatching on identity:

```
src/examples/multimethods.clj
(defmulti my-class identity)
(defmethod my-class nil [_] nil)
(defmethod my-class :default [x] (.getClass x))
```

Any nil-check could be rewritten this way. But I find the original class function easier to read than the multimethod version. This is a nice "exception that proves the rule." Even though class branches on type, the branching version is easier to read.

Use the following general rules when deciding whether to create a function or a multimethod:

- If a function branches based on a type, or multiple types, consider a multimethod.

- Types are whatever you discover them to be. They do not have to be explicit Java classes or data tags.

- You should be able to interpret the dispatch value of a defmethod without having to refer to the defmulti.

- Do not use multimethods merely to handle optional arguments or recursion.

When in doubt, try writing the function in both styles, and pick the one that seems more readable.

8.6 Wrapping Up

Multimethods support arbitrary dispatch. Usually multimethods work based on type relationships. Sometimes these types are formal, as in Java classes. Other times they are informal and ad hoc and emerge from the properties of objects in the system.

CHAPTER 9

Java Down and Dirty

Clojure's Java support is both powerful and lean. It's powerful, in that it brings the expressiveness of Lisp syntax, plus some syntactic sugar tailored to Java. It's lean, in that it can get right to the metal. Clojure code compiles to bytecode and does not have to go through any special translation layer on the way to Java.

Clojure embraces Java and its libraries. Idiomatic Clojure code calls Java libraries directly and does not try to wrap everything under the sun to look like Lisp. This surprises many new Clojure developers but is very pragmatic. Where Java isn't broken, Clojure doesn't fix it.

In this chapter, you will see how Clojure access to Java is convenient, elegant, and fast:

- Calling Java is simple and direct. Clojure provides syntax extensions for accessing anything you could reach from Java code: classes, instances, constructors, methods, and fields. Although you will typically call Java code directly, you can also wrap Java APIs and use them in a more functional style.

- Clojure is *fast*, unlike many other dynamic languages on the JVM. You can use custom support for primitives and arrays, plus type hints, to cause Clojure's compiler to generate the same code that a Java compiler would generate.

- Clojure's exception handling is easy to use. Better yet, explicit exception handling is rarely necessary. Clojure's exception primitives are the same as Java's. However, Clojure does not require you to deal with checked exceptions and makes it easy to clean up resources using the with-open idiom.

9.1 Exception Handling

In Java code, exception handling crops up for three reasons:

- Wrapping checked exceptions (see *Checked Exceptions*, on page 205 if you are unfamiliar with checked exceptions)

- Using a finally block to clean up nonmemory resources such as file and network handles

- Responding to the problem: ignoring the exception, retrying the operation, converting the exception to a nonexceptional result, and so on

In Clojure, things are similar but simpler. The try and throw special forms give you all the capabilities of Java's try, catch, finally, and throw. But you should not have to use them very often, for the following reasons:

- You do not have to deal with checked exceptions in Clojure.
- You can use macros such as with-open to encapsulate resource cleanup.

Let's see what this looks like in practice.

Keeping Exception Handling Simple

Java programs often wrap checked exceptions at abstraction boundaries. A good example is Apache Ant, which tends to wrap low-level exceptions (such as I/O exceptions) with an Ant-level build exception:

```
// Ant-like code (simplified for clarity)
try {
  newManifest = new Manifest(r);
} catch (IOException e) {
  throw new BuildException(...);
}
```

In Clojure, you are not forced to deal with checked exceptions. You do not have to catch them or declare that you throw them. So, the previous code would translate to the following:

```
(Manifest. r)
```

The absence of exception wrappers makes idiomatic Clojure code easier to read, write, and maintain than idiomatic Java. That said, nothing prevents you from explicitly catching, wrapping, and rethrowing exceptions in Clojure. It simply is not required. You *should* catch exceptions when you plan to respond to them in a meaningful way.

> ## Checked Exceptions
>
> Java's checked exceptions must be explicitly caught or rethrown from every method where they can occur. This seemed like a good idea at first: checked exceptions could use the type system to rigorously document error handling, with compiler enforcement. Most Java programmers now consider checked exceptions a failed experiment, because their costs in code bloat and maintainability outweigh their advantages. For more on the history of checked exceptions, see Rod Waldhoff's article[a] and the accompanying links.
>
> ___
>
> a.   http://tinyurl.com/checked-exceptions-mistake

Cleaning Up Resources

Garbage collection will clean up resources in memory. If you use resources that live outside of garbage-collected memory, such as file handles, you need to make sure that you clean them up, even in the event of an exception. In Java, this is normally handled in a finally block.

If the resource you need to free follows the convention of having a close method, you can use Clojure's with-open macro:

```
(with-open [name init-form] & body)
```

Internally, with-open creates a try block, sets name to the result of init-form, and then runs the forms in body. Most important, with-open always closes the object bound to name in a finally block.

A good example of with-open is the spit function in clojure.string:

```
(clojure.core/spit file content)
```

spit simply writes a string to file. Try it:

```
(spit "hello.out" "hello, world")
-> nil
```

You should now find a file at hello.out with the contents hello, world.

The implementation of spit is simple:

```
; from clojure.core
(defn spit
  "Opposite of slurp.  Opens f with writer, writes content, then
  closes f. Options passed to clojure.java.io/writer."
  {:added "1.2"}
  [f content & options]
  (with-open [^java.io.Writer w (apply jio/writer f options)]
    (.write w (str content))))
```

spit creates a PrintWriter on f, which can be just about anything that is writable: a file, a URL, a URI, or any of Java's various writers or output streams. It then prints content to the writer. Finally, with-open guarantees that the writer is closed at the end of spit.

If you need to do something other than close in a finally block, the Clojure try form looks like this:

```
(try expr* catch-clause* finally-clause?)
; catch-clause -> (catch classname name expr*)
; finally-clause -> (finally expr*)
```

It can be used thusly:

```
(try
  (throw (Exception. "something failed"))
(finally
  (println "we get to clean up")))
| we get to clean up
-> java.lang.Exception: something failed
```

The previous fragment also demonstrates Clojure's throw form, which simply throws whatever exception is passed to it.

Responding to an Exception

The most interesting case is when an exception handler attempts to respond to the problem in a catch block. As a simple example, consider writing a function to test whether a particular class is available at runtime:

```
src/examples/interop.clj
; not caller-friendly
(defn class-available? [class-name]
  (Class/forName class-name))
```

This approach is not very caller-friendly. The caller simply wants a yes/no answer but instead gets an exception:

```
(class-available? "borg.util.Assimilate")
-> java.lang.ClassNotFoundException: borg.util.Assimilate
```

A friendlier approach uses a catch block to return false:

```
src/examples/interop.clj
(defn class-available? [class-name]
  (try
   (Class/forName class-name) true
   (catch ClassNotFoundException _ false)))
```

The caller experience is much better now:

```
(class-available? "borg.util.Assimilate")
-> false

(class-available? "java.lang.String")
-> true
```

Clojure gives you everything you need to throw and catch exceptions and to cleanly release resources. At the same time, Clojure keeps exceptions in their place. They are important but not so important that your mainline code is dominated by the exceptional.

Clojure is designed to let you get things done and have fun while doing it. However, an important part of getting things done is being able to use your platform to its full potential. Throughout the rest of the book, we have looked at doing things the idiomatic Clojure way. In this chapter, we will do it Java style.

To provide the full power of the Java platform, Clojure does several things:

- Type hinting and inference, where needed, give the performance that people (incorrectly) associate with statically typed languages.

- Ahead-of-time (AOT) compilation lets Clojure programs participate in the binary-artifact-centric Java ecosystem as an equal player.

- While reify, defrecord, and deftype are preferable as flexible implementation tools, Clojure also provides interop forms that give you access to the ugly parts of Java interop.

- Clojure (and Clojure Contrib) have a rapidly expanding set of "batteries included" libraries for common tasks. (But, you can always call the raw Java libraries if these libraries do not include something you need.)

- If the techniques in this chapter seem ugly or unnecessary for the problem you are solving, that's great! Run with it. But if you need to squeeze out that last bit of performance or play well with an ancient, ugly library, this chapter is for you.

9.2 Wrestling with the Integers

Clojure provides three different sets of operations for integer types:

- The unchecked operators
- The default operators
- The promoting operators

The following table gives a sampling of these operator types.

Unchecked	Default	Promoting
unchecked-add	+	+'
unchecked-subtract	-	-'
unchecked-multiply	*	*'
unchecked-inc	inc	inc'
unchecked-dec	dec	dec'

The unchecked operators correspond exactly with primitive math in Java. They are fast but terrifically dangerous in that they can overflow silently and give incorrect answers. In Clojure, the unchecked operators should be used only in the rare situation that overflow is the desired behavior or when performance is paramount and you are certain overflow is impossible or irrelevant.

```
(unchecked-add 9223372036854775807 1)
-> -9223372036854775808
```

The default operators use Java primitives where possible for performance but always make overflow checks and throw an exception.

```
(+ 9223372036854775807 1)
-> ArithmeticException integer overflow
```

The promoting operators will automatically promote from primitives to big numbers on overflow. This makes it possible to handle an arbitrary range but at significant performance cost. Because primitives and big numbers share no common base type, math with the promoting operators precludes the use of primitives as return types.

```
(+' 9223372036854775807 1)
-> 9223372036854775808N
```

Clojure relies on Java's BigDecimal class for arbitrary-precision decimal numbers. See the online documentation[1] for details. BigDecimals provide arbitrary precision but at a price: BigDecimal math is significantly slower than Java's floating-point primitives.

Clojure has its own BigInt class to handle BigInteger conversions. Clojure's BigInt has some performance improvements over using Java's BigInteger directly. It also wraps some of the rough edges of BigInteger. In particular, it properly implements hashCode. This makes equality take precedence over representation, which you will see in almost every abstraction in the language.

---

1. http://docs.oracle.com/javase/6/docs/api/java/math/BigDecimal.html

Under the hood, Clojure uses Java's BigInteger. The performance difference comes in how BigInt treats its values. A BigInt consists of a Long part and a BigInteger part. When the value passed into a BigInt is small enough to be treated as a Long, it is. When numerical operations are performed on BigInts, if their result is small enough to be treated as a Long, it is. This gives the user the ability to add the overflow hint (N) without paying the BigInteger cost until it is absolutely necessary.

9.3 Optimizing for Performance

In Clojure, it is idiomatic to call Java using the techniques described in Section 2.5, *Calling Java*, on page 43. The resulting code will be fast enough for 90 percent of scenarios. When you need to, though, you can make localized changes to boost performance. These changes will not change how outside callers invoke your code, so you are free to make your code work and then make it fast.

Using Primitives for Performance

In the preceding sections, function parameters carry no type information. Clojure simply does the right thing. Depending on your perspective, this is either a strength or a weakness. It's a strength, because your code is clean and simple and can take advantage of duck typing. But it's also a weakness, because a reader of the code cannot be certain of datatypes and because doing the right thing carries some performance overhead.

Consider a function that calculates the sum of the numbers from 1 to n:

```
; performance demo only, don't write code like this
(defn sum-to [n] (loop [i 1 sum 0]
  (if (<= i n) (recur (inc i) (+ i sum)) sum)))
```

You can verify that this function works with a small input value:

```
(sum-to 10)
=>  55
```

Let's see how sum-to performs. To time an operation, you can use the time function. When benchmarking, you'll tend to want to take several measurements so that you can eliminate start-up overhead plus any outliers; therefore, you can call time from inside a dotimes macro:

```
(dotimes bindings & body)
```

dotimes will execute its body repeatedly, with the name bound to integers from zero to n-1. Using dotimes, you can collect five timings of sum-to as follows:

```
(dotimes [_ 5] (time (sum-to 10000)))
|  "Elapsed time: 0.149 msecs"
|  "Elapsed time: 0.126 msecs"
|  "Elapsed time: 0.194 msecs"
|  "Elapsed time: 0.279 msecs"
-> "Elapsed time: 0.212 msecs"
```

To speed things up, you can hint the argument and return type as long. Clojure's type inference will flow this hint to all the internal operations and function calls inside the function.

```
(defn ^long integer-sum-to [^long n]
  (loop [i 1 sum 0]
    (if (<= i n)
      (recur (inc i) (+ i sum))
      sum)))
```

The integer-sum-to is indeed faster:

```
(dotimes [_ 5] (time (integer-sum-to 10000)))
|  "Elapsed time: 0.044 msecs"
|  "Elapsed time: 0.023 msecs"
|  "Elapsed time: 0.025 msecs"
|  "Elapsed time: 0.023 msecs"
-> "Elapsed time: 0.02 msecs"
```

Clojure's primitive math is still correct, in that it will check for overflow and throw an exception. Is that as fast as things can get? Java programmers have access to super-fast busted math: arithmetic operations that have the maximum possible performance but can silently overflow and corrupt data.

Clojure provides access to Java's arithmetic semantics through the unchecked family of functions. Maybe you can get an even faster function by using the unchecked version of +, unchecked-add:

```
(defn ^long unchecked-sum-to [^long n]
  (loop [i 1 sum 0]
    (if (<= i n)
      (recur (inc i) (unchecked-add i sum))
      sum)))
```

The unchecked-sum-to is not significantly faster:

```
(dotimes [_ 5] (time (unchecked-sum-to 10000)))
|  "Elapsed time: 0.039 msecs"
|  "Elapsed time: 0.018 msecs"
|  "Elapsed time: 0.014 msecs"
|  "Elapsed time: 0.015 msecs"
-> "Elapsed time: 0.015 msecs"
```

Orders of magnitude are important! Primitive hinting can make certain operations significantly faster. However, switching to Java's unchecked semantics is generally a losing proposition. You get a trivial performance gain on average, with the possibility of data corruption tomorrow.

So, why does Clojure provide these operations at all? Two reasons:

• Sometimes you actually want Java semantics. The primary use case for the unchecked operations is when you need to interoperate with other libraries that expect this behavior.

• Without trying them, nobody would know (or believe) that they weren't faster.

Prefer accuracy first and then optimize for speed only where necessary. integer-sum-to will throw an exception on overflow. This is bad, but the problem is easily detected:

```
(integer-sum-to 10000000000)
-> java.lang.ArithmeticException: integer overflow
```

unchecked-sum-to will fail silently on overflow. In a program setting, it can quietly but catastrophically corrupt data:

```
(unchecked-sum-to 10000000000)
-> -5340232216128654848 ; WRONG!!
```

Given the competing concerns of correctness and performance, you should normally prefer simple, undecorated code such as the original sum-to. If profiling identifies a bottleneck, you can force Clojure to use a primitive type in just the places that need it.

The sum-to example is deliberately simple in order to demonstrate the various options for integer math in Clojure. In a real Clojure program, it would be more expressive to implement sum-to using reduce. Summing a sequence is the same as summing the first two items, adding that result to the next item, and so on. That is exactly the loop that (reduce + ...) provides. With reduce, you can rewrite sum-to as a one-liner:

```
(defn better-sum-to [n]
  (reduce + (range 1 (inc n))))
```

The example also demonstrates an even more general point: pick the right algorithm to begin with. The sum of numbers from 1 to n can be calculated directly as follows:

```
(defn best-sum-to [n]
  (/ (* n (inc n)) 2))
```

Even without performance hints, this is faster than implementations based on repeated addition:

```
(dotimes [_ 5] (time (best-sum-to 10000)))
|  "Elapsed time: 0.029 msecs"
|  "Elapsed time: 0.0040 msecs"
|  "Elapsed time: 0.0040 msecs"
|  "Elapsed time: 0.0040 msecs"
-> "Elapsed time: 0.0030 msecs"
```

Performance is a tricky subject. Don't write ugly code in search of speed. Start by choosing appropriate algorithms and getting your code to work correctly. If you have performance issues, profile to identify the problems. Then, introduce only as much complexity as you need to solve those problems.

Adding Type Hints

Clojure supports adding type hints to function parameters, let bindings, variable names, and expressions. These type hints serve three purposes:

- Optimizing critical performance paths
- Documenting the required type
- Enforcing the required type at runtime

For example, consider the following function, which returns information about a Java class:

```
(defn describe-class [c]
  {:name (.getName c)
   :final (java.lang.reflect.Modifier/isFinal (.getModifiers c))})
```

You can ask Clojure how much type information it can infer, by setting the special variable *warn-on-reflection* to true:

```
(set! *warn-on-reflection* true)
-> true
```

The exclamation point on the end of set! is an idiomatic indication that set! changes mutable state. set! is described in detail in *Working with Java Callback APIs*, on page 130. With *warn-on-reflection* set to true, compiling describe-class will produce the following warnings:

```
Reflection warning, line: 87
- reference to field getName can't be resolved.

Reflection warning, line: 88
- reference to field getModifiers can't be resolved.
```

These warnings indicate that Clojure has no way of knowing the type of c. You can provide a type hint to fix this, using the metadata syntax ^Class:

```
(defn describe-class [^Class c]
  {:name (.getName c)
   :final (java.lang.reflect.Modifier/isFinal (.getModifiers c))})
```

With the type hint in place, the reflection warnings will disappear. The compiled Clojure code will be exactly the same as compiled Java code. Further, attempts to call describe-class with something other than a Class will fail with a ClassCastException:

```
(describe-class StringBuffer)
  {:name "java.lang.StringBuffer", :final true}

(describe-class "foo")
-> java.lang.ClassCastException: \
   java.lang.String cannot be cast to java.lang.Class
```

If your ClassCastException provides a less helpful error message, it is because you are using a version of Java prior to Java 6. Improved error reporting is one of many good reasons to run your Clojure code on Java 6 or newer.

When you provide a type hint, Clojure will insert an appropriate class cast in order to avoid making slow, reflective calls to Java methods. But if your function does not actually call any Java methods on a hinted object, then Clojure will not insert a cast. Consider this wants-a-string function:

```
(defn wants-a-string [^String s] (println s))
-> #'user/wants-a-string
```

You might expect that wants-a-string would complain about nonstring arguments. In fact, it will be perfectly happy:

```
(wants-a-string "foo")
-> foo

(wants-a-string 0)
-> 0
```

Clojure can tell that wants-a-string never actually uses its argument as a string (println will happily try to print any kind of argument). Since no string methods need to be called, Clojure does not attempt to cast s to a string.

When you need speed, type hints will let Clojure code compile down to the same code Java will produce. But you won't need type hints that often. Make your code right first, and then worry about making it fast.

9.4 Creating Java Classes in Clojure

Clojure's objects all implement reasonable Java interfaces:

- Clojure's data structures implement interfaces from the Java Collections API.
- Clojure's functions implement Runnable and Callable.

In addition to these generic interfaces, you will occasionally need domain-specific interfaces. Often this comes in the form of callback handlers for event-driven APIs such as Swing or some XML parsers. Clojure can easily generate one-off proxies or classes on disk when needed, using a fraction of the lines of code necessary in Java.

Creating Java Proxies

To interoperate with Java, you will often need to implement Java interfaces. A good example is parsing XML with a Simple API for XML (SAX) parser. To get ready for this example, go ahead and import the following classes. We'll need them all before we are done:

```
(import '(org.xml.sax InputSource)
        '(org.xml.sax.helpers DefaultHandler)
        '(java.io StringReader)
        '(javax.xml.parsers SAXParserFactory))
```

To use a SAX parser, you need to implement a callback mechanism. The easiest way is often to extend the DefaultHandler class. In Clojure, you can extend a class with the proxy function:

```
(proxy class-and-interfaces super-cons-args & fns)
```

As a simple example, use proxy to create a DefaultHandler that prints the details of all calls to startElement:

```
(def print-element-handler
  (proxy [DefaultHandler] []
    (startElement [uri local qname atts]
      (println (format "Saw element: %s" qname)))))
```

proxy generates an instance of a proxy class. The first argument to proxy is [DefaultHandler], a vector of the superclass and superinterfaces. The second argument, [], is a vector of arguments to the base class constructor. In this case, no arguments are needed.

After the proxy setup comes the implementation code for zero or more proxy methods. The proxy shown earlier has one method. Its name is startElement, and it takes four arguments and prints the name of the qname argument.

Now all you need is a parser to pass the handler to. This requires plowing through a pile of Java factory methods and constructors. For a simple exploration at the REPL, you can create a function that parses XML in a string:

```
(defn demo-sax-parse [source handler]
  (.. SAXParserFactory newInstance newSAXParser
      (parse (InputSource. (StringReader. source)) handler)))
```

Now the parse is easy:

```
(demo-sax-parse "<foo>
  <bar>Body of bar</bar>
  </foo>" print-element-handler)
| Saw element: foo
| Saw element: bar
```

The previous example demonstrates the mechanics of creating a Clojure proxy to deal with Java's XML interfaces. You can take a similar approach to implementing your own custom Java interfaces. But if all you are doing is XML processing, the clojure.data.xml library already has terrific XML support and can work with any SAX-compatible Java parser.

The proxy mechanism is completely general and can be used to generate any kind of Java object you want, on the fly. Sometimes the objects are so simple you can fit the entire object in a single line. The following code creates a new thread and then creates a new dynamic subclass of Runnable to run on the new thread:

```
(.start (Thread.
  (proxy [Runnable] [] (run [] (println "I ran!")))))
```

In Java, you must provide an implementation of every method on every interface you implement. In Clojure, you can leave them out:

```
(proxy [Callable] []) ; proxy with no methods (??)
```

If you omit a method implementation, Clojure provides a default implementation that throws an UnsupportedOperationException:

```
(.call (proxy [Callable] []))
-> java.lang.UnsupportedOperationException: call
```

The default implementation does not make much sense for interfaces with only one method, such as Runnable and Callable, but it can be handy when you are implementing larger interfaces and don't care about some of the methods.

So far in this section, you have seen how to use proxy to create implementations of Java interfaces. This is very powerful when you need it, but often Clojure is already there on your behalf. For example, functions automatically implement Runnable and Callable:

```
; normal usage: call an anonymous function
(#(println "foo"))
foo
; call through Runnable's run
(.run #(println "foo"))
foo
; call through Callable's call
(.call #(println "foo"))
foo
```

This makes it very easy to pass Clojure functions to other threads:

```
(dotimes [i 5]
  (.start
    (Thread.
      (fn []
        (Thread/sleep (rand 500))
        (println (format "Finished %d on %s" i (Thread/currentThread)))))))
```

For one-off tasks such as XML and thread callbacks, Clojure's proxies are quick and easy to use. If you need a longer-lived class, you can generate new named classes from Clojure as well.

Using Java Collections

Clojure's collections supplant the Java collections for most purposes. Clojure's collections are concurrency-safe, have good performance characteristics, and implement the appropriate Java collection interfaces. So, you should generally prefer Clojure's own collections when you are working in Clojure and even pass them back into Java when convenient.

If you do choose to use the Java collections, nothing in Clojure will stop you. From Clojure's perspective, the Java collections are classes like any other, and all the various Java interop forms will work. But the Java collections are designed for lock-based concurrency. They will not provide the concurrency guarantees that Clojure collections do and will not work well with Clojure's software transactional memory.

One place where you will need to deal with Java collections is the special case of Java arrays. In Java, arrays have their own syntax and their own bytecode instructions. Java arrays do not implement any Java interface. Clojure collections cannot masquerade as arrays. (Java collections can't either!) The Java platform makes arrays a special case in every way, so Clojure does too.

Clojure provides make-array to create Java arrays:

```
(make-array class length)
(make-array class dim & more-dims)
```

make-array takes a class and a variable number of array dimensions. For a one-dimensional array of strings, you might say this:

```
(make-array String 5)
-> #<String[] [Ljava.lang.String;@45a270b2>
```

The odd output is courtesy of Java's implementation of toString() for arrays: [Ljava.lang.String; is the JVM specification's encoding for "one-dimensional array of strings." That's not very useful at the REPL, so you can use Clojure's seq to wrap any Java array as a Clojure sequence so that the REPL can print the individual array entries:

```
(seq (make-array String 5))
-> (nil nil nil nil nil)
```

Clojure also includes a family of functions with names such as int-array for creating arrays of Java primitives. You can issue the following command at the REPL to review the documentation for these and other array functions:

```
(find-doc "-array")
```

Clojure provides a set of low-level operations on Java arrays, including aset, aget, and alength:

```
(aset java-array index value)
(aset java-array index-dim1 index-dim2 ... value)
(aget java-array index)
(aget java-array index-dim1 index-dim2 ...)
(alength java-array)
```

Use make-array to create an array, and then experiment with using aset, aget, and alength to work with the array:

```
(defn painstakingly-create-array []
  (let [arr (make-array String 5)]
    (aset arr 0 "Painstaking")
    (aset arr 1 "to")
    (aset arr2 "fill")
    (aset arr 3" in")
    (aset arr 4 "arrays")
    arr))

(aget (paintakingly-create-array) 0)
-> "Painstaking"

(alength (painstakingly-create-array))
-> 5
```

Most of the time, you will find it simpler to use higher-level functions such as to-array, which creates an array directly from any collection:

```
(to-array sequence)
```

to-array always creates an Object array:

```
(to-array ["Easier" "array" "creation"])
-> #<Object[] [Ljava.lang.Object;@1639f9e3>
```

to-array is also useful for calling Java methods that take a variable argument list, such as String/format:

```
; example. prefer clojure.core/format (String/format "Training Week: %s Mileage: %d"
(String/format "Training Week: %s Mileage: %d"
               (to-array [2 26]))
-> "Training Week: 2 Mileage: 26"
```

to-array's cousin into-array can create an array with a more specific type than Object.

```
(into-array type? seq)
```

You can pass an explicit type as an optional first argument to into-array:

```
(into-array String ["Easier", "array", "creation"])
-> #<String[] [Ljava.lang.String;@391ecf28>
```

If you omit the type argument, into-array will guess the type based on the first item in the sequence:

```
(into-array ["Easier" "array" "creation"])
-> #<String[] [Ljava.lang.String;@76bfd849>
```

As you can see, the array contains Strings, not Objects. If you want to transform every element of a Java array without converting to a Clojure sequence, you can use amap:

```
(amap a idx ret expr)
```

amap will create a clone of the array a, binding that clone to the name you specify in ret. It will then execute expr once for each element in a, with idx bound to the index of the element. Finally, amap returns the cloned array. You could use amap to uppercase every string in an array of strings:

```
(def strings (into-array ["some" "strings" "here"]))
-> #'user/strings

(seq (amap strings idx _ (.toUpperCase (aget strings idx))))
-> ("SOME" "STRINGS" "HERE")
```

The ret parameter is set to _ to indicate that it is not needed in the map expression, and the wrapping seq is simply for convenience in printing the result at the REPL. Similar to amap is areduce:

```
(areduce a idx ret init expr)
```

Where amap produces a new array, areduce produces anything you want. The ret is initially set to init and later set to the return value of each subsequent invocation of expr. areduce is normally used to write functions that "tally up" a collection in some way. For example, the following call finds the length of the longest string in the strings array:

```
(areduce strings idx ret 0 (max ret (.length (aget strings idx))))
-> 7
```

amap and areduce are special-purpose macros for interoperating with Java arrays.

9.5 A Real-World Example

While it's great to talk about the different interop cases and learn how to eke out some additional performance using Java's primitive forms, you still need to have some practical, hands-on knowledge. In this example, we will be building an application to test the availability of websites. The goal here is to check to see whether the website returns an HTTP 200 OK response. If anything other than our expected response is received, it should be marked as unavailable.

Again, we will use the Leiningen build tool. Refer to Section 1.2, *Clojure Coding Quick Start*, on page 11 if you don't have Leiningen installed already. Let's start by creating a new project:

```
lein new pinger
```

Open your project.clj file and modify the contents to match what we are going to be working on. Be sure to update Clojure to the latest version:

```
(defproject pinger "0.0.1-SNAPSHOT"
  :description "A website availability tester"
  :dependencies [[org.clojure/clojure 1.3.0]])
```

Grab the dependencies by running lein deps:

```
lein deps
```

First we need to write the code that connects to a URL and captures the response code. We can accomplish this by using Java's URL class.

```
(ns pinger.core
  (:import (java.net URL HttpURLConnection)))

(defn response-code [address]
  (let [conn ^HttpURLConnection (.openConnection (URL. address))
        code (.getResponseCode conn)]
    (when (< code 400)
      (-> conn .getInputStream .close))
    code))
```

Give it a try in the REPL:

```
(response-code "http://google.com")
-> 200
```

Now let's create a function that uses response-code and decides whether the specified URL is available. We will define available in our context as returning an HTTP 200 response code.

```
(defn available? [address]
  (= 200 (response-code address)))

(available? "http://google.com")
-> true

(available? "http://google.com/badurl")
-> false
```

Next we need a way to start our program and have it check a list of URLs that we care about every so often and report their availability. Let's create a -main function.

```
(defn -main []
  (let [addresses '("http://google.com"
                    "http://amazon.com"
                    "http://google.com/badurl")]
    (while true
      (doseq [address addresses]
        (println (available? address)))
      (Thread/sleep (* 1000 60)))))
```

In this example, we create a list of addresses (two good and one bad) and use a simple while loop that never exits to obtain a never-ending program execution. It will continue to check these URLs once a minute until the program is terminated. Since we are exporting a -main function, don't forget to add :gen-class to your namespace declaration.

```
(ns pinger.core
  (:import (java.net URL))
  (:gen-class))
```

Now that we have the fundamentals in place, we need to tell Leningen where our main function is located. Open project.clj and add the :main declaration:

```
(defproject pinger "0.0.1-SNAPSHOT"
  :description "A website availability tester"
  :dependencies [[org.clojure/clojure "1.3.0"]]
  :main pinger.core)
```

It's time to compile our program into a JAR file and run it. To do this, run the following:

```
lein uberjar
java -jar pinger-0.0.1-SNAPSHOT-standalone.jar
true
false
true
```

You should see your program start and continue to run until you press Ctrl-C to stop it.

Adding Real Continuous Loop Behavior

A while loop that is always true will continue to run until terminated, but it's not really the cleanest way to obtain the result because it doesn't allow for a clean shutdown. We can use a scheduled thread pool that will start and execute the desired command in a similar fashion as the while loop but with a much greater level of control. Create a file in the src directory called scheduler.clj and enter the following code:

```
(ns pinger.scheduler
  (:import (java.util.concurrent ThreadPoolExecutor
            ScheduledThreadPoolExecutor TimeUnit)))
(defn scheduled-executor
  "Create a scheduled executor."
  ^ScheduledThreadPoolExecutor [threads]
  (ScheduledThreadPoolExecutor. threads))

(defn periodically
  "Schedules function f to run on executor e every 'delay'
   milliseconds after a delay of 'initial-delay' Returns
   a ScheduledFuture."
  ^ScheduledFuture [e f & {:keys [initial-delay delay]}]
  (.scheduleWithFixedDelay
    e f
    initial-delay delay
    TimeUnit/MILLISECONDS))
(defn shutdown-executor
  "Shutdown an executor."
  [^ThreadPoolExecutor e]
  (.shutdown e))
```

This namespace provides functions to create and shut down a Java ScheduledEx-ecutor. It also defines a function called periodically that will accept an executor, a function, an initial-delay, and a repeated delay. It will execute the function for the first time after the initial delay and then continue to execute the function with the delay specified thereafter. This will continue to run until the thread pool is shut down.

Let's update pinger.core to take advantage of the scheduling code as well as make the -main function responsible only for calling a function that starts the loop. Replace the old -main with the following functions:

```
(defn check []
  (let [addresses '("http://google.com"
                    "http://google.com/404"
                    "http://amazon.com")]
    (doseq [address addresses]
      (println (available? address)))))

(def immediately 0)
(def every-minute (* 60 1000))

(defn start [e]
  "REPL helper. Start pinger on executor e."
  (scheduler/periodically e check
                          :initial-delay immediately
                          :delay every-minute))

(defn stop [e]
  "REPL helper. Stop executor e."
  (scheduler/shutdown-executor e))

(defn -main []
  (start (scheduler/scheduled-executor 1)))
```

Make sure to update your namespace declaration to include the scheduler code:

```
(ns pinger.core
  (:import (java.net URL))
  (:require [pinger.scheduler :as scheduler])
  (:gen-class))
```

Not everything in the previous sample is necessary, but it makes for more readable code. Adding the start and stop functions makes it easy to work interactively from the REPL, which will be a huge advantage should you choose to extend this example. Give everything one last check by running lein uberjar and executing the JAR file. The program should function exactly as it did before.

Logging

So far, we have produced a program capable of periodically checking the availability of a list of websites. However, it lacks the ability to keep track of what it has done and to notify us when a site is unavailable. We can solve both of these issues with logging. There are a lot of logging options for Java applications, but for this example we will use log4j. It gives us a real logger to use, and it gives us an email notification. This is great because we will have the ability to send email alerts when a website isn't available. To do this, we will need to pull the log4j and mail libraries into our application. To make it easier to take advantage of log4j, we will also pull in clojure.tools.logging. Open your project.clj file and add clojure.tools.logging, log4j, and mail:

```
(defproject pinger "0.0.1-SNAPSHOT"
  :description "A website availability tester
  :dependencies [[org.clojure/clojure "1.3.0"]
                 [org.clojure/tools.logging "0.2.3"]
                 [log4j "1.2.16"]
                 [javax.mail/mail "1.4.1"]]
  :main pinger.core)
```

Also pull the dependencies in with Leiningen:

```
lein deps
```

The great part about the Clojure logging library is that it will use any standard Java logging library that is on the classpath, so there is no additional wiring required between log4j and your application. Create a folder in the root of your project called resources. Leiningen automatically adds the contents of this folder to the classpath, and you will need that for your log4j properties file. Create a file under the resources directory named log4j.properties and add the following contents:

```
log4j.rootLogger=info, R, email
log4j.appender.R=org.apache.log4j.RollingFileAppender
log4j.appender.R.File=logs/pinger.log
log4j.appender.R.MaxFileSize=1000KB
log4j.appender.R.MaxBackupIndex=1
log4j.appender.R.layout=org.apache.log4j.PatternLayout
log4j.appender.R.layout.ConversionPattern=%d{ISO8601} %-5p [%c] - %m%n
log4j.appender.email=org.apache.log4j.net.SMTPAppender
log4j.appender.email.SMTPHost=localhost
log4j.appender.email.From=system@yourapp.com
log4j.appender.email.To=recipient@yourapp.com
log4j.appender.email.Subject=[Pinger Notification] - Website Down
log4j.appender.email.threshold=error
log4j.appender.email.layout=org.apache.log4j.PatternLayout
log4j.appender.email.layout.conversionPattern=%d{ISO8601} %-5p [%c] - %m%n
```

This sets up standard logging to pinger.log and will send an email notification for anything logged to the error log level, which in our case is when a website doesn't respond with an HTTP 200 response or when an exception is thrown while checking the site. Make sure to change the email information to something that works in your environment.

Let's update the code and add logging. The goal here is to replace any println statements with log messages. Open core.clj, add the info and error functions from clojure.tools.logging into your namespace declaration, and create a function to record the results.

```
(ns pinger.core
  (:import (java.net URL))
  (:require [pinger.scheduler :as scheduler]
            [clojure.tools.logging :as logger])
  (:gen-class))
...


(defn record-availability [address]
  (if (available? address)
    (logger/info (str address " is responding normally"))
    (logger/error (str address " is not available"))))
```

Also update check to reflect the changes:

```
(defn check []
  (let [addresses '("http://google.com"
                    "http://google.com/404"
                    "http://amazon.com")]
    (doseq [address addresses]
      (record-availability address))))
```

Rebuild to try your program again. You should notice a newly created logs directory that you can check for program execution. You should also notice an email come in with an error message. If you get a "connection refused" error on port 25, you will need to set up a mail transport agent on your machine to enable mail sending. You now have a way to notify people of a website failure!

Configuration

We have hard-coded our list of websites to monitor, and that simply won't work! We need a way to give a list of sites to monitor from some external source. We could use a properties file, database, or web service to accomplish this. For ease of explanation, we will go with a properties file. Create a file named pinger.properties in the root directory of the application and add the following to it:

```
urls=http://google.com,http://amazon.com,http://google.com/badurl
```

We need a way to load this file and create a collection of sites to feed into the check function. Create a file named config.clj in the src directory:

```
(ns pinger.config
  (:use [clojure.java.io :only (reader resource)])
  (:require [clojure.string :as str])
  (:import (java.util Properties)))

(defn load-properties [src]
  (with-open [rdr (reader src)]
    (doto (Properties.)
      (.load rdr))))

(defn config
  []
  (load-properties (resource "pinger.properties")))
```

As long as pinger.properties is on the classpath, the config function will read pinger.properties into a Java properties object. All we have left to do is get the urls attribute and put it into a list. Add the following function into the config namespace:

```
(defn urls [conf]
  (str/split (.get conf "urls") #","))
```

Finally, update the check function in core.clj to use the new configuration function.

```
(ns pinger.core
  (:import (java.net URL))
  (:require [pinger.scheduler :as scheduler]
            [clojure.tools.logging :as logger]
            [pinger.config :as config])
  (:gen-class))

...

(defn check []
  (doseq [address (config/urls (config/config))]
    (record-availability address)))
```

Rebuild your application with Leiningen and try it. Remember to put the root directory on the classpath so that the application can find pinger.properties.

```
java -cp .:pinger-0.0.1-standalone.jar pinger.core
```

We now have what we need to succeed. In this example, we covered the following:

- Using Java's URL to check a website to see whether it was available
- Using Java's ScheduledTheadPoolExecutor to create a periodically running task
- Using log4j with clojure.tools.logging to send error notifications
- Using Java's property system for configuration
- Using Leiningen to create stand-alone executable JAR files

We could do quite a few things to expand this example. We could redefine what it means for a website to be available by adding requirements for certain HTML elements to be present or for the response to return in a certain time to cover an SLA. Try adding to this example and see what you can come up with.

9.6 Wrapping Up

We just covered a good chunk of how Clojure and Java get along. We even mixed the two up in some interesting ways. Since we have started to experiment with things outside of the Clojure language, it is probably a good time to start talking about different libraries you can use to build real-world Clojure applications. We will do just that in the next chapter.

CHAPTER 10

Building an Application

Now that you have learned the basics of the Clojure language, it is time for you to begin using Clojure in your own projects. But when you run out the door to start work on your killer Clojure app, you quickly discover that language knowledge is only part of what you need to work effectively in an ecosystem. You have questions like these:

- What tools do I use to organize projects and dependencies?
- What is a good workflow for writing code?
- How do I make sure that my code is correct?
- How do I keep code flexible and maintainable?
- What libraries do I need?
- How do I put Clojure on the Web?

There will never be a single, one-size-fits-all answer to these questions. Clojure runs on the JVM, a huge ecosystem where hundreds of approaches have flourished. But you have to start somewhere. In this chapter, we will give you temporary answers to these questions. These answers have worked well for us, and you can use them for a short while. As your own preferences and sensibilities evolve, you can adapt or abandon the approaches in this chapter in favor of approaches that work best for you.

As our sample application, we will implement a web version of the Clojure-breaker game. In Clojurebreaker, a code-maker (the program) creates a secret code of N-ordered colored pegs. A code-breaker (the human player) then submits a guess. The code-maker scores the guess as follows:

- One black peg for each peg of the right color in the right position
- One white peg for each peg of the right color but not in the right position

The game ends with a correct guess or after reaching some predetermined limit on the number of guesses.

While we will show you all the code as we go, this chapter is not really about code. It is about a style of attacking problems and about the details of delivering solutions within the Clojure ecosystem. Let's get started.

10.1 Scoring a Clojurebreaker Game

As a Clojure programmer, one question you will often ask is, "Where do I need state to solve this problem?" Or, better yet, "How much of this problem can I solve *without* using any state?"

With Clojurebreaker (and with many other games), the game logic itself is a pure function. It takes a secret and a guess and returns a score. Identifying this fact early gives us two related advantages:

- The score function will be trivial to write and test in isolation.
- We can comfortably proceed to implement score without even thinking about how the rest of the system will work.

Scoring itself divides into two parts: tallying the exact matches and tallying the matches that are out of order. Each of these parts can be its own function. Let's start with the exact matches. To make things concrete, we will pick a representation for the pegs that facilitates trying things at the REPL: the four colors :r (red), :g (green), :b (blue), and :y (yellow). The function will return the count of exact matches, which we can turn into black pegs in a separate step later. Here is the shell of the function we think we need:

```
clojurebreaker/snippets.clj
(defn exact-matches
  "Given two collections, return the number of positions where
   the collections contain equal items."
  [c1 c2])
```

Hold the phone—that doc string doesn't say anything about games or colors or keywords. What is going on here? While some callers (e.g., the game) will eventually care about the representation of the game state, exact-matches doesn't need to care. So, let's keep it generic. A key component of responsible Clojure design is to think in data, rather than pouring object concrete at every opportunity.

When described as a generic function of data, exact-matches sounds like a function that might already exist. After searching through the relevant namespaces (clojure.core and clojure.data), we discover that the closest thing to exact-matches is clojure.data's diff. diff recursively compares two data structures, returning a three-tuple of things-in-a, things-in-b, and things-in-both. The things-in-both is nothing other than the exact matches we are looking for. Try it at the REPL:

```
(require '[clojure.data :as data])
(data/diff [:r :g :g :b] [:r :y :y :b])
-> [[nil :g :g] [nil :y :y] [:r nil nil :b]]
```

The non-nil entries in [:r nil nil :b] are the exact matches when comparing r/g/g/b and r/y/y/b. With diff in hand, the implementation of exact-matches is trivial:

clojurebreaker/src/clojurebreaker/game.clj

```
(defn exact-matches
  "Given two collections, return the number of positions where
   the collections contain equal items."
  [c1 c2]
  (let [[_ _ matches] (data/diff c1 c2)]
    (count (remove nil? matches))))
```

Again, we test at the REPL against an example input:

```
(exact-matches [:r :g :g :b] [:r :y :y :b])
2
```

Now let's turn our attention to the unordered matches. To calculate these, we need to know how many of each colored peg are in the secret and in the guess. This sounds like a job for the frequencies function:

```
(def example-secret [:r :g :g :b])
(frequencies example-secret)

-> {:r 1, :g 2, :b 1}

(def example-guess [:y :y :y :g])
(frequencies example-guess)

-> {:y 3, :g 1}
```

To turn those two frequencies into the unordered-matches, we need to do two additional things:

- Consider only the keys that are present in both the secret and the guess
- Count only the overlap (i.e., the minimum of the vals under each key)

Again, we hope these operations already exist, and happily they do. You can keep the keys you need with select-keys:

```
(select-keys (frequencies example-secret) example-guess)
-> {:g 2}

(select-keys (frequencies example-guess) example-secret)
-> {:g 1}
```

And you can count the overlap between two frequency maps using merge-with:

```
(merge-with min {:g 1} {:g 2})
-> {:g 1}
```

Combining frequencies and select-keys and merge-with gives the following definition for unordered-matches:

clojurebreaker/src/clojurebreaker/game.clj
```
(defn unordered-matches
  "Given two collections, return a map where each key is an item
   in both collections, and each value is the number of times the
   value occurs in the collection with fewest occurrences."
  [c1 c2]
  (let [f1 (select-keys (frequencies c1) c2)
        f2 (select-keys (frequencies c2) c1)]
    (merge-with min f1 f2)))
```

which, of course, we should verify at the REPL:

```
(unordered-matches [:r :g :g :b] [:y :y :y :g])
-> {:g 1}
```

That's nice, with one subtlety. unordered-matches counts matches *regardless* of order, while the game will want to know only the matches that are *not* in the right order. Even though the game doesn't seem to need unordered-matches, writing it was a win because of the following:

- unordered-matches does exactly one thing. To write a not-ordered match, we would have to reimplement exact-matches inside unordered-matches.

- The two simple functions we just wrote are exactly the functions we need to compose together to get the not-ordered semantics. Just subtract the results of exact-matches from the results of unordered-matches.

With the two primitives in place, the score operation simply compounds them:

clojurebreaker/src/clojurebreaker/game.clj
```
(defn score
  [c1 c2]
  (let [exact (exact-matches c1 c2)
        unordered (apply + (vals (unordered-matches c1 c2)))]
    {:exact exact :unordered (- unordered exact)}))
```

And the REPL rejoices:

```
(score [:r :g :g :b] [:r :y :y :g])
-> {:exact 1, :unordered 1}
```

At this point, we have demonstrated a partial answer to the question, "What is a good workflow for writing code?" In summary:

- Break apart the problem to identify pure functions.
- Learn the standard library so you can find functions already written.
- Pour no concrete (use data as data).
- Test inside out from the REPL.

In our experience, programmers trying this workflow for the first time make two typical mistakes:

- Coding too much
- Complicating the tests

You have written too much code whenever you don't understand the behavior of a form, but you haven't yet tested and understood all of its subforms. Many developers have an intuition of "write X lines of code and then test," where X is the smallest number of lines that can do something substantial. In Clojure, X is significantly smaller than one, which is why we emphasize building functions inside out at the REPL.

"Complicating the tests" is more subtle, and we will take it up in the next section.

10.2 Testing the Scorer

In the previous section, we developed the score function iteratively at the REPL and saw it work correctly with a few example inputs. It doesn't take much commitment to quality to want to do more validation than that! Let's begin by teasing apart some of the things that people mean when they say "testing." Testing includes the following:

- Thinking through whether the code is correct
- Stepping through the code in a development environment where you can see everything that is happening
- Crafting inputs to cover the various code paths
- Crafting outputs to match the crafted inputs
- Running the code with various inputs
- Validating the results for correctness
- Automating the validation of results
- Organizing tests so that they can be automatically run for regression purposes in the future

This is hardly an exhaustive list, but it suffices to make the point of this section. In short, testing is often complex, but it can be simple.

Traditional unit-testing approaches complect many of the testing tasks listed earlier. For example, input, output, execution, and validation tend to be woven together inside individual test methods. On the other hand, the minimal REPL testing we did before simply isn't enough. Can we get the benefit of some of the previous ideas of testing, without the complexity of unit testing? Let's try.

Crafting Inputs

We have already seen the score function work for a few handcrafted inputs. How many inputs do we need to convince ourselves the function is correct? In a perfect world, we would just test all the inputs, but that is almost always computationally infeasible. But we are lucky in that the problem of scoring the game is essentially the same for variants with a different number of colors or a different number of pegs. Given that, we actually can generate *all* possible inputs for a small version of the game.

The branch of math that deals with the different ways of forming patterns is called *enumerative combinatorics*. It turns out that the Clojure library math.combinatorics has the functions we need to generate all possible inputs. Add the following form under the :dependencies key in your project.clj file, if it is not already present:

```
[org.clojure/math.combinatorics "0.0.1"]
```

The selections function takes two arguments (a collection and a size), and it returns every structure of that size made up of elements from that collection. Try it for a tiny version of Clojurebreaker with only three colors and two columns:

```
(require '[clojure.math.combinatorics :as comb])
(comb/selections [:r :g :b] 2)
-> ((:r :r) (:r :g) (:r :b)
    (:g :r) (:g :g) (:g :b)
    (:b :r) (:b :g) (:b :b))
```

So, selections can give us a possible secret or a possible guess. What about generating inputs to the score function? Well, that is just selecting two selections from the selections:

```
(-> (comb/selections [:r :g :b] 2)
    (comb/selections 2))
 -> (81 pairs of game positions omitted for brevity)
```

Let's put that into a named function:

clojurebreaker/src/clojurebreaker/game.clj
```
(defn generate-turn-inputs
  "Generate all possible turn inputs for a clojurebreaker game
```

```
    with colors and n columns"
  [colors n]
  (-> (comb/selections colors n)
      (comb/selections 2)))
```

All right, inputs generated. We are going to skip thinking about outputs (for reasons that will become obvious in a moment) and turn our attention to running the scorer with our generated inputs.

Running a Test

We are going to write a function that takes a sequence of inputs and reports a sequence of inputs and the result of calling score. We don't want to commit (yet) to how the results of this test run will be validated. Maybe a human will read it. Maybe a validator program will process the results. Either way, a good representation of each result might be a map with the keys secret, guess, and score.

All this function needs to do is call score and build the collection of responses:

clojurebreaker/src/clojurebreaker/game.clj
```
(defn score-inputs
  "Given a sequence of turn inputs, return a lazy sequence of
   maps with :secret, :guess, and :score."
  [inputs]
  (map
   (fn [[secret guess]]
     {:secret (seq secret)
      :guess (seq guess)
      :score (score secret guess)})
   inputs))
```

Try it at the REPL:

```
(->> (generate-turn-inputs [:r :g :b] 2)
     (score-inputs))
-> ({:secret (:r :r), :guess (:r :r),
     :score {:exact 2, :unordered 0}}
    {:secret (:r :r), :guess (:r :g),
     :score {:exact 1, :unordered 0}}
    ;; remainder omitted for brevity
```

If a human is going to be reading the test report, you might decide to format a text table instead, using score print-table. While we are at it, let's generate a bigger game (four colors by four columns) and print the table to a file:

```
(use 'clojure.pprint)
(require '[clojure.java.io :as io])
(with-open [w (io/writer "scoring-table")]
  (binding [*out* w]
```

```
          (print-table (->> (generate-turn-inputs [:r :g :b :y] 4)
                            (score-inputs)))))
-> nil
```

If you look at the scoring-table file, you should see 65,536 different secret/guess combinations and their scores.

Validating Outputs

At this point, it is obvious why we skipped crafting the outputs. The program has done that for us. We just have to decide how much effort to spend validating them. Here are some approaches we might take:

- Have a human code-breaker expert read the entire output table for a small variant of the game. This has the advantage of being exhaustive but might miss logic errors that show up only in a larger game.

- Pick a selection of results at random from a larger game and have a human expert verify that.

Because the validation step is separated from generating inputs and running the program, we can design and write the various steps independently, possibly at separate times.

Moreover, the validator knows nothing about how the inputs were generated. With unit tests, the inputs and outputs come from the same programmer's brain at about the same time. If that programmer is systematically mistaken about something, the tests simply encode mistakes as truth. This is not possible when the outputs to validate are chosen exhaustively or randomly.

We will return to programmatic validation later, but first let's turn to regression testing.

Regression Testing

How would you like to have a regression suite that is more thorough than the validation effort you have made? No problem.

- Write a program whose results should not change.
- Run the program once, saving the results to a (well-named!) file.
- Run the program again every time the program changes, comparing with the saved file. If anything is different, the program is broken.

The nice thing about this regression approach is that it works even if you never did *any* validation of results. Of course, you should still do validation, because it will help you narrow down where a problem happened. (With no validation, the regression error might just be telling you that the old code was broken and the new code fixed it.)

How hard is it write a program that should produce exactly the same output? Call only pure functions from the program, which is exactly what our score-inputs function does.

Wiring this kind of regression test into a continuous integration build is not difficult. If you do it, think about contributing it to whatever testing framework you use.

Now we have partially answered the question, "How do I make sure that my code is correct?" In summary:

- Build with small, composable pieces (most should be pure functions).
- Test forms from the inside out at the REPL.
- When writing test code, keep input generation, execution, and output validation as separate steps.

This last idea is so important that it deserves some library support. So, before we move on, we are going to introduce test.generative, a library that aspires to bring simplicity to testing.

10.3 test.generative

The test.generative library divides testing into three key steps:

- Generating test inputs
- Invoking test functions
- Validating results

Each of these three steps is implemented via functions, which are then composed into tests via the defspec form.

Let's install test.generative and take it for a spin. Add the following line to your project.clj:

```
[org.clojure/test.generative "0.1.3"]
```

Now execute whatever steps you use to reload project code and meet us at the REPL to generate some test data.

Generating Data

From the REPL, require the generators namespace as follows:

```
(require '[clojure.test.generative.generators :as gen])
```

The generators namespace contains functions to generate pseudorandom values for different common datatypes. For example, for every Java primitive, there is a generator function with the same name. Try a few of them:

```
(gen/int)
-> 977378563

(gen/char)
-> \A

(gen/boolean)
-> true
```

Note that your results will likely not be identical to those shown earlier, since the point of these values is to be random.

You can also generate random values for different Clojure collection types. These functions are parameterized by the type of collection to make. For example:

```
(gen/vec gen/boolean)
-> [false false true true true false]

(gen/hash-map gen/byte gen/int)
-> {32 -504310803, 100 424501842, 5 1439482147, 37 1161641068}
```

In addition to the basic types, you can use several knobs to control how the types are generated. You can choose a probability distribution:

```
(gen/geometric 0.02)
-> 10
```

And you can control how collections are sized, with either a constant or a distribution:

```
(gen/list gen/int 2)
-> (-1029960512 1985289448)

(gen/list gen/int (gen/uniform 0 5))
-> (315829211)
```

There are several other goodies, but we won't spoil all the fun of discovery. Do a dir of the namespace, and familiarize yourself with the other standard generators that are available.

To test the Clojurebreaker scorer, we will want a function that generates a random secret (or guess). Sticking with the keyword representation for peg colors, such a function could be as follows:

```
clojurebreaker/test/clojurebreaker/game_test.clj
(defn random-secret
  []
  (gen/vec #(gen/one-of :r :g :b :y) 4))
```

Don't forget to try random-secret at the REPL before moving on to think about validation.

Programmatic Validation

Programmatic validation should be more than just a hand-coded spot-check of specific values. Such spot-checks are a poor use of time when we can easily review a set of outputs for validity and then save them as a regression test. Instead, programmatic validators should enforce logical invariants about the input and output data.

Here are some invariant properties of the Clojurebreaker scoring function:

- Scoring is symmetric. If you invert the secret and guess arguments, the score should be the same.

- The sum of the exact and unordered matches must be greater than or equal to zero and less than or equal to the number of pegs.

- If you scramble the order of pegs in a guess, the sum of exact and unordered matches in the score will not change.

Let's encode each of these invariants as a boolean function of secret, guess, and score:

```
clojurebreaker/test/clojurebreaker/game_test.clj
(ns clojurebreaker.game-test
  (:use [clojure.test.generative :only (defspec) :as test])
  (:require [clojure.test.generative.generators :as gen]
            [clojurebreaker.game :as game]
            [clojure.math.combinatorics :as comb]))

(defn matches
  "Given a score, returns total number of exact plus
   unordered matches."
  [score]
  (+ (:exact score) (:unordered score)))

(defn scoring-is-symmetric
  [secret guess score]
  (= score (game/score guess secret)))

(defn scoring-is-bounded-by-number-of-pegs
  [secret guess score]
  (< 0 (matches score) (count secret)))
```

```
(defn reordering-the-guess-does-not-change-matches
  [secret guess score]
  (= #{(matches score)}
     (into #{} (map
                #(matches (game/score secret %))
                (comb/permutations guess)))))
```

While we often type code at the REPL and then paste it into the appropriate file, we went the other way with the invariant functions earlier, adding them to the source file first. But this doesn't mean we have to lose the immediacy of the REPL. From the REPL, we can reload the namespace and then move into the namespace with in-ns:

```
(require :reload 'clojurebreaker.game-test)
(in-ns 'clojurebreaker.game-test)
```

Now that we are in the namespace we want to use, we have access to all of its public names and aliases. This makes it convenient to handcraft some sample data as a quick sanity check for the validation functions:

```
(def secret [:r :g :g :b])
(def guess [:r :b :b :y])

(scoring-is-symmetric secret guess
  (game/score secret guess))
-> true

(scoring-is-bound-by-number-of-pegs
  secret guess (game/score secret guess))
-> true

(reordering-the-guess-does-not-change-matches
  secret guess (game/score secret guess))
-> true
```

With a test data generator and some validation functions in hand, we are now ready to wire everything together in a defspec.

defspec

The defspec takes three required arguments:

- A name for the spec
- The function to test
- The arguments to generate

After the arguments come zero or more body forms, which perform validations. Here is a trivial example:

clojurebreaker/snippets.clj
```
(defspec closed-under-addition
  +'
  [^long a ^long b]
  (assert (integer? %)))
```

The arguments look like normal Clojure arguments, but there is a twist. Normal function arguments can optionally be tagged with type hints. Spec arguments *must* be tagged, with hints that tell how to *generate* the arguments.

The test.generative function generate-test-data takes an argument spec and generates an infinite sequence of test data. You can call generate-test-data directly to generate arguments separately from any test execution:

```
(take 3
  (test/generate-test-data '[long long]))

-> ([-5025562857975149833 -5843495416241995736]
    [5694868678511409995 5111195811822994797]
    [-6169532649852302182 -1782466964123969572])
```

The body of a defspec has access to the arguments by name, just like a normal function. In addition, it also has access to %, which holds the return values from calling the test function. In the closed-under-addition example, the single validator form checks that the result of addition is an integer, without even bothering to look at the input arguments:

```
(assert (integer? %))
```

More sophisticated validators will typically refer to both the input arguments and the result.

Running Tests

Specs are still functions, so you can run them by simply invoking the function. If you evaluated the closed-under-addition spec at the REPL while reading the previous section, you can invoke it now, passing in some integers:

```
(closed-under-addition 1 2)
-> nil
```

But the more interesting thing is to run the spec with generated inputs. There are three helpers in test.generative for this purpose:

- test-vars takes one or more vars and runs the specs referenced by the vars.

- test-dirs takes one or more directories and reflectively finds all specs in those directories and runs them.

- test-namespaces takes on more namespaces and reflectively finds all specs in those namespaces and runs them.

Let's run the closed-under-addition spec:

```
(require '[clojure.test.generative :as test])
(test/test-vars #'closed-under-addition)

-> [#<core$future_call$reify__5684@603a3e21: :pending>
    #<core$future_call$reify__5684@fc519e2: :pending>]
```

The call to test-vars returns some number of futures (two in the earlier output). Then nothing happens for about ten seconds, followed by REPL output similar to this:

```
{:iterations 179766,
  :msec 10228,
  :var #'clojurebreaker.game-test/closed-under-addition,
  :seed 43}
{:iterations 156217,
  :msec 10249,
  :var #'clojurebreaker.game-test/closed-under-addition,
  :seed 42}
```

Behind the scenes, test.generative has created a future per processor on your local hardware. Each future runs the tests as many times as possible in ten seconds. The output then shows how many iterations ran on each thread, how much wall-clock time each thread took to finish, and the random seed used to generate the data for each var that was tested.

test.generative exposes several dynamic vars to customize a test run. You can bind test/*msec* to change the length of the test run, or you can bind test/*cores* to change the number of cores utilized by the test run. You can also bind test/*verbose* to have all the inputs printed to *out* during the test run.

When a Spec Fails

When a spec fails, test.generative provides additional output to assist you in reproducing the problem. Let's write a spec that will fail by asserting that the sum of two numbers is less than either:

clojurebreaker/snippets.clj
```
(defspec incorrect-spec
  +'
  [^long a ^long b]
  (assert (< a %))
  (assert (< b %)))
```

If you run incorrect-spec, it will fail quickly with an error like this:

```
{:form (#'clojurebreaker.game-test/incorrect-spec
        -5025562857975149833 -5843495416241995736),
 :iteration 0,
 :seed 42,
 :error "Assert failed: (< a %)",
 :exception #<AssertionError java.lang.AssertionError:
            Assert failed: (< a %)>}
```

The :form key gives you the input that failed, and the iteration tells what iteration of the input generator caused the failure. Because the test data generation is pseudorandom with a well-known seed, you can get the failure to repeat by simply rerunning the entire test (possibly after adding logging or attaching a debugger).

If you do not want to repeat the entire run to get back to the point of a failure, you can access a collection of the forms that caused errors by calling the failures function:

```
(test/failures)
-> ({:form
     (#'clojurebreaker.game-test/incorrect-spec
      -5025562857975149833 -5843495416241995736)}
    {:form
     (#'clojurebreaker.game-test/incorrect-spec
      -5027215341191833961 -2715953330829768452)}
```

From here, it is a simple matter of collection traversal to reevaluate past failing inputs:

```
(eval (:form (first (test/failures))))
-> AssertionError Assert failed: (< a %)
```

We have now written and run specs and seen how to explore when things go wrong. Next we will put these techniques to use testing the Clojurebreaker score function.

Generative Testing the score Function

In *Programmatic Validation*, on page 237, we created several functions that validated invariants in Clojurebreaker scoring. Now let's add them to a spec:

clojurebreaker/test/clojurebreaker/game_test.clj
```
(defspec score-invariants
  game/score
  [^{:tag `random-secret} secret
   ^{:tag `random-secret} guess]
  (assert (scoring-is-symmetric secret guess %))
  (assert (scoring-is-bounded-by-number-of-pegs secret guess %))
  (assert (reordering-the-guess-does-not-change-matches secret guess %)))
```

This spec shows one new bit of defspec semantics: the use of the syntax quote
(`) character. The syntax quote on random-secret indicates that the generator
function is a custom one written by us. There are two rules for quoting names
in an argument spec:

- If a name is not syntax-quoted, then that name is interpreted against the
  built-in generators from the namespace clojure.test.generative.generators. These
  names happen to be shadow types and factory names from clojure.core,
  which is why the built-in generators look like type hints.

- If a name is syntax-quoted, then the name is interpreted by the rules of
  the namespace the defspec resides in. This allows you to use all the normal
  namespace tools to manage your own generators.

And now, the moment of truth. When we run the spec, do the invariants
actually hold?

```
#'clojurebreaker.game-test/score-invariants
-> [#<core$future_call$reify__5684@590e130c: :pending>
    #<core$future_call$reify__5684@2b04a681: :pending>]

;; ten seconds pass
{:iterations 1794, :msec 10002, :seed 42,
 :var #'clojurebreaker.game-test/score-invariants}
{:iterations 1787, :msec 10001, :seed 43,
 :var #'clojurebreaker.game-test/score-invariants}
```

Looks good. Can you think of other interesting invariants to test?

At this point, we have only scratched the surface of test.generative. And, while
we like the separation of input generation, execution, and validation, it is
certainly possible to use more familiar unit testing, TDD, and BDD
approaches in Clojure. If you are interested in these, you should check out
the following libraries:

- clojure.test[1] is a modest unit testing library that is built into Clojure's own
  test suite.

- Lazytest[2] is a generic library that supports different testing styles atop a
  few generic representations of tests.

- Midje[3] emphasizes readable tests, while allowing for both top-down and
  bottom-up testing.

---

1. http://clojure.github.com/clojure/clojure.test-api.html
2. https://github.com/stuartsierra/lazytest
3. https://github.com/marick/Midje

Many of the ideas in test.generative are inspired by QuickCheck,[4] a testing library originally written in Haskell but now ported to many languages. If you find test.generative interesting, you should definitely check out QuickCheck, which has a long development history and many capabilities not yet found in test.generative.

Now that we have some confidence in our scoring function, let's see about running a game of Clojurebreaker on the Web.

10.4 Creating an Interface

With a solid foundation, introducing an interface and a playable version of the game should be a breeze. Let's start with a basic web application. The *noir* web framework will serve as a nice base for us to build our application. Creating a new noir project is easy.

First, you will need to install the lein-noir plug-in to leiningen:

```
$ lein plugin install lein-noir 1.2.0
```

Now we can generate our application and launch it:

```
$ lein noir new clojurebreaker
$ cd clojurebreaker
$ lein run
```

Point your browser to http://localhost:8080. You will get the default noir landing page, which isn't interesting to you at the moment, but it will ensure that you have things set up correctly.

It's Finally Time for Some State

This is where we will introduce our one and only piece of state. Since we want multiple players to be able to enjoy our game at once and we want to be able to maintain the game's solution between requests, we will need to store this value somewhere. The great part is that we don't have to manage it in our code. We can just put it in the browser's session, leaving our application code free of state management.

Let's start by opening src/clojurebreaker/views/welcome.clj. Change the /welcome page to just /. We need a way to put something in the session if it isn't already there. Luckily, noir has session/put! and session/get. Let's use them.

```
(defpage "/" []
  (when-not (session/get :game)
    (session/put! :game (.nextInt (java.util.Random.) 1000000)))
```

---

4. http://en.wikipedia.org/wiki/QuickCheck

```
(common/layout
 [:p "Welcome to clojurebreaker.
      Your current game id is " (session/get :game)]]))
```

If you refresh your browser, you will now see that you have a game ID in your session. If you continue to refresh, it shouldn't change. If you clear your sessions and refresh, you should see a new game ID. We will use this technique going forward, but we won't need a randomly generated ID anymore. That was just to demonstrate that the session store is working properly.

Create a new file named game.clj in src/clojurebreaker/models. Here we will put the function we need to generate a new game secret and return it to the view.

```
(ns clojurebreaker.models.game)
```

```
(defn create []
  (vec (repeatedly 4 (fn [] (rand-nth ["r" "g" "b" "y"])))))
```

Let's give this a try in the REPL just to make sure it is producing what we need.

```
(in-ns 'clojurebreaker.models.game)
clojurebreaker.models.game=> (dotimes [_ 5] (println (create)))
| [g y g b]
| [g r r r]
| [r y g r]
| [b y y b]
| [b g r g]
-> nil
```

This is everything we need to start our game. We just need to go back to our view and wire up the code. Remember that test.generative can also create your game secret, so feel free to use it instead of the earlier function. This just demonstrates another way of creating a secret.

```
(defpage "/" []
  (when-not (session/get :game)
    (session/put! :game (game/create)))
  (common/layout
    [:p "Welcome to clojurebreaker.
         Your current game solution is " (session/get :game)]]))
```

Also, don't forget to require clojurebreaker.models.game :as game in your namespace declaration. When you refresh your browser, you will see your game solution printed. If the solution is still an ID, you will need to clear your browser's session data and refresh. Try opening a different browser and visiting the application. You should see a different game solution.

The Player Interface

Now that we have game state, we need an interface for the players. Let's start by creating a game board. We will need to add the hiccup.form-helpers namespace into our namespace declaration with the rest of the hiccup imports. We will now take advantage of noir's defpartial macro.

```
(defpartial board []
  (form-to [:post "/guess"]
   (text-field "one")
   (text-field "two")
   (text-field "three")
   (text-field "four")
   (submit-button "Guess")))
```

The defpartial macro is quite useful here, because it is used just like a regular Clojure function. This will come in handy later when we wire in scoring. Give it a try at the REPL:

```
clojurebreaker.models.game=> (in-ns 'clojurebreaker.views.welcome)
clojurebreaker.views.welcome=> (board)
| "<form action=\"/guess\" method=\"POST\">
|  <input id=\"one\" name=\"one\" type=\"text\" />
|  <input id=\"two\" name=\"two\" type=\"text\" />
|  <input id=\"three\" name=\"three\" type=\"text\" />
|  <input id=\"four\" name=\"four\" type=\"text\" />
|  <input type=\"submit\" value=\"Guess\" /></form>"
```

Now we just need to wire it in:

```
(defpage "/" []
  (when-not (session/get :game)
    (session/put! :game (game/create)))
  (common/layout (board)))
```

Since we have verified that the session bits are working, we can just remove their display and replace them with the actual game. We now have a way for users to guess. Well, at least we have a way for users to type into a browser. Let's wire up the server side.

Back in the view, we need to create another page to respond to the post to /guess. Here we will need to do the following:

- Accept the four inputs and send them to the scorer.

- Determine whether the player has won the game (four exact matches). If so, congratulate them on winning and add a button to start a new game.

- If the user has not won, return the number of exact and unordered matches, as well as the last set of inputs, and display them to the user.

To score the request, we need to add the game-scoring functions we created earlier in the chapter. Let's add exact-matches, unordered-matches, and score to our model. With our scoring functions in place, we can wire up our post handler and complete the first phase of the game.

clojurebreaker/src/clojurebreaker/views/welcome.clj

```clojure
(defpage [:post "/guess"] {:keys [one two three four]}
  (let [result (game/score (session/get :game) [one two three four])]
    (if (= (:exact result) 4)
      (do (session/remove! :game)
          (common/layout
           [:h2 "Congratulations, you have solved the puzzle!"]
           (form-to [:get "/"]
                    (submit-button "Start A New Game"))))
      (do (session/flash-put! result)
          (render "/" {:one one
                       :two two
                       :three three
                       :four four
                       :exact (:exact result)
                       :unordered (:unordered result)})))))
```

OK, so this is a bit of a REPL-full. Here we are able to determine whether the player has won the game and handle it appropriately. There are a couple of new things pulled in from noir here that haven't been introduced yet, though. The :keys destructuring after defpage is dealing with the arguments passed in from the browser. session/remove! does exactly what you think it might do. The interesting bits start with session/flash-put!. This will add something to the session for the request immediately following to consume, and then it will disappear. It is similar to the Ruby on Rails flash method. Finally, the render function calls the route with the arguments that follow.

With just a few modifications, we will be ready to give the game a try. Our / route needs to be able to accept the arguments that it is passed via the call to render that we just wrote. Let's fix that. First modify the board partial to accept and destructure arguments passed to it and render results:

clojurebreaker/src/clojurebreaker/views/welcome.clj

```clojure
(defpartial board [{:keys [one two three four exact unordered]}]
  (when (and exact unordered)
    [:div "Exact: " exact " Unordered: " unordered])
  (form-to [:post "/guess"]
           (text-field "one" one)
           (text-field "two" two)
           (text-field "three" three)
           (text-field "four" four)
           (submit-button "Guess")))
```

Here we have changed the rendering of the board to respond to the player's guesses. We will display the results of the guess and place the player's previous guess back onto the board so that they can modify it and continue. Experiment with this at the REPL to see what output is yielded given certain inputs:

```
clojurebreaker.views.welcome=> (board {:one "r"
                                        :two "b"
                                        :three "y"
                                        :four "g"})

|   "<form action=\"/guess\" method=\"POST\">
|     <input id=\"one\" name=\"one\" type=\"text\" value=\"r\" />
|     <input id=\"two\" name=\"two\" type=\"text\" value=\"b\" />
|     <input id=\"three\" name=\"three\" type=\"text\" value=\"y\" />
|     <input id=\"four\" name=\"four\" type=\"text\" value=\"g\" />
->   <input type=\"submit\" value=\"Guess\" /></form>"

clojurebreaker.views.welcome=> (board {:one "r"
                                        :two "b"
                                        :three "y"
                                        :four "g"
                                        :exact 2
                                        :unordered 0})

|   "<div>Exact: 2 Unordered: 0</div>
|     <form action=\"/guess\" method=\"POST\">
|       <input id=\"one\" name=\"one\" type=\"text\" value=\"r\" />
|       <input id=\"two\" name=\"two\" type=\"text\" value=\"b\" />
|       <input id=\"three\" name=\"three\" type=\"text\" value=\"y\" />
|       <input id=\"four\" name=\"four\" type=\"text\" value=\"g\" />
->     <input type=\"submit\" value=\"Guess\" /></form>"
```

Just one minor change to the / page definition, and we are ready to start playing!

clojurebreaker/src/clojurebreaker/views/welcome.clj
```
(defpage "/" {:as guesses}
  (when-not (session/get :game)
    (session/put! :game (game/create)))
  (common/layout (board (or guesses nil))))
```

Here we are just accepting the arguments from render so that we can pass them along to the board partial. Since board works like a standard Clojure function, this process is trivial.

There is just one more thing to do before we can take the game for a spin. We need to add math.combinatorics to the project.clj file in our noir project.

```
clojurebreaker/project.clj
(defproject clojurebreaker "0.1.0-SNAPSHOT"
            :description "Clojurebreaker game for Programming Clojure 2nd Edition"
            :dependencies [[org.clojure/clojure "1.3.0"]
                           [org.clojure/math.combinatorics "0.0.1"]
                           [org.clojure/test.generative "0.1.3"]
                           [noir "1.2.0"]]
            :main clojurebreaker.server)
```

Rerun lein deps and lein run, and you can now play Clojurebreaker to your heart's content.

10.5 Deploying Your Code

Now that you have a complete application, it's time to put it somewhere for the world to enjoy! Deploying an application to production can be a long and arduous task that involves adding code or moving parts to your application. Luckily, we are going to skip all of those steps and just get to the point. There is a service available that fully supports Clojure application deployment and makes it drop-dead easy. They call themselves Heroku.[5]

There are a few initial steps to getting an account set up at Heroku, but the deployment process is as easy as checking code into a source control repository. In fact, that is all you have to do. A simple git push is how you deploy.

To get to the deployment step, you will need to sign up for an account at Heroku. It is fairly straightforward and is completely free. Heroku does have paid offerings, but this example should not cost you a dime. After signing up, you will need to create an application on the Heroku platform.

The Procfile

Heroku uses a special file in your program to let it know how the program should be started. It is called the Procfile. Add this to the root of the project.

```
web: lein run
```

If you want to ensure that things are set up properly, you can install the foreman gem and run foreman start. If that successfully starts your application, you should have no trouble on Heroku.

```
foreman start

14:35:28 web.1 | started with pid 34538
14:35:33 web.1 | Starting server...
```

---

5. http://heroku.com

```
14:35:33 web.1 | 2011-12-09 14:35:33.042:INFO::Logging to STDERR
14:35:33 web.1 | Server started on port [5000].
14:35:33 web.1 | You can view the site at http://localhost:5000
14:35:33 web.1 | #<Server Server@63ce15f6>
14:35:33 web.1 | 2011-12-09 14:35:33.044:INFO::jetty-6.1.26
14:35:33 web.1 | 2011-12-09 14:35:33.070:INFO::Started SocketConnector@0.0.0.0:5000
```

The Heroku Library

Heroku provides a nice way to programmatically interact with its platform. The only gotcha here is that it requires some additional setup if you don't already have it. You will need the Ruby programming language along with RubyGems. Your systems package manager should be able to provide you with these items. If not, you can always visit http://ruby-lang.org.

Installing the Heroku library is done via RubyGems:

```
gem install heroku
```

Git

This will provide a heroku command that you will use for all of your Heroku-based interactions.

The next step is to create a git repository inside of your Clojurebreaker codebase. Again, your system's package manager should be able to provide you with a suitable version of git. If not, you can visit http://git-scm.org.

Once you have git installed, simply run git init in the root of the clojurebreaker application:

```
git init
-> Initialized empty Git repository in ~/clojurebreaker/.git/
```

This will create the initial git shell for your application. Next you need to locally commit your code:

```
git add .
git commit -m "Initial commit"

[master (root-commit) dd4f8a8] initial commit
13 files changed, 65860 insertions(+), 0 deletions(-)
create mode 100644 .gitignore
create mode 100644 project.clj
create mode 100644 resources/public/css/reset.css
create mode 100644 src/clojurebreaker/game.clj
create mode 100644 src/clojurebreaker/models/game.clj
create mode 100644 src/clojurebreaker/server.clj
create mode 100644 src/clojurebreaker/views/common.clj
create mode 100644 src/clojurebreaker/views/welcome.clj
```

Housing Your Application

At this point, you have staged your code locally to be pushed up to Heroku. Now it's time to create a Heroku application to house your program:

```
heroku create --stack cedar

Creating freezing-waterfall-3937... done, stack is cedar
http://freezing-waterfall-3937.herokuapp.com/ |
git@heroku.com:freezing-waterfall-3937.git
Git remote heroku added
```

The --stack argument specifies the platform on Heroku that supports Clojure applications. The application will get a random name provided by Heroku with a URL that you can visit to see your running program. You can rename this later if you want.

The Deployment

The last step is to run git push, and Heroku will take care of the rest.

```
git push heroku master

Counting objects: 24, done.
Delta compression using up to 4 threads.
Compressing objects: 100% (15/15), done.
Writing objects: 100% (24/24), 230.67 KiB, done.
Total 24 (delta 0), reused 0 (delta 0)

-----> Heroku receiving push
-----> Clojure app detected
-----> Installing Leiningen
       Downloading: leiningen-1.5.2-standalone.jar
       Downloading: rlwrap-0.3.7
       Writing: lein script
-----> Installing dependencies with Leiningen

... Output elided ...

-----> Discovering process types
       Procfile declares types -> web
-----> Compiled slug size is 12.8MB
-----> Launching... done, v4
       http://stormy-water-3888.herokuapp.com deployed to Heroku
```

You can visit your application using the heroku command as well:

```
heroku open
```

This will open a browser and send you right to your deployed application. It might take some time to load on the first visit, but subsequent requests will get faster. You can find an additional Heroku/Clojure tutorial on Heroku's dev center at http://devcenter.heroku.com/articles/clojure-web-application.

Have fun with your new Clojure web application. Make it better, give it some personality, and share it with the world!

10.6 Farewell

Congratulations. You have come a long way in a short time. You have learned the many ideas that combine to make Clojure great: Lisp, Java, functional programming, and explicit concurrency. And in this chapter, you saw one (of a great many) possible workflows for developing a full application in Clojure.

We have only scratched the surface of Clojure's great potential, and we hope you will take the next step and become an active part of the Clojure community. Join the mailing list.[6] Hang out on IRC.[7] The Clojure community is friendly and welcoming, and we would love to hear from you.

---

6. http://groups.google.com/group/clojure
7. #clojure on irc.freenode.net

Editor Support

Editor support for Clojure is evolving rapidly, so some of the information here may be out-of-date by the time you read this. For the latest information, see the Getting Started[1] page in the community wiki, which has child pages for a number of different dev environments.

Clojure code is concise and expressive. As a result, editor support is not quite as important as for some other languages. However, you will want an editor that can at least indent code correctly and can match parentheses.

While writing the book, we used Emacs plus Jeffrey Chu's clojure-mode.[2] Emacs support for Clojure is quite good, but if you are not already an Emacs user, you might prefer to start with an editor you are familiar with from among those shown here:

Editor	Project Name	Project URL
Eclipse	Counterclockwise	http://code.google.com/p/counterclockwise/
Emacs	clojure-mode	http://github.com/jochu/clojure-mode
IntelliJ IDEA	La Clojure	http://plugins.intellij.net/plugin/?id=4050
jEdit	jedit modes	http://github.com/djspiewak/jedit-modes/tree/master/
NetBeans	enclojure	http://enclojure.org
TextMate	textmate-clojure	https://github.com/swannodette/textmate-clojure
Vim	VimClojure	http://www.vim.org/scripts/script.php?script_id=2501

---

1. http://dev.clojure.org/display/doc/Getting+Started
2. http://github.com/jochu/clojure-mode

Bibliography

[Goe06]   Brian Goetz. *Java Concurrency in Practice*. Addison-Wesley, Reading, MA, 2006.

[Hof99]   Douglas R. Hofstadter. *Gödel, Escher, Bach: An Eternal Golden Braid*. Basic Books, New York, NY, USA, 20th Anniv, 1999.

[McC06]   Steve McConnell}. *Software Estimation: Demystifying the Black Art*. Microsoft Press, Redmond, WA, 2006.

Index

Long Live the Command Line!

Use tmux for incredible mouse-free productivity, and learn how to create profession com-mand-line apps.

Your mouse is slowing you down. The time you spend context switching between your editor and your consoles eats away at your productivity. Take control of your environment with tmux, a terminal multiplexer that you can tailor to your workflow. Learn how to customize, script, and leverage tmux's unique abilities and keep your fingers on your keyboard's home row.

Brian P. Hogan
(88 pages) ISBN: 9781934356968. $11.00
http://pragprog.com/titles/bhtmux

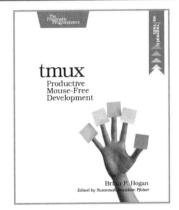

Speak directly to your system. With its simple com-mands, flags, and parameters, a well-formed command-line application is the quickest way to automate a backup, a build, or a deployment and simplify your life.

David Bryant Copeland
(200 pages) ISBN: 9781934356913. $33
http://pragprog.com/titles/dccar

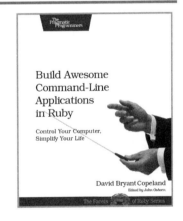

Welcome to the Better Web

You need a better JavaScript and more expressive CSS and HTML today. Start here.

CoffeeScript is JavaScript done right. It provides all of JavaScript's functionality wrapped in a cleaner, more succinct syntax. In the first book on this exciting new language, CoffeeScript guru Trevor Burnham shows you how to hold onto all the power and flexibility of JavaScript while writing clearer, cleaner, and safer code.

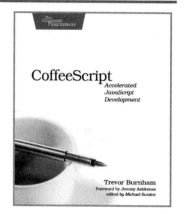

Trevor Burnham
(160 pages) ISBN: 9781934356784. $29
http://pragprog.com/titles/tbcoffee

CSS is fundamental to the web, but it's a basic language and lacks many features. Sass is just like CSS, but with a whole lot of extra power so you can get more done, more quickly. Build better web pages today with *Pragmatic Guide to Sass*. These concise, easy-to-digest tips and techniques are the shortcuts experienced CSS developers need to start developing in Sass today.

Hampton Catlin and Michael Lintorn Catlin
(128 pages) ISBN: 9781934356845. $25
http://pragprog.com/titles/pg_sass

Learn a New Language This Year

Want to be a better programmer? Each new programming language you learn teaches you something new about computing. Come see what you're missing.

You should learn a programming language every year, as recommended by *The Pragmatic Programmer*. But if one per year is good, how about *Seven Languages in Seven Weeks*? In this book you'll get a hands-on tour of Clojure, Haskell, Io, Prolog, Scala, Erlang, and Ruby. Whether or not your favorite language is on that list, you'll broaden your perspective of programming by examining these languages side-by-side. You'll learn something new from each, and best of all, you'll learn how to learn a language quickly.

Bruce A. Tate
(328 pages) ISBN: 9781934356593. $34.95
http://pragprog.com/titles/btlang

Bill Karwin has helped thousands of people write better SQL and build stronger relational databases. Now he's sharing his collection of antipatterns—the most common errors he's identified out of those thousands of requests for help.

Most developers aren't SQL experts, and most of the SQL that gets used is inefficient, hard to maintain, and sometimes just plain wrong. This book shows you all the common mistakes, and then leads you through the best fixes. What's more, it shows you what's *behind* these fixes, so you'll learn a lot about relational databases along the way.

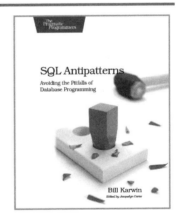

Bill Karwin
(352 pages) ISBN: 9781934356555. $34.95
http://pragprog.com/titles/bksqla

The Pragmatic Bookshelf

The Pragmatic Bookshelf features books written by developers for developers. The titles continue the well-known Pragmatic Programmer style and continue to garner awards and rave reviews. As development gets more and more difficult, the Pragmatic Programmers will be there with more titles and products to help you stay on top of your game.

Visit Us Online

This Book's Home Page
http://pragprog.com/titles/shcloj2
Source code from this book, errata, and other resources. Come give us feedback, too!

Register for Updates
http://pragprog.com/updates
Be notified when updates and new books become available.

Join the Community
http://pragprog.com/community
Read our weblogs, join our online discussions, participate in our mailing list, interact with our wiki, and benefit from the experience of other Pragmatic Programmers.

New and Noteworthy
http://pragprog.com/news
Check out the latest pragmatic developments, new titles and other offerings.

Save on the eBook

Save on the eBook versions of this title. Owning the paper version of this book entitles you to purchase the electronic versions at a terrific discount.

PDFs are great for carrying around on your laptop—they are hyperlinked, have color, and are fully searchable. Most titles are also available for the iPhone and iPod touch, Amazon Kindle, and other popular e-book readers.

Buy now at *http://pragprog.com/coupon*

Contact Us

Online Orders:	*http://pragprog.com/catalog*
Customer Service:	*support@pragprog.com*
International Rights:	*translations@pragprog.com*
Academic Use:	*academic@pragprog.com*
Write for Us:	*http://pragprog.com/write-for-us*
Or Call:	+1 800-699-7764